LAMPS OF WESTERN MYSTICISM

LAMPS OF
WESTERN MYSTICISM

by
ARTHUR EDWARD WAITE

Introduction by
PAUL M. ALLEN

ILLUSTRATED

"Independent Writers"
P.O. Box 104
Woods Hole, MA 02543

RUDOLF STEINER PUBLICATIONS
151 North Moison Road
Blauvelt, New York 10913, U.S.A.
1973

INTRODUCTION

The spiritual striving of humanity takes many, often apparently contradictory forms. However, beneath this external diversity are certain fundamentals which all will recognize who wish to bring order and purpose into their experience, raising the latter from a condition of mere existence to a life worthy of the dignity and potentialities of a human being.

A truly modern path to the spirit as described by the author of this book does not imply alienation from the demands and requirements of everyday life, but rather enhances man's ability to live that life more fully, earnestly and fruitfully. From an existence motivated primarily by selfishness and egotistical desires, the individual comes to live more intensively in terms of his fellow-man, of environing nature, of the present and future social and spiritual well-being of humanity.

This development follows certain definite steps which have as their preliminary goal the harmonizing and balancing of the inner life in terms of objective, ultimate reality. Beyond this, the path opens out to a still higher attainment, ultimating in that sublime, conscious oneness with the divine, described in the writings of those men and women who have attained at least a first experience of this highest of all goals.

This book was written in order to open before us the prospect of this goal, to outline at least the first steps on the path leading to it, and to introduce us to some of these human beings who have achieved noteworthy results in this quest, particularly in the Western World.

INTRODUCTION

The author is convinced—and rightly—that "there was never an age when the doors of the human mind stood open so widely as they stand now," and this conviction motivates his presentation. In simple, straightforward language he outlines the ideals and practice of the spiritual life from the standpoint of the man of the West as he is today, a description entirely free of asceticism and the restrictions of theological dogma.

Basing himself first of all upon his own conscious spiritual strivings and the perspectives made visible by the light streaming from the lamps of those Westerners who achieved much in this same area of experience, the author reveals in this book what he terms "the secret dealings between the soul and God."

This presentation of eminently valid, modern esoteric strivings, experiences and goals is certain to evoke appreciative echo in the heart of every reader who in one way or another prepares to set out upon the mystical path leading to the heights where is fulfilled the longing so widespread among humanity today, the longing for the spirit, the age-old quest for the Holy Grail.

Paul M. Allen

Botton,
Danby / Whitby
Yorkshire, England.

January, 1972

CONTENTS

INTRODUCTION . . . . **v**

PART I

LAMPS OF QUEST

THE PATH OF REALITY: AN EX-PARTE STATEMENT . . . 3
OBLATION AND SERVICE 17
CONSECRATIONS OF LIFE AND THOUGHT 23
THE HIGHER UNDERSTANDING 32
THE SENSE OF THE INFINITE 43
LIFE AND DOCTRINE 52
A STUDY IN CONTRAST 61
THE HIGHER ASPECT 72
SPIRITISM AND THE MYSTIC QUEST 83
OFFICIAL CHURCHES AND SPIRITISM 90
THE PATH OF THE MYSTERIES 97

PART II

LAMPS OF LIFE

OF CROWNED MASTERS 127
THE DIONYSIAN HERITAGE 134
THE EVERLASTING GOSPEL 145
THE MESSAGE OF ECKEHART 151
RUYSBROECK'S JOURNEY IN THE DIVINE DISTANCE . . . 158
A BRIDE OF CHRIST 163
VOICES FROM CARMEL 172
POST-REFORMATION MYSTICS 178
MOLINOS AND THE QUIETISTS 184
LATER WITNESSES TO THE LIFE OF LIFE 198
IN THE SHADOW OF REVOLUTION 211
A MODERN DAUGHTER OF DESIRE 231

CONTENTS

PART III

LAMPS ON HEIGHTS

	PAGE
MYSTICAL REALISATION	239
FAITH AND VISION	245
THE PATH OF CONTEMPLATION	255
THE WORLD TO COME AND THE WORLD OF THE HOLY ONE	277
GROUNDS OF UNITY IN GRACE AND NATURE	290
THE POET'S GLASS OF VISION	298
A STUDY IN CHRISTIAN PANTHEISM	308
THE GRADES OF LOVE	320
THE INWARD HOLY OF HOLIES	325
INDEX	331

Fig. 1 Jacob Boehme

Fig. 2 *Angelus Silesius, 1624-1677*

Fig. 3 *Emanuel Swedenborg*

Fig. 4 F. M. Van Helmont

Fig. 5 Louis Claude de St. Martin

Fig. 6 Duns Scotus

Fig. 7 Giordano Bruno

Fig. 8 Nicholas of Cusa

Fig. 9 Jamblicus

Fig. 10 Ideal Figure of Hermes Trismegistus

Fig. 11 St. Thomas Aquinas

Fig. 12 Meister Eckhardt and Uta, 1260-1328

PART I

LAMPS OF QUEST

THE PATH OF REALITY

AN EX-PARTE STATEMENT

THERE are subjects which some years ago it would have been
nearly impossible to discuss with any expectation of a hearing;
but now, saving in the purlieus and "low-life deeps" of thought,
they will find an auditory everywhere, and in several quarters
an increasing recognition that ultimately there are no other
subjects. The time-immemorial conventions of thought and
mental habit survive, as they will, under the hallowing of general
assent; but the minds of the age are disposed to new ways,
which we have a poet's authority for saying that the world loves,
and also to those others which are so old as to be for them new.
It is not only possible now to speak of things which concern the
philosophy but also the practice of religion, from that standpoint
which can be called universal because it embraces all, without
being dependent on any of the official ecclesiastical systems.
The standpoint in question, at the beginning of the present
studies, cannot of course be devotional; intellectual and critical
considerations must lead on to deeper things. It is after this
manner in any case that it seems desirable, in the first instance, to
offer those whom I address some preliminary intimations concerning that reflective system which is here termed mystical, and even
so it will be prudent to begin by assuring them that they are
approached only at the outset as those who may be indifferently
interested in such a field of thought, because in recent years it
has received a certain vogue and is hence one of those topics of
which an informed person may be assumed to know something
slightly. It is for this reason also that I have termed this particular essay an *ex-parte* statement, that I may not deal
ungenerously, as it so happens that I have travelled a good
distance along these uncommon paths of thought, and have

got to know where they lead. As the subject-matter of this volume unfolds it is to be presumed that it will find those for whom it is intended and that others will fall away.

One critical writer, who had, however, very little sympathy with the subject of which he was treating, has told us that, strictly speaking, the mystical sentiment in man has no history : it is an attitude, a condition of mind, a pathological state, if you will, common to certain temperaments in all places and at nearly all times. On the contrary, or from the alternative standpoint, that state or sentiment is coincident with the history of the human soul, which, from all time, and in all places, has striven towards the consciousness of its source, and has aspired to return whence it came. This desire and its passionate endeavour have, for the rest, been objectified sufficiently on the external plane to make them count for something not inconsiderably important in the world's history ; and it is practically a commonplace— which, for the rest, does not specially concern us—that in their lesser manifestations at least they have been almost invariably among the active phenomena heralding or accompanying great crises in the life of humanity ; as for example at the dawn of the Christian era, at the beginning of the French Revolution and, I may perhaps add, at the present day.

Now, it is desirable that we should make one or two further distinctions on the subject of Mysticism—what it is and what it is not—quite clear to our minds, but more especially how it is to be understood as regards the Western world, with which we are exclusively concerned. We are apt to use words interchange-ably which are either not interchangeable at all, or, if to some extent synonymous, they have been subjected, for more or less cogent reasons, to a conventional distinction which must bring ourselves and others into confusion if we come now to disregard it. But outside questions that belong to the meaning of words, several lessons of experience teach other precautions, for example, that we must separate in our minds certain things from Mysticism which are liable to be identified therewith. This paper may be classed also as an historical consideration, partly because it does follow a certain order of time and partly because it does deal, in a broad manner, with events in the history of the mind within the limits of its subject-matter. It is thus formally a protest against any attempt to minimise the importance of the mystic object because it has been alleged to be of little vital consequence for historical purposes, or in connection, let us say, with the constitutional history of England and the date of the Norman Conquest.

Before approaching Western Mysticism, I must establish one distinction which is peculiar and personal to myself: it is not of a flattering kind, for it is a distinction of ignorance. We are dealing admittedly with a subject which is essentially religious, and the sum of real religion, and I wish to shew presently that all Mysticism worthy of the title had in the West for many centuries its home and abiding place within the Sanctuaries of the Church. But I am not able to say whether there has been, since the division between East and West, any philosophical development of importance in the Greek Church. This is worth mentioning in passing as an instance of one of those important questions which must some day be cleared up by research. I speak therefore with a certain reservation, remembering that the subject generally, including its literature, is even in external and historical aspects, to adapt the words of Dean Stanley, behind the mountains of the ignorance of us all.

In respect of Western Mysticism, up to the fifteenth or sixteenth century, it is almost wholly a heritage from the Church. This is not an adventitious statement, but a concise summary of an indisputable case. For the most part, I am speaking admittedly of a period when to differ from that institution was frequently to incur a great risk, and there is no need to add that there was throughout it much smouldering hostility towards the central authority which occasionally burst up into flame. But it is necessary to say that such hostility was scarcely on the part of the mystics, nor can most doctrines and teachers that were from time to time condemned and persecuted be regarded as mystics, if we except such signal instances as Eckehart, Molinos and Fénelon. It is preferable to accentuate this, because of a tendency on the part of incautious writers in sympathy with popular transcendentalism to identify Mysticism with every revolt against the ecclesiastical authority. As an example in point, we may, I think, take the case of Abelard. He was a liberal theologian of his period and not in any sense a theosophist; but he clashed with his masters in theology, and partly on account of this opposition, and partly because of his brilliance, and for the rest by reason of the tragical episodes of his life, and in spite of its fatal story of a none too mystic love, he has been somehow set down as a mystic. Let us endeavour on our part to avoid these mistakes of classification and, in a certain sense, of prejudice. The case for the ecclesiastical character of mediæval Mysticism in the Western world centres in the simple point that there was no other kind, and there is also no evidence that the mystics who illuminated the Church were in it and not of it. They may have deviated almost unawares on certain deeper and more obscure aspects of doctrinal theology, but there is, indeed, as it seems to me, full and direct evidence of the contrary, and that they did not, as is sometimes suggested, remain there from considerations of prudence, or otherwise against their will. The *via prudentiæ* which they studied had no relation to any time-serving and material discretion. They, less than any, as the heroes of a strange enterprise of sanctity, would have been actuated by a mere question of personal safety.

Let us take three names in their order, Bernard, Ruysbroeck and Tauler—names which are typical for our subject, standing for much that had gone before and much also that was to come after. If there is one thing which issues clearly from the many writings that they have each of them left us, it is that it is wholly untrue, as some have advanced unthinkingly, that these mystics were not faithful members of their Church, as that Church was understood by herself at their period, and not by the liberalising tendencies of modern thought, within or without its pale, seeking to explain the Church. In matters of doctrine and practice there was nothing that they held or did which differed from the ortho-dox practice or doctrine. We do not find Solomon's temple spiritualised, so to speak; dogma did not evaporate into allegory or transfigure into symbol, and the method of these thinkers was simply the method of accepted religious life, exalted to the heroic point. Furthermore, there is no trace of a secret doctrine, as we now understand this phrase, behind the official doctrine of which they remained exponents upon a higher plane. A serious mistake is being made at the present day by writers who endeavour to identify obscure Manichæan and pseudo-Manichæan sects of Southern Europe with an apostolate of Mysticism, and with the teachings and lives of mystics. It would seem as if hatred of the Church, and, if I understand the matter rightly, of all ecclesiastical Christianity, should be regarded as a test of inward spiritual life, and as one of the true marks by which we may know it. The mistake to which I am adverting is not less indiscriminate in its details than it is baseless in its general notion. Albigensian or Vaudois, it matters not; if it is to be found in Southern Europe at a certain period, it receives the distinguished title of Manichæan, and if it loathes the yoke of the Church, it is part of a hidden tradition; while if these sects were opposed by great doctors and shining lights of the Church, it was not through a sincere conviction that they were contrary to the truth, but because, for example, Saint Augustine had failed to attain the higher grades of the initiation which was dispensed by them. Insensate nonsense on this subject has been talked by modern theosophists and has helped to make this bewrayed movement a byword and scorn of scholarship. These points, and many others which might be mentioned, are not illustrations of malice but rather of imperfect equipment and of uncritical adherence to biassed or exploded authorities. No one acquainted with his subject would say that the Vaudois were either followers of Manes or esoteric philosophers, or seekers in this life for the attainment of the Beatific Vision; or that Peter Lombard the Nominalist, who maintained that universals have no real existence outside the mind, must be classed with Ruysbroeck, Tauler, St. John of the Cross and Molinos, any more than with Trithemius, Raymond Lully, Cornelius Agrippa or Paracelsus.

It must be observed, in the next place, that there is no trace, doctrinal or otherwise, in the Christian mystics with whom we are concerned here of the existence of any Secret Church, or of a Church within the Church. As it must be held that Councillor Eckartshausen bore true witness in his CLOUD ON THE SANCTUARY concerning a Holy Assembly or Hidden Church in Christ, the silence of the great mystics on this subject may seem, at first sight, a grave difficulty, and I could wish to report that there were indications of the kind, but I have found none, while there is also no real attempt to get behind sacrament or doctrine. We must remember, however, that Eckartshausen's Assembly signifies the communion of souls in the Christhood and by no means an incorporated body with places of meeting and a defined form of procedure. For the rest, there is absolutely no reason to suppose that the mystics just mentioned, or any others of whom they are typical representatives, made use of doctrine and sacrament by way of economy or symbol, except in the sense of the sacraments. The end of Western Mysticism was the return of the many into the One, and the means of that reunion did not differ from the lesser means of sanctification. They were, so to speak, the higher mathematics of the soul, and the last words of Ruysbroeck in the last chapter of the ADORNMENT OF THE SPIRITUAL MARRIAGE, where he promises to those who can so prepare themselves by the pursuit of virtue, that out of the flesh, and to some extent before it is set aside, they shall attain *in vastissimum divinitatis pelagus navigare*, are simply the formal guarantee of the last vital consequence in a closely knit chain of cause and effect, the first links of which are still to be found in all the elementary religious catechisms.

As this paper is explanatory and not polemical, and, in respect of the ecclesiastical system, is less than anything to be regarded as a confession of official faith, I need not touch till later upon the question whether Western mystics were right in being thus content with their Church, and with its *summa totius theologiæ*. It will seem to the simple senses that if any of us are disposed to accept Christian theosophy as the best guide to the Hidden Life in God, they should not, if they are logical, shrink from anything that follows reasonably from such disposition. The alternatives, however, are not of this clear kind, for the distinction between essences and accidents would intervene to cloud the issues. Happily my sole province is to record, at the fact's value, that the men who aspired to the possession of the essential unity by the way of fruition, and to attain the dilucid contemplation of the Trinity in Unity, did, without evasion, equivocation or mental reservation of any kind, believe in

Baptism, Confirmation, Repentance, the Holy Eucharist, Extreme Unction, Holy Orders and Matrimony—yes, even in Matrimony as the outward sign of an inward grace, and, let us dare to trust, without any *arrière-pensée* in their mind to suggest that they considered it, like the young lady mentioned by Coventry Patmore, as rather a wicked sacrament. I must add also, that I may not spare the whole truth, that they believed in eternal punishment and in the resurrection of the body with the same firmness as in the life everlasting. On this whole question I cannot do better than refer my readers to the celebrated INSTITUTIONS of Tauler, which treatise deals generally with the manner of returning to our First Source and with the transmutation of the human into the Divine Will, but is at the same time a method of preparation for receiving the Eucharist worthily.

Another point which assumes, in certain respects, an aspect of comparative magnitude is the question whether, positively or by implication, we can trace in these Christian thinkers any one of the modern speculations concerning the soul and its destiny. There is no opportunity here to go over the whole ground, but there is one of them which, I think, may be taken to stand for the rest, because it has entered more into the life of modern metaphysical reveries than perhaps any other that we can name. I refer to Reincarnation. This belief has had a chequered career in recent times; but not only is the Metempsychosis, in any of its forms, quite outside the horizon of early Christian mystics, but, by inference at least, it seems impossible to their system. It is, of course, open to modern theosophists and others to regard the experience of the Beatific Vision as belonging to the Devachanic Plane, or, in other words, not what it was thought by those who aspired to reach it and did in their belief enjoy a certain foretaste of its ecstasy. About this I must disclaim jurisdiction, admitting that, on his part, no Christian mystic would contend that Devachanic experience, if any, was or is an experience of the Beatific Vision.

If we were to follow the indication offered by this one doctrine into all paths, parallel and connected, we should reach a much clearer distinction between pseudo-theosophist and mystic than could reside in the variation of the words. The dual purpose of this brief excursus has, however, been served reasonably when it is added that, after all occult theorems and occult practical formulæ, there remains the true object which is external to these, and is that of the Western mystic, which we can express, if we please, in the words of the dying Plotinus : " I take the Divine within me to the Divine in the universe." And Christian Mystic or Grecian Philosopher, or Spanish Kabalist, putting the traditions of Israel into the great book of the ZOHAR, it is all one as regards the path to that object, which is wholly and simply, as the ZOHAR calls it, the path of ecstasy. If outside this union with the Divine and this state of " still rest and of changeless simplicity " which bears uninterruptedly the consciousness of the whole Reality within it, there is any other mystic object, I do not know what it is.

That Mysticism is not only a great but also an exact science is the first and will be the last contention of the present book, and to state this does not exceed the principles of exposition and of criticism laid down already in my opening words as proper guides in a study which is the reverse of apologetic in its character. And for the rest I have established one point, the exactitude of which remains above challenge. The history of the mystics is conclusive, and this absolutely, thereon ; the literature is also conclusive, and books without number remain which every doubtful mind may consult at need. Upon any merely polemical consideration, that consultation is perhaps a little less than desirable, but there are better motives possible, and for those who possess them, in spite of certain impediments, it is not really and unreasonably difficult for anyone to become acquainted at least with the rumours of the depths and the heights of mystical doctrine and of the experience which lies behind it. At present, I fear that the greater mystics are in the position of certain poets mentioned by Dr. Johnson, who were quoted but not read—or they are read perhaps casually and here and there. Those who will be at the pains of abiding with them in the deep reflection which they demand will not, I think, look up from their pages without an overflowing conviction that, far removed from ordinary paths and interests, even in the domain of psychology, there is a grand experiment possible, and that some have achieved it.

So many misconceptions being about us, it is well to reiterate that the mystic life does not carry with it any divorce from the spirit within the Churches. Some of them may seem, and some of them, I think, are more fully in consonance with that life, but it is because the lesser among the various academies have not entered so fully into their higher consciousness. Mysticism is, in one sense, like Kabalism ; it is a liberal education in religion, as that was a liberal education in Israel ; but the roots of the mystic subject are, in the last resource, as native to the Bethel in its foundations as they are to the City of the Seven Hills.

And now it is necessary to make in conclusion two further distinctions : again they are explanatory and not polemical, and they will obtain throughout these essays. We have seen that the Latin Church was the general nursing mother of Christian Mysticism in the West, even if it was also the scourge when certain individual mystics drifted or seemed to drift outside the chartered circle of authorised thought and practice. It is inevitable that those who read will question the relation in which I stand thereto for the clearance of their own issues before they proceed further. My position is therefore that of a Christian mystic who venerates the sacraments of doctrine in the sense of their essential truth as symbolism and who regards the chief Church of the Western world as the keeper of the Mystery of Faith defined in sacramental forms. The title to existence on the part of other Churches, as that which is called Anglican, is valid, but so only in proportion as it maintains and promulgates the Mystery of Faith in sacrament without reducing the sacraments. In so far as the thing called Protestantism is not too dead to count it is condemned herein and hereby, with all its surviving ragfair of divisional sect and school. As regards the Greek Church it is a witness also in the world but with a sleep of the ages on it, and the time is not yet—if indeed it shall be called to awaken.

We know that a sacrament is the outward sign of an inward grace in the hiddenness, and as regards the *symbolum* it is a body of doctrine which vests a holy spirit within the doctrine. The spirit is not the body and the grace is not the sign, but because of Divine Truth, and because also of the holy spirit which penetrates and dissolves the veils according to gifts of understanding, there is a valid correspondence between them, even as I believe that the adjustment between our physical senses and the external universe communicates sacramentally to the soul within the body a valid and operative notion of that reality within the universe which is shadowed forth in its beauty and splendour. The office of the Church is to maintain the outward signs with such fidelity to the inward spirit as can be postulated of an institution which in the sacred nature of things can have no jurisdiction over the spirit. The office of the faithful who are under the Church-obedience is to accept the representative tokens, but the living realisation of the inward grace and spirit lies between the soul and God, in I know not what far reaches of the light-winning soul of man. The spirit moves where it wills and the Church is not its custodian, though in ages of open vision it knows of an Eternal Presence. There is haply a vision to come at the end of the age that is and of those long centuries when it has seen through a glass and darkly, when it has imposed the outward signs as the sole reality, when it has forgotten St. Augustine and his key-note dictum on the Trinity—to which we shall come in due course.

There is surely no need to say more on this side of the subject, and I have written so far of necessity, as one who shrinks from personal confession. All this is sufficient—over and above—to indicate what great waters divide me from official religion, as it is content to understand itself. In every other respect than that to which I have certified, the official Canterbury is to me an *amabilis insania* and Rome is a *caput mortuum*. We acknowledge them, each on its own degree, because they serve while they last, because of the sleep of Greece, because in the last resource it seems that the day is far spent and after the sunset and night-time we look to another morning.

There is a sense in which we are their children—I am speaking now also for others in my own school—and in Greater and Lesser Mysteries we are pledged to defend them against " unprovoked attacks of the infidels," to which end we are armed and ready till the day of battle is over and the peace comes down. But in so far as the keepers of doctrine testify to Trinity in Unity, the virgin birth, redemption by fleshly blood, transubstantiation, apostolic succession *et hoc genus omne* as otherwise than holy and living sacraments which must be realised in its own way by each receiving soul, to such extent are there scales on the eyes of the keepers and a yoke on the teaching tongue. Hell, Purgatory and Paradise are as another heap of symbols put into our hands, and it is for us to understand them in the justification of the ways of God to man. Our duty as mystics is to " love the highest," in doctrine as in all things else, and the highest message that we can read into any doctrine is the truest meaning for us and the only true.

In this sense is the private judgment of the inward mind betrothed to the Divine Judgment, in the hope of a marriage that is to come. And above all the sacraments, above all symbols, above all offices of dogma there remains God in the Highest. There remains also that path which God has opened to the soul for its return to Him. *Apologia pro fide mea ;* and if the essence of sincere intention has escaped in the attempt to formulate, I ask to be regarded at least as one who loves the highest so far as it has been conceived in his heart, and however words may fail. In the leading of this love we are brought to a plenary conviction that there is only one doctrine which matters in fine to that mystical experiment which produces the mystical science, and it is this—" that God is and that He recompenses those who seek Him out." Here is the root beneath of all the growth above ; but after what manner God is and what is the peculiar nature of the mystical relation to God, beyond that of seeker to object, so long as the search lasts, are other questions. They are points of debate on which the schools have originated ; but the quest goes on and the end is reached, out of the schools and in, whatever the findings thereon.

The fact that one is a Latin of his period, subscribing to all the councils and the last dogmas comprised by Vatican decrees does not prevent him from becoming " a mystic citizen of the Eternal Kingdom " : it is the state in which he is called and the path by which he goes up. I have loved Eckehart from the beginning, but the path of Ruysbroeck is also a way to God. The fact that another is of Canterbury, confessing his obedience to a Primate of all England, shall be assuredly his starting-point, and valid when the call has come. From such a beginning, and in the path which leads therefrom, I think that Traherne and others come to the gates of the city and beheld the Vision which is He. But because the time is long dead and gone when we can class the Christianity which we love, and in which we are rooted, as other than chief among several great faiths which rule in this world of ours, and because the time has gone by also when we could deny at our peril the reality of attainment except within a single circle of external religion, one bond of sacramental doctrine, the fact that a third is Hindu or Buddhist, holding to the Law of Karma and the age-long cycle of rebirths, shall not prevent him either. It follows that there is a path in the East for those who are called therein : it is recognised here and now, that it may be left out of consideration hereafter, by us who have received another vocation, being called in Christ, and by those also for whom these essays are written, because if they or any of them should receive a mandate, it will be from that which lies nearest, even at their own doors, and " that is best."

There remains now the second and last point of distinction belonging to the present essay. As I write, the time draws near the death of Christ, and that time will melt into the dawn of Easter. Remembering many mysteries of experience, we are called to realise in what sense, if any, our mystic scheme, as it is conceived and formulated here, may differ from official Christianity concerning the Personal Christ and the Christ-Spirit, while cleaving to all that is vital, to all that is of the essence therein. The concern, the dedication, the end for which we exist, and towards which we work and look, is the realisation of the Christ-Spirit within us—otherwise, Divine Life and the part of God in our nature. It is so called because the peculiar mode of realisation to which Christ is the witness is the highest and most catholic of all. It represents a great experiment which must be carried greatly to its term, and in comparison therewith the personality of Jesus of Nazareth is less important in our eyes than it is in the holy Churches. At the same time we do not reduce the personality, its actuality, its historic side, its accepted place and time, or the luminous body of symbolism which has grown up around it in Christendom.

The palmary mystical sacrament of the Church Catholic is that of the Holy Eucharist, in which the communicant receives Christ according to the body and blood of His manifestation here on earth. I believe that the time of His presence is held to be fifteen minutes, for which reason the Eucharist is not taken once and for all, like Baptism or Holy Orders, but is renewable at need daily, according to devotion and the state of grace in the soul. Now, the Church recites periodically the Divine maxim which tells us that God is within. The great commentators have said great things concerning it, and the great mystics of the West have known and declared some part of the mystery shadowed forth by the brief verbal formula; but in official circles, and by the faithful at large, there is little understanding of that which is expressed, and of that which is implied less. So also, by the Eucharistic hypothesis, the *corpus naturale et supernaturale* of Christ is received into the body of the communicant; but in most cases the realisation, if any, is only in the emotion of a vague will to believe. To receive Christ in this manner is one thing but to find the Christ within is an attainment of another order. He must be born and live and suffer and die and rise gloriously within us before the work of our redemption is fulfilled in each. Herein is the distinction between receiving and becoming, between gifts of grace and election to Divine Sonship.

So also, according to another symbolism of Christian mystical experience, Christ is the Spouse of the soul, and He is saluted as such in many mystical devotions: it is the teaching also of mystical theology in that part where doctrine dissolves into experience. It is, however, the personal Christ on the human side as the glorified Son of Mary, and it is submitted in all reverence that this is not what is to be understood at its highest of attainment in the Christ-Spirit, the attainment in each one of us of that Spirit in each, or its marriage with the soul-part, whereby all that is capable of redemption is redeemed in the personality of all. It is not the last end of Mysticism, because there are deeper states, but of that which remains beyond it can be said only that it is of the life dissolved with the Christ-part of us in God.

There is a hidden mind of the Church which knows of this high research and its endless term in the Mystery of Divine Being ; the waters of life have come to us from that source ; but they have no overt part in the consciousness of official Sanctuaries or in the sacramental system dispensed thereby. On the other hand, the sequence of mystical symbolism which formulates Divine experience in the great literature of the quest is even as a single sacrament which exists only to communicate the graces of the second birth, the spiritual life that follows, the glory of mystical death, as an earnest of union realised, and thereafter that which is termed truly the resurrection of the soul in God. Herein is the path of attainment, whereby the soul enters into Christhood, or according to the alternative and wholly synonymous symbolism into the marriage-state in God. If only their words of power, which are also words of love, can so awaken us within that we may know and understand that which is to be received in these symbolisms, we shall find that many Christs have gone before us, that many will come after, and in a deeper sense than official Churches dream we shall acknowledge that Jesus of Nazareth is the first-begotten of the dead, Who has borne to us a faithful witness, on the evidence of which we may proceed also ourselves on the great journey, that we may see for ourselves and know.

It follows that we belong to the Churches in the root and spirit which is behind them ; their root is as our root ; it is no other spirit than ours which is within their form or letter ; and a day may come when the wardens of their holy temples may see the light that we carry and find that it has become again their own.

OBLATION AND SERVICE

As it is not every one who saith : Lord, Lord, that shall enter into the Kingdom of Heaven, so it is not every high allusion, whether in philosophy or poetry, which, for that reason, has any office in the mystic life. With an intellectual licence which by some minds might be held to exhaust the entire privilege of the poet and to infringe even on the ecclesiastical prerogative of the indulgence, Matthew Arnold gives permission in one of his poems to leave the Cross, if necessary, as we have left the idols of the Gentiles, but he counsels us to "guard the fire within." By putting to heart this recommendation, or its more popular substitutes and analogies, as a kind of golden rule in conduct, many people of to-day and of days and years behind it have contrived to remain apart, "holding no form of creed," and perhaps contemplating all with a tolerance which is not invariably unmingled with impatience.

A certain looseness and indetermination of culture has increased our capacity for discerning superficial analogies to which no great consequence attaches, and by which we are assisted, it may be even disposed, to miss the actual and vital relations. We "sit and play with similes," which is pleasant and easy : in current thought, in books, in Nature, and in so much of the things of Grace as we may be prepared to acknowledge, we recognise with fatal facility suggestions almost innumerable, but the real consanguinities are too deep for us. We do not see, for example, that to "guard the fire within" is a direction that does not differ essentially from some old ordinances which have claimed, and have been allowed in the past, a more sacred authorisation than his who has told us, at some far away distance, how "The Master sat upon the mount and taught." As a guide of conduct, it is not more valid or wholesome than that which would persuade us to let our light so shine before men that they may glorify the source of all light.

Moreover, the " new commandment " which Matthew Arnold has given us may appear on reflection to lack one saving quality which belongs to the older ordination ; it does not involve that passage from subject to object which is necessary for man in the measure of his ordinary stature, if only to shew him that he does not stand alone—either in his salvation or his loss. It is true that there are certain states of consciousness which have been descried by highest theosophy wherein there is no such passage ; it is true that they are very high states ; and it is true further that man, when he has reached them, does, in respect of humanity, appear to stand alone. He is neither under the old nor under the new law, but is in the freedom of another rule, about which it has not entered into the heart of normal man to conceive. These states are, however, outside the field intended to be covered by the recommendation of Matthew Arnold, which is a recipe for enabling a cultured person to rescue from the shipwreck of his faith a certain salvage, on the proceeds of which he may subsist without being actually starved or frozen to death. Failing this,

> Each will have one anguish—his own soul
> Which perishes of cold.

It is not, therefore, a recipe for the benefit of man in the heights, but for man in his diurnal environment, with a certain example to set and a certain duty of transmission on the intellectual side to his children. As a rule of life, the older instruction is the better, because it provides what is here called the passage from subject to object ; it directs us to guard the fire within, that the light of it may shine before men. It will continue to be chosen in preference by those who believe that among the first intentions of personal goodness is the design of being good to others. It embodies the reasonable altruism which is the proper corrective of the impassioned and hysterical self-sacrifice, for the sake of self-sacrifice, which is preached by some devotees, and even practised occasionally, in spite of the law and the order.

To these the poet's injunction has, of course, never been commended, and its suggested alternative may not have fared much better, because, in place of flame and perfervour, it is moderate and sweetly reasonable, and because, like Matthew Arnold, it implies that the first consideration is to save one's own soul alive. That of his brother, Arnold tells us, no man is able to save, which at once divorces altruism from the most momentous field of its activity and disqualifies its apology in chief.

This point connects with the subject in hand more closely than may appear on a first reference. Arnold's precept concerning the inward guardianship is imperfect precisely because it rests upon this his other dogma, against which the true order, the universal experiences and the right analogies cry out with one voice. Not only is man continually saving both the souls and the bodies of his brethren ; not only is all rule of manifest goodness and loving kindness grounded on this fact, but even that extreme view of the subject which is embodied in the idea of vicarious atonement has the whole creation for its witness. That is to say, the entire system of animate nature is founded on the vicarious sacrifice of one to another and of all to all. It is only in the human kingdom and in those kingdoms which are above it that this involuntary and inevitable renunciation becomes an expiation, an atonement, a willing sacrifice, an intent of union with the cosmic law and order.

It should be remembered, however, that if man must make an offering of himself, it is not less essential that he must not throw himself away. If in the last resource he loses his life for others, it is in order that he may find his life, not that it may be wasted. It is a question not of suicide but of service, and the highest quality of this service, like other institutes of universal chivalry, is not without an honourable and scrupulous regard for the consideration and dignity of him who offers it. It is in his own person, as a fact, that the service and the sacrifice must first begin, lest it should become of no account. Before a man can do real good in the world he must have learned the great secret of his own healing. That is a very good maxim which says : " Be the eye of the blind, and the arm of the poor, and the stick of the aged, and God shall give you a master-key to the life of man." But the final object after all is the possession of the key; the race is not entirely without some consideration of the crown; the legendary hero may cast himself all armed into the abyss, but he has at least the design of filling it. Those who argue otherwise overshoot their mark because they outstep their measure.

It follows therefore that a man's first concern is with himself. We may express it how we will; we may call it the care for our own salvation, or the sacrifice of ourselves to ourselves for the purgation of our coarser part, but in either case we must be enkindled before we can give light. Therefore Arnold's mandate is a right and just one, and it is eternally just and right, but it falls short of perfection because it falls short of fruition, and is one side only of the equation of human life, which is found more perfectly in the older precept, contained in a threefold division—(1) that the light must shine from within us; (2) that it must shine before men, that they also may shine in their turn; and (3) that the final consideration is neither the glory of the one nor the service of the other, but is ostensibly extrinsic and separate; the third act of the mystery is transferred outside of humanity, to that region where the passage from subject to object becomes suspended because it is the repose of both. And herein lies the secret of all high ruling in conduct and the ultimate redemption of ethics, by the transfer of the final consideration, which lies no longer either between man and himself or between man and man, but between universal humanity, under all aspects of individualism and solidarity, and that which is the term of all, as it is also the source of all.

In these reflections, somewhat solicitously sustained, a few matters have been suggested which do not lie otherwise openly on the surface of the contrasted maxims of conduct, at least for those who think lightly, whence it may occur to some on reflection that one or two old teachings suffer rather than gain by their later restatements, and that while it is possible to extend the interpretations, it is not always wise to vary the text of the discourses. This is only another way of saying what perhaps can be stated more obviously, if this is indeed an advantage, namely, that we are scarcely in need of new maxims of conduct within the conventional limits any more than of new doctrines, but rather of a better understanding of old doctrines and maxims. And this understanding lies to some extent, though not fully or exactly, outside the logical processes, entering through other avenues by which the catholic life of transcendent Nature is communicated to the mind as the first working of that law of integration in virtue whereof the soul of man, after many morganatic marriages, enters at last into the royal union.

There remains a further question to open the heart of this subject, and if in the last resource it must be answered by each for himself, there is a response in the high places which is catholic and obtains for all who go up the Mountain of the Lord. What is this fire within which we are called upon to guard by the poet ? What is that light which the earlier and higher counsel bids us lift up—as if from within ourselves—in order that it may shine before men ? They may answer well enough in the lower ranges to the light of conduct, the torch of good example and the " virtuous thought " of Spenser, all that which in an ordinary sense might be counted by St. Paul to " the praise of them that do well," for there is an ethical and social standard which is presupposed at the foot of the Mountain in those who would ascend to the summit. And this is well, God knows, for the many who abide on the spiritual plains, by their pleasant streams or in quiet glades and glens. But the state of virtuous thought which testifies concerning itself in its own silence unawares, and which carries its own warrants, led up for Spenser to something which he affirms indeed, but does not attempt to expound. He calls it " glorious great intent," which brings forth an " eternal brood," as if a light shining in very truth before the face of the whole world. Who shall say what it signified to him, the immortal poet in his rapture ? But that which it means to the mystics, wheresoever dispersed through the paths of the great religions, is and can be one thing only. It is the glory of the Inward Presence, and this also is the light which, although it is meant to shine before men and can in no wise help shining when it dwells in the heart of man, is of no human kindling. It is sought, it is found within, but it is there and is not made. It is brought forth, however, in the leading of mystical life, as if a certain lamp of the Sanctuary were carried to the Western door and displayed on the Church steps in the darkness, or the Sacred Host in the monstrance above the tabernacle were borne through the streets in procession, the Supreme Mystery of Faith displayed before the eyes of all for recognition and worship in the world. I testify that the light of the Presence, raised up by realisation in the soul from a state of immanence to the state of manifestation, is the only light of the world; that the inward maintenance of the Presence is the guarding of the fire within; and that when it shines before men—I have said that it cannot help shining—all those who have eyes to see will glorify the Father Who is in Heaven.

CONSECRATIONS OF LIFE AND THOUGHT

As it is necessary in the last resource to distinguish between the elections and dedications of the mystic life and that which has been termed conventionally an interest in the claims of Mysticism, or a predilection towards the literature of the mystics ; and as between the two classes represented by these leanings there is that other and very large class with whom the spirit is weak but willing and the world strong ; it seems desirable to say something which will not be set aside by those who receiving the call have obeyed it, and which yet may assist others who have turned in their hearts towards Zion, at however great a distance. It must be admitted, I suppose, that there are people for whom a conception of the mystic life is more hopeless than speaking with tongues ; they might less improbably raise the dead than enter themselves into life. They are not of necessity ignorant or even unintellectual ; they may fill high offices in their particular sphere, but the world is closed within them more utterly than is the world without to one who is congenitally blind. Accepting them at their best, mentally and otherwise, they are rather in the position of the man who has become rich without the personal qualifications to support it. We know that large revenues may gild artificially and externally, but we know also that the peasant is still a peasant, and that the " Carynthian boor " of Goldsmith has no place in the king's palace. These also have otherwise their uses, as those have to whom the avenues of spiritual perception are sealed by a limitation of their nature. Experience, I think, teaches that the last class are not so large as the initial lessons of association would seem to indicate, while there are certainly many who late in life may begin to learn the alphabet, and this is good, though they may never be able to write.

What is much more important is that the weakness of the will, already mentioned, though it signifies a clear incapacity, does not in any sense mean absence of all faculty. It is certainly incapacity which finds the world too strong for all the high intention : that environment is strong enough and it is also insistent enough, but it is just because of the world that the soul is able to attain. The city is not less Jerusalem because the hills stand round it, and, when all has been said, the world is not so much our hindrance as a material to be adapted for our ends ; it is indeed no hindrance at all in the sense that is usually attributed thereunto. But let us take it for all that it is worth, making every concession that is needful to excuse the disabilities of weakness, and let us acknowledge also that there are impediments which seem outside what is understood by the world, as, for example, that there are barriers to sanctity which arise out of the notions of sanctity. By this means we may come into contact at once with the middle class which I have mentioned —that class which confesses to a peculiar attraction towards the inward life—which acknowledges within it a certain quality of desire, which is in part at least conscious of a faculty—if only in vestige—designed for ministration thereto. Such persons fail, however, in the attainment of any mystic term, even of the intellectual order, and there are two reasons—firstly, because they meet the difficulties of environment more than half way ; and secondly, because they regard themselves as constitutionally unable to lead that kind of life which alone is supposed to give knowledge of mystic doctrine, that is to say, a vital and personal knowledge as distinct from a literary conversance or a simple persuasion of mind.

Now, without speaking dogmatically upon a point which is mystically far too important for any new views to be tolerated lightly, it is possible to offer a simple leading which may be helpful to minds of this habit. It is possible, in the first place, to say something which, though it is not the keynote of the present paper, may lead up to the keynote. Within the sanctuary of the Latin Church, during sacrificial celebration, there is, or may be, in addition to the celebrant in chief, a considerable concourse of inferior ministers, some of whom perform an extremely unimportant part, yet each of them fulfils a function to him assigned, and all are necessary for the complete development of the sacred pageant. The office of the Crucifer or Acolyte is generically distinct from that of the High Priest, but both enter into the public ministry, and, although it is in every respect a perilous quotation, we may remember in this sense that "they also serve who only stand and wait." The peasant torch-bearer who appears at the consecration and departs at the *benedictus qui venit*, supposing him to be devout and recollected, is serving God at His altar even as the Cardinal Archbishop or the Pope himself, and this because each in his own degree is taking his part in that sphere of ecclesiastical duty to which it has pleased God to call him. There would be no office for the Sacristan if there were no priestly office, but the Sacristan is necessary to the Priest.

So in the life of the mystic, and in the interior service which constitutes mystic life, there are duties of order and degree; and even as it is a normal practice in the Latin Church for laymen to serve in the sanctuary, so within the mystic chancel it is not needful that all who are called to reception shall become epopts of the mystery, or even in this life consciously on the road to the realised mystic term. There are consecrations of life and thought, an interior attitude, a direction of spiritual aspiration, an obedience to spiritual promptings, which are essential to every mystic; but by these a man may be vitalised and yet may live in the world, not in any sense isolated, not here and now expecting Divine Union; and so living, from the highest mystic standpoint, he may be doing a good and that his proper work, not for himself alone but for many who are around him. If anyone is therefore called by some inherent desire to look towards Zion of the Blessed, he has no need to hesitate because, for any reason, he may appear otherwise prohibited from the greater things.

If there were not in the intellectual attitude, already named, even in the simple and perhaps unspecialised interest, a reward in itself, for example such a reward as the pupil in a school of philosophy finds in his scheme of the universe, there is perhaps no need to say that there would be no phase of mystic life on this planet at all. The illumination which follows from accepted mystical doctrine and the consciousness of the heights which are opened out to aspiration can be enjoyed, according to the measure of their interior stature, by many men and women who have nothing within them which would respond to the great counsels of mystical perfection.

But in the second place, there is what has been termed above an intellectual difficulty which hinders certain people. In the old literature of Christian sanctity, and in some at least of its latest developments, they find the notion of spiritual progress connected with an advanced type of asceticism, by which alone the neophyte,

> His soul well-knit and all his battles won,
> Mounts, and that hardly, to eternal life.

But the whole spirit of the age has long since agreed to set aside asceticism—especially in its extreme degrees—as one of the errors of religious enthusiasm ; and though in a matter of this kind a concession to the spirit of the age carries with it a suggestion of unwisdom, there is yet sufficient efficacy in the sentiment to command sincere assent. I mean to say that man has come, and correctly on the whole, to see that it is not a religious act to practise barbarism on his body, and that he is not approximating towards the Divine by despising, hating and applying gross epithets to the physical environment with which he has been endowed in his exile. That environment is the temple of a Holy Presence and not the prison of a malefactor ; but, supposing it to be the prison of a malefactor, there does not seem a reasonable purpose in destroying or even defacing the house of the criminal.

The reason is that the changes which are begun from without and the measures which have their province externally are of comparatively little account in the processes of the inward school, for they begin at the wrong side of the subject. The soul which is seeking its native term of attainment and the fulfilment of that destiny to which from all time the soul alone has been called, has already its proper path assigned to it, and will in its own advancement carry with it into necessary reconstruction whatever yokes belong to it at this present time. If the body is the cross of the soul, that is an old truth which long ago told us to carry the cross willingly, that in the end it may carry us. It is by such an ascent of Calvary, and so alone, that the cross, whatever it is, becomes ultimately glorified.

There is no doubt that every man who is dedicated to the mystic life must, as a part of that dedication, forsake what is termed sin, though he will stand to be guided by other specific motives than those which obtain commonly in the simple conduct of life. There is also no doubt that this abandonment signifies, in a certain restricted sense, the life of the ascetic; but here the term is understood rationally and not in any instituted sense. The eradication of evil from our nature can never be a painless process, except when the House of the Lord has utterly eaten us up; but after all it is an operation which has its roots in our interior side, and is not to be confused with such asceticism of the external class as was practised, for example, by Marianna of Geso, whose life has been described as "nothing but one unbroken series of the most startling austerities, which make us shudder at the inventive cruelty which they display." The dispensation of this kind of asceticism as an aid to religious progress seems to be passing away even within the precincts of the Latin Church, and if it contributed once in the soul's development towards the mystic end, that time too, it may be hoped, has also gone by.

This is not to say therefore, or at least in a decisive manner, that the process has never been useful in the past, or that one should speak of it slightingly now if the period of its validity has elapsed. What is no longer necessary is regarded too commonly as having been always unreasonable.

In these as in the other ministries, we have to remember that the soul has entered into its rest not only by more than one path but by all paths that are open, including many byways and some particular roads which at first sight might look as if they led to destruction. We have further to remember, and this also in the past perhaps more than in these days, that the first matter on which the mystery of Christ was put to work in the world was largely an animal matter, and that the religious animal, although he has been brought under the rule, is, in spite of that rule—and sometimes almost because of it—superstitious, dogmatic, sectarian, intolerant, persecuting. When man, so limited, set out after the Divine Union, he felt called to avenge terribly the inadequacies of his own nature before he could expect to make progress.

There is nothing about or within us to suggest that we are eradicating the animal man, but in a measure we are perhaps civilising him, and we have reached that point at least when it may be allowed that the race more generally has travelled some little distance nearer to the Divine by the mediation of kindness and charity, together with all the other softening influences of our increasing complexity of life. If there was ever therefore an ascetic rule of Mysticism which could not then be abrogated, we can regard it now as at least a mitigated rule, much as the High Grades of Masonry having once established the Rite of the Strict Observance, at some later day are said to have modified it by establishing a Lax Observance. If we can take as our exemplars such instances as Jacob Böhme and Saint-Martin, we know that they were neither of them ascetics in the ordinary sense of the word, and yet both were seers who advanced a considerable distance in the higher knowledge of Divine things and in complete dedication thereto. I do not mean that they were heralds of a new and milder dispensation, but they are notable instances of their time.

I should like, if it were possible, to add that the existing interest in the higher aspects even of official religion, the progress made by many people now living in the world, above all, the desire after Divine Union which is found occasionally in quarters antecedently unlikely, are all significant that man is coming closer to God ; that the goal is nearer, the way simpler ; and that we are passing, moreover, into the living recognition of Divine Unity. But there is nothing so easy to misread as such surface signs of the times, and we must be content rather with appreciating at their proper value those traces of awakening and quickening which it is possible to descry around us. There is in any case no easy way to perfection, but there is one which can be cleared of unnecessary difficulties, to encourage which hope is not to countenance laxity, to make willing evil less impossible for the mystic, or to condone the life of luxury, even the life of ease. The perfect way must be ever a *Via Dolorosa* to the material part of our nature ; but as the term is to be raised with Christ, any crucifixion by the way is transitory, and in the last resource it is perhaps of the sacramental kind rather than a literal passion.

The beginning of the inward life is such a concern with spiritual things that what is at first performed by the work of applied attention—as in the study of any given subject—becomes a habit of the mind. In the growth of this habit an interior condition is reached, of which it can be affirmed validly that the thought of God and of Divine Things is implied always when it is not expressed within us. This is dedication of the mind, which connotes the heart's dedication, and the practical duty therein is that of maintaining the high honour of the work in all the ways of life. Herein is the faith of dedication, and the keeping of this faith becomes itself a habit. As in the code of the world, the relations and affairs of man, those to whom honourable action is, so to speak, native do not have to be reminding themselves and watching over their deeds incessantly lest suddenly they should decline from honour, so it comes about on a time that those in this faith of dedication are ever in the state of honour towards God and His inward light. It must not be understood that there are no declensions whatever, because the flesh is weak, or that temptation ceases, but the will towards evil is reduced to a vanishing point. There is also a stage when the desire after God has broken up all the barriers and has burnt all the traps and snares which encompass our daily ways ; but we are far on the path then, while I am speaking now of initial states and things which lead up to proficiency. That is reached, I think, when in the midst of all its activity—and it may be very active indeed, in and without the world—our life has become a contemplation, and we know of the Presence within. Beyond this there are deeper and yet deeper stages, of which something must be said hereafter.

By those who stand on the threshold it must be realised that the mystic path is followed in a work of the will, which is applied in one direction only, being that of conformity with Divine Will.

If it be asked what is the test of knowledge concerning Divine Will, there is one answer only, namely, that it becomes known in love. Conformity is a work of love. The business of the path at its beginning makes no demand on knowledge, reposing upon a single postulate, that the soul can find God if the soul seeks, with undivided purpose turned thereto. We may call it, if we please, a working hypothesis, and in the naked simplicity of the statement it will be found that it does work. No one desiring to do the Will of the Eternal shall fail to find a means or shall abide for a period in doubt as to what the Will is. This is on the faith of the records, with no appeal therefrom.

It is to be held that this is enough, because it is the marrow of the whole alchemy of the path, from the state of neophyte even to that of epopt. But it is to be understood that the quest is within, for the institution of those relations between God and the soul which unfold the Divine Purpose, in harmony with that which is human, to fulfil the work of the union. But seeing that we are established now in the order of manifested things, the work within cannot be followed apart from a work without, since we do not stand alone, and the God Who abides is also He Who encompasses. The mission is not to ourselves merely but to all about us, and it is so only that we shall truly find ourselves or the Spirit within.

We have been told that the whole creation " groaneth and travaileth," awaiting the " manifestation of the Sons of God." It is the realisation within and the manifestation without of our own Divine Son which is the purpose of mystic life. For this we go up unto the Altar of God and for this, as indeed thereby, we enter into the Joy of the Spirit, when the hidden and empty places of the soul are filled with its Divine Presence. We shall be then as channels of grace through which the Divine Will may flow over the will of others, that the heart may be changed in its substance. If our light shines in this true sense of light before man upon such an Altar of Burnt Offerings in the great temple of the universe, it may happen that they also shall turn, as from many ways of misdirection, to glorify their Father Who is in Heaven, and not only as those who in His light have beheld light but in His glory have become glory.

Now, it is said in fine that "there remaineth a rest for the people of God," and the disciple of this dual path shall ever in a most hidden temple, which no man knoweth save he who has entered therein, repose in the Presence that is He and renew the life therein, because of the perfect union.

THE HIGHER UNDERSTANDING

TRUE Mysticism cannot be said to possess in reality any controversial side, seeing that the great men of all ages on the things which are of all the greatest have borne the same witness, so that there is the least possible appeal from East to West, as from authority to counter-authority. In speaking therefore throughout of Christian Mysticism, as distinguished from other mysteries of the inward life, it must be remembered that we are not proposing a diversity either in the root-matter or the term attained, because term and root are the same. This notwithstanding, since I am intending to shew forth some part of the valid science which is in Christ, I must not stultify my convictions by recourse to any spurious universalism and identify the great masters as if they were indeed but one master, or the sanctuaries as if they were a single holy place. It is known in fine that they may lead into one only state, yet seeing that the masters are many it must be said that there are various and higher grades; that there is also one paramount Captain of our Salvation, though the legions have other leaders; and that as regards external and official sanctuaries there is no Lamp of any Eastern Temple which is like the Lamp of the Church of Christ. The thesis as thus formulated arises from the old axiom that " simplicity is the seal of Nature and Art ": it is especially the seal of Grace and Divine Life. The main epochs of the manifested Christhood were Birth, Life, Death, Resurrection and Ascension, which are also epochs in the story of every soul on its return to God, and there is no simpler delineation anywhere in records of attainment. Hereof is the Way in Christ and an elemental path of sacrament unfolded in all clearness. Yet the end is reached by those who delineate its epochs in other manners of symbolism, and this is the ground of union between all aspects of the Great

Work everywhere. The keynote is always union and the end is always God.

Now, it has been put forward at various but comparatively recent times, and under more than one form, that the keynote of Christian Mysticism—obviously from an intellectual standpoint—is to be sought in a doctrine of interpretation, understood, on the one hand, as a faculty of insight which claims to discern the secret law that underlies the mystery of being and, on the other, the secret meaning which subtends the written word of sacred literature. In modern developments it is concerned more particularly with the second of these divisions, but there is an admixture of both.

It is not on the surface, or as thus formulated crudely, a very wise or acceptable suggestion, seeing that all Mysticism, Christian or not, is a science of life and is neither a philosophical research as such nor the analysis of documents. At the same time it does connote, as we have seen, at least from my own standpoint, an interior mode of understanding doctrine and sacrament from which it follows that interpretation is or may be a light upon Christian sacred literature and the external science of faith. They call to be regarded from this standpoint, but on the understanding that the office in its exercise is a side issue of mystical experience and that it is one of personal judgment in the absence of an agreed and therefore authorised method.

Once—it is now long ago—an utterance of Matthew Arnold put the position of his period in a way which appealed at the period concerning Christianity in general. He said : " At the present moment there are two things about the Christian Religion which must be obvious to every percipient person—one, that men cannot do without it ; the other, that they cannot do with it as it is." In so far as the position has changed, it has changed only by the occasional recognition of another form of understanding, which is in fact the conditional and sometimes dogmatic substitution of a mystical construction for that of liberal theology. The kind of understanding may be new but the principle itself is old, alike in Israel and Christendom. The literal problems are the same and their difficulties are otherwise the same, under whatever reserves we speak of their proper and final value. If it happens

D

that a few of the old are removed from time to time their place is taken by the new. We shall see shortly that Arnold's statement obtains not only in the original sphere of its application, namely, in connection with external Christianity, but in other fields, and a little thought must make evident that much of it would apply not only to doctrine as it is understood by the official Churches, but also to views which find expression, almost on every side, in much of the current and popular teaching which passes as mystic literature, notwithstanding the change which I have mentioned.

To say this is to modify largely the application to that literature of the keynote characteristic which has been affirmed regarding the science itself, and it must be recognised that the ascription, though it contains a truth, has been advanced so far in considerable confusion of mind. We must move therefore with considerable care on our own part, if we would avoid several pitfalls. In the first place, the older voice of mystic thought, in so far as literature and written teaching are concerned, is by no means a voice of interpretation, while the modern schools in which that voice is heard appear, consciously or otherwise, to be setting aside by one rule not only the official Churches but the masters of inward life. Those who have recourse to the older mystics for hypermathematical formulæ of Trinity in Unity or the hyperphysics of virginal conception will not find what they want, as they are knocking at a gate behind which these difficulties have dissolved, or at least have passed out of view. Secondly, it will be found that the records of modern mystic schools—from the eighteenth century onward—call for interpretation quite as much as this is, by the hypothesis, required for our assistance in respect of the sacred scriptures.

Let us recognise therefore in fuller illustration of Matthew Arnold's dictum, that it is found difficult now, as in his day, to " do with " the legend of the fall of man, or the history of the garden and the apple, as these things are inscribed upon the cortex of Genesis ; it is similarly difficult to " do with " the picture of the new Jerusalem, a ready-made city coming down four-square out of heaven, as it is understood literally in the last splendour of the Apocalyptic Vision. Between the covers of that great Book of the Mysteries which begins and ends thus, there is much more that man can scarcely " do with," as he is now posed for our consideration, though he has been taught it in the literal sense for nineteen centuries. The Church which is called of Christ has administered it bodily, as the angel administered the book to St. John the Evangelist, and though it may have been sweet in the mouth for a time, since there is a certain sweetness even in the husk of Christianity, yet in the belly of humanity it has been bitter, because the body of the Bible, like the body of Christ, does not, in the last resource, provide essential sustenance for our interior nature, since that is not of the flesh but the spirit.

Now, the office of mystic interpretation should be, on its own hypothesis, to shew that, beneath the surface, there is another and higher understanding in the annunciation of these mysteries, because it is impossible to advance that the external side of such doctrine does not require the light of a fuller understanding. The recognition of this necessity, if not so old as the written word itself, has been among us from time immemorial. So far as the Old Testament is concerned, it is at least as old in Israel as any date to which we may refer the Jewish literature of the Christian era, which literature, from the ZOHAR downwards, not to speak of the TALMUD and the general storehouse of MIDRASHIM, is concerned with nothing else.

But the luminous body of Christian mystic literature on the doctrinal side enters into the same category as the sacred scriptures themselves. With that also in its external presentation man will do scarcely at this day. The student who determines to approach it for the first time is often apt to suppose that he will enter forthwith into some full light of a higher theology, but he finds only a similar cloud on the sanctuary. In its doctrinal parts the surface difficulties of the mystic treasury are precisely those of authorised dogmatic theology, possessing, in fact, every intellectual hindrance which attaches thereto, as well as a few other barriers which may be held peculiar to itself.

This is the position which confronts us, as an answer to any supposition that the Christian mystics were possessors of a deeper doctrinal wisdom.

One is met at the outset therefore by the fact that the old masters maintain, as we have seen, in those of their books which have come down to us, those very dogmas for which many serious minds are urgently desiring interpretation. Dionysius the Areopagite teaches them, though there is something of Gnostic involution in his estimate of the celestial hierarchies. They were taught by St. Thomas, though he has filled a folio with avowed mystical theology. Every one cites Bonaventure and his ITINERARY OF THE MIND'S JOURNEY IN GOD as a notable manual of the life within, but he also teaches them. Eckehart and Tauler and Molinos all taught them, and if in some things they have been charged with heresy, it is not because they disagreed with any central doctrine, while their heresies are not only of no account as to vital consequence but are largely matters of imputation. It is certain that for them the Word of Life was held within the circle of knowledge set forth by that school to which they belonged personally. They do not offer it with an explanatory subsurface sense ; they do not in their accounts of spiritual progress give any indication of a period when the doctrines will be suspended or substituted, or even subjected to a process of transmutation through the working of some canon of criticism provided by inward experience.

If we turn from the mystics of the Latin Church to such an example of the later schools as Jacob Böhme, there, in like manner, the same characteristics meet us, the same construction precisely of admitted doctrine, including things which it is now almost agreed to hold as intellectual scandals. Certain mystic views, for instance, in respect of everlasting punishment, will come through these channels with an additional force of repulsion because the student has expected another quality of light than that which is diffused from the gates of hell. It is not therefore to the literature itself that we must refer for any canons of interpretation, and this must be made quite plain, lest postulants and neophytes should have recourse for the issues of interpretation to those who, at least on the surface, do not in their sense interpret at all. That which the mystics give us is the annals of experience in the life of sanctity. Is it therefore only the novices who require interpretation, not the enlightened men of old who had entered into direct knowledge, suffusing the old forms, and had, of all artists, the least reason to quarrel with their tools ? As to these, did they know and were they silent ?

It is no part of my concern to affirm or disclaim any express pretence of sympathy with current strictures on doctrine. The actuating spirit throughout may be often that which suffered the displeasure of St. Paul when he reproached those who did not discern the Body of the Lord. The process of selection in dogma is above all the very last which leads into truth. The real difficulties are not the current difficulties ; though as much, in the final resource, can be said perhaps of those who have mismanaged the symbolism as of those who think to improve it by reducing the numerical proportion. Moreover, the external aspect or outward body of doctrine is proportionately more important as any mode of transliteral interpretation is deeper and rings more truly. It is desirable and needful therefore to preserve the veils of that faith which was once delivered to the saints, remembering always that common difficulties of doubt are the defects of untrained minds and the stumblings of mere children.

Having found that the old mystics were at need content with what they had, the fact does not cancel the present demand for inward understanding, because there are many awakenings in those days, and the morning redness never looks precisely the same to different eyes. There were great saints to whom the unity of the Trinity constituted an intellectual problem which to us is now scarcely conceivable, and they had *ex hypothesi* special inward lights vouchsafed them. Some part of the raw material of sanctity at this day may be hindered not less genuinely by the doctrine of a virginal conception. The true way is neither to dissolve nor foreshorten, but, if it be possible, to increase experience by deep inward searching and to ensure direct ministry, which is the way of all the mystics. The mode of interpretation is not in any case to be regarded as a certain canon of criticism. It is, at its best in literature, an analogical manifestation of doctrine ; and if it does not sustain and increase the light of the doctrine, it is thereby made void.

It calls to be understood otherwise that the things which are of all truth and high above all others are attained outside of doctrine, yet from doctrine they do not differ, that is to say, in its symbolical reception. The first thing to recognise is that through many avenues God enters into the soul, though it is through those rarely which count for paths of progress before the face of the world. No statement ever went to the root of the matter as that utterance of Christ in the fourth Gospel— that " the Prince of this World cometh and in Me he hath not anything "—not even in natural goodness, not in commercial honour, not in any canon of integrity, not in qualified purity, not also in the promptings of natural love towards brethren. I do not mean that these things are under condemnation ; they are under all blessings of which they can receive the ministry, but until they are integrated in Christ they cannot have part in Him ; they do not count in the numerical formulæ of eternal life, for there is one minus sign against all. They have their proper course and direction, but being in the world they are of it, and being of it they are without God in the world. They enter into another heritage when the soul is called to Him in paths of sanctification and paths of inward grace.

It is not to be denied that the great teaching Churches, notwithstanding their accredited external odour of sanctity and their halo belonging to the traditional and historical past, are under an analogous category of limitation. The spirit of the world has inducted itself into the stalls and thrones of the Holy Places. There has been no sale of divine birthrights for the pottage which is offered in the markets of this visible kingdom ; but an obscure process of inoculation has gone on secretly through the centuries, and the spirit of the world is there. It does not, in any sense, follow that the Shekinah has departed, and yet there are other clouds on the sanctuary than those merely of official doctrine and its literal sense substituted for that of the spirit. It comes about therefore that the light which should be indubitable before men is now seen only through glasses and darkly.

Moreover, there is no transformation of outward doctrine and there is no inreading of sacred texts which of themselves will work on the soul or raise the veil of its sanctuary for the exposition of the Inward Presence. The Shekinah remains in the hiddenness while the spirit of the world dwells in the courts of our temple. It is only the life of the mystic which can reflect light on the doctrine; it is only the Christ within Who communicates the spirit of His gospel. Interpretations which are products of mental skill and subtlety are from the brain rather than the soul of man, while those which originate through psychic gifts and inspirations outside the life of the union are like partial "intimations of immortality," reflected lights of suggestion amidst clouds and fantasia congregated about a closed palace of spiritual things.

These are insuperable difficulties which encompass the whole subject, but there are yet others which call for notice. There has not only been never a time when the inward sense of doctrine can be said to have had the Church for its mouthpiece, because it is the custodian only of the outward forms, but there has been never a time when it has had accredited schools for its keepers. Accredited or otherwise, there have been no such schools throughout the Christian centuries, but in place of them there have been individual voices, because—as I have said—hermeneutics of this kind are of necessity the outcome of private illumination, personal inspiration, independent mental searching. This is at their best and highest, with Swedenborg and Böhme standing in the first rank. But at their lowest they are reveries and outpourings of emotional hearts, and it may be that Maria d'Agreda could be named in this connection.

It is for this reason that in affirming the sacramental nature of official doctrine I have been careful not to indicate, except along broadest lines, that which may lie behind, lest I should be adding another revelation to the scores or hundreds which have accumulated in the past behind us. It follows that there are many exponents, but there is no science of interpretation respecting dogmatic theology or the text of Scripture, unless and until a soul in the state of the union is led into all truth by the Divine Witness within. Outside and awaiting this, the only valid canon is that which discerns in outward doctrine an analogy with the soul's experience in the states and stages of return to God, as we know of them in the long annals of mystic life. The doctrine concerning a Divine Birth in Bethlehem corresponds to the second birth of man into spiritual life; the Word is made flesh because our human nature is a temple of the Divine Presence. From such points does the great old story unfold through all its epochs.

I am not intending to suggest that those who are seekers for deep spiritual life have nothing to gain from the old hermeneutical writers or the old psychic seers, any more than I should dissuade them from exploring many great books which doctors of the Latin Church have left as a dower to all the ages after them. The commentaries of the ZOHAR on the five books of the PENTA-TEUCH shine with innumerable stars of strange light, though they are clouded by special embarrassments particular to secret doctrine put forth, in this case, under exceedingly cumbersome veils. The MYSTERIUM MAGNUM of Böhme, whom I have mentioned, is another theosophical commentary on part of the same text and, as it seems to me, of the same value, though there is little other likeness between them. There is even a sense in which Martines de Pasqually's LA RÉINTÉGRATION DES ÊTRES has rays of Divine Grace shining through its veil of fantasy, but there is no work of interpretation belonging to past or present which is tolerable, and much less valid, taken as a whole.

These things and others that are like them are part of our heritage, because we are the heirs of the ages in things mystic as in those of the outside world, and amidst all imperfections and fallacies, sometimes indeed because of them, they may hold up a lamp on our way. They will not tell us, like the solar mythologists, that Christ was only crucified in the starry heavens, but they may help us, even unawares, to realise that the secret of the Word of God is contained within the soul of man and how its proper understanding is to be sought there, seeing that it is part of the soul's experience.

The invitation of the mystic life is to come and see; the promise of the mystic life is that we shall attain to see. We shall find possibly, if we follow on this call, that some things which appeared to us and have been held as essential, and even central, look differently in the broader light; but at no stage shall we find that grace has made void either her sacraments or symbols. As it is not by the pruning of doctrine that we shall get to the truth which is of God, so it is not by the substitution of Z for X, more especially if Z, in the last resource, remains, like X, an unknown quantity. Interpretations of this order are not less unprofitable to the soul than the enlightenments of the higher criticism—which are understood to have failed. Very likely the lower criticism—if that means ordinary Church teaching—has failed after its own manner; but there are greater issues outside these alternatives.

The study of the stellar universe is not without its difficulties, but the broad universal laws under the aspect of which it manifests are not less in the possession of man as the reward for his ages of toil; and anyone who, because of those difficulties, should attempt to make a fresh start, ignoring all precedents of know-ledge, would have a vain labour for his only reward. This is one counsel of caution, and another is that the study of the spiritual life has, in like manner, proceeded for ages and ages; it has taken us a certain distance amidst many troubles and imper-fections; it will profit nothing to repudiate it and attempt to begin again—whether on the path of the union or in lesser ways of advancement. Furthermore, as we are grounded most easily in the knowledge of the outer world by incorporation in its schools of learning, though ultimately we must follow our own path if we would be truly men of science, so also in the old schools of spiritual life we shall make our best beginning, even if a time may come when we shall be called in ways that are almost beyond their ken. Moreover, the expert man of science does not leave his schools but contributes to their progress, and advancement in spiritual knowledge is not without its duty, if it can be fulfilled, to the source from which it originated. As it is necessary that here and now we should live in the world, yet desirable that we should not be of it, so also the proper place of most is in those Churches and institutions wherein Providence has installed us, though it is above all things desirable that, being in them, we should be of them in respect only of that which is highest within them, and should in our individual persons so sustain the light of spiritual life that it shall shine not only before men incorporated in the sodality of the natural world, but shall glorify the great confraternities which glorify the Father of Lights, looking for that time when the Orient from on high shall once again revisit them.

For the rest, it is the fuller light of the wider life which brings the gifts of interpretation—that light which comes into the heart as the result of real life—that gift by which we see under the Divine guidance, according to the measure of our reception, the spirit and the truth which are behind the symbolism of doctrine. It is this which I have chosen to term the Higher Understanding, accepting those words in the sense of wisdom. It is the inspiration and the leading which took the Kings of the East, who were called Magi, in the old luminous tradition, from their unknown land into that place of sacrament and mystery where the Kingdom of Heaven was manifested within space and time.

I conclude now as follows : (1) The secret law which underlies manifested being is that of the Presence of God. (2) There is an immanence of God in doctrine which draws its crude extremes into a perfect mode. (3) The sacred texts are great books of the world, and they unfold their deeper meanings in the light of His union. (4) There comes a time when mere dogma signifies no longer, when Ritual passes away, when holy books close up of themselves, for the peace of God in love has filled the soul with knowledge. (5) So are we drawn in fine within the Church behind the Church, and this is the Church of the Union.

THE SENSE OF THE INFINITE

AN undesigned divagation of reason sought in Victorian days to expound spiritual law, not by the illuminating analogies of law in the natural world, but by an extension from the lower to the higher. It is unnecessary to enter the path of the saint and the mystic before we can recognise that it is Grace which explains Nature, or that the mystery of man is understood only in its relation to the mystery of God. This notwithstanding, and because of the analogy of things, it is no unprofitable course which takes us at times from the reflection on that which is above to the study of that which is below. Thus, in the consideration of mystic life and doctrine it is wise here and there to reflect on our present environment, including that spirit of the age which is a persistent part thereof.

In pursuance of this purpose, let us realise that if the multiplication of interests can be shewn truly to increase the value of life, then it must be confessed that the last hundred years have added almost incalculably to the goodwill of human industry, regarded as a going concern. It has become almost trite to say that every department of activity is nowadays specialised highly in view of these interests, and tends to become further divided and subdivided. The minute philosopher and practitioner are called for more and more, and such higher mental abilities as are qualified for the profession of the specialist, in whatever department of effort, are not likely to lie idle or to go without their reward for many generations to come. Knowledge adds to the complexities of civilisation, and civilisation, as it increases the complexities, makes further demand upon knowledge. We have really very little need to ask, if we are concerned in such matters, what we shall do with the more intelligent and capable of our children, whether boys or girls. The answer might well be : Train them for specialists in that subject wherein you observe that their interest has been awakened, or along the lines of which it seems possible to awaken their interest. The departments are innumerable ; they are all wage-earning, and in many of them there are high rewards possible. Naturally, they lie outside the common fields of the educational curriculum ; they are not comprised in the classical or commercial course ; but education itself, as it rises to meet the demand for particular and extraordinary knowledge in given directions, will tend to become specialised, as it is indeed already tending.

Outside the practical advantage that knowledge means daily bread, there is one of a higher order, since it is purely intellectual. The field of discovery is always in front of the specialist, and he can scarcely fail to enter its promised land, by whatever path he travels. He is ever on the threshold of that unknown which is also for ever passing into the known and acquired. There is, however, unfortunately another side to the picture. The eye which looks in one direction only loses sight too often of the wide horizon ; the mind which works solely upon a single department of knowledge misses the greater issues ; and it is to this extent an open question whether the multiplication of concerns has added capital value to life, or has simply split up its investments, the return on which, moreover, must depend upon the concerns themselves, and these are too often depreciating securities, or short leases with heavy repairing covenants.

The speculative question, in any case, is not without importance at this day, when side by side with the specialisation of knowledge, of research and all industry, there are found also increasing convictions that man's highest interests do not lie in these directions. In the old times of the schoolmen there were those who argued from particulars to universals, following what was then called the Aristotelian method, and there were those who argued from universals to particulars, which they used to call the Platonic method. These two classes find their representatives even in the modern spirit of this twentieth century, and by taking a glance at the age as it is, it may be possible to forecast somewhat broadly and very roughly, bearing these two tendencies in mind, how matters are likely to stand in respect of them after the lapse of another hundred years.

There is a safe assumption at the outset, and this is that in those fields which are now licensed for research, the really gigantic tasks have been achieved already : in science, in literature, in art the statement holds equally. The possibilities of differentiation seem infinite, but the great things have been discovered, and, within limits, they have been said as well as done. To affirm this is not to put a bound upon human capacity, by which I mean in the known fields, but to define the unavoidable confines of the existing order of things. Once and for all— unless another flood could again reduce the race to the unit of a single family and all knowledge perish in the catastrophe— earth and sea have had their Christopher Columbus, and the new world cannot be discovered for a second time. An illustration is ready to our hand. The North Pole has been reached in our own day and generation, and those who achieved the task are counted among immortal adventurers ; but they cannot be held for a moment so great in discovery as Columbus, though the latter's task was infinitely more simple, because their success means less to the world. In a word, earth and sea have been so far reduced within the province of our knowledge that all further explorations are necessarily of secondary importance, and in two or three generations it seems reasonable to suppose that nothing worth speaking of will remain to be done in this direction ; yet the differentiation and specialisation of our knowledge in every corner of the world will, of course, go on indefinitely.

In all departments of science the same stage appears to have been reached, subject to one important qualification. The surface of the globe is so well known that there is no reason why it should not be explored ultimately from end to end, but along the broad tracks of the general sciences a certain great progress brings us to limits which the human mind cannot overstep. Biology, for example, is practically a creation of the nineteenth century, but all brilliant discoveries notwithstanding, it may yet prove that its irremovable landmarks have been established, its great attainments reached, and though enormous differentiation is still possible, and innumerable byways are still open to research, the mystery of life has been pursued in one sense to its source, to the point, that is to say, where we lose it, at that beginning for which we cannot account and which bids fair to remain unaccountable, because it is the Secret of the King and is therefore unsearchable, except in the Palace of the King.

In astronomical observation it may well seem perilous to take another instance, when a great new field has been laid open by the Hooker telescope, and when the interferometer is revealing the incredible dimensions of stars like Betelgeuse and Arcturus. But whether these momentous additions to the world of knowledge will help us towards a better theory of the stellar universe is that which remains to be seen. We have put back in a given direction but have not removed that term of investigation at which the word Impassable is written. The ultimate constitution of matter may still baffle us. However widely distinguished in themselves, there are other sciences which convey the same doubtful message. I will not speak of mathematics, while the Einstein theory is still being put to the test. In physiology, the barriers rise up everywhere. It is, however, in the domain of the chemist, if anywhere, and in the investigation of the latent and concealed forces of the universe, that the great hope of official invention lies.

That which is true of science seems true also of literature, of history, of religion—understood in their ordinary senses—and of the field of speculation which assumes to itself in a more particular manner the name of philosophy.

No questioning of culture would elicit an expectation of another Homer or of a second Shakespeare ; as literary monuments the scriptures of Jewry and Christendom are so great that a right instinct regards them—outside all theological considerations—as not only for their own age but all time, and this in such a manner that time is unlikely to produce their parallel. At this period in particular we are not in the day of great names, but in that of differentiation and specialisation of literary gifts, with a highly increased standard of average talent everywhere ; while round about the horizon of literature the old Titans loom impassable as those barriers which say to the biologist, the astronomer, the chemist: Thus far shalt thou go and no farther.

If other records of the past be challenged, it will be found that as little hope of great things to come is cherished by the historian, although the yearning eye may be turned beyond Lhassa of Thibet for treasures still unearthed, and the heart still hope for something, so far undemonstrable, in the land of the Pharaohs. The voices of the records are in all men's ears; they have been made to speak everywhere; but beyond this there is the dumbness of the great unknown, which looks so mournfully unknowable. There is, however, that lesser unknown, ever responding to research and mutiplying minute knowledge in the hands of particular investigation—like other specialities, highly important in its way, profoundly interesting, but offering nothing to the intellectual notion of greatness.

If we touch for the moment upon matters of religion in those aspects which lie outside the realm of its divine sanction, it becomes thus a part of history, a part of literature, a domain of criticism, a controversial region, a science of the higher laws of conduct, the principles and limits of which have been fixed long ago, leaving only departmental issues, but these innumerable, in which it is possible to create new epochs. Around the whole horizon of these issues, far above and beyond them, stand the giants which were on earth in those days, the great theologians, the great commentators, the great controversialists, and—may it be added respectfully?—the great saints of old, to compel reverence if they do not inspire obedience or engage assent, and to offer an overwhelming assurance that the force of soul can scarcely further go.

It would seem almost idle to mention a second time that arrogant word philosophy, because the mantle of this Elijah has not passed to later servants; but avoiding the enumeration of names, and admitting that important schools of thought have originated in the last two centuries, the highest tribunal of ultimate appeal can only confirm the judgment of the mere wayfaring man, that on all the great speculations the schools of thought change, but the problems remain, and that the root-questions are unanswered in those academies which dispense the admitted degrees.

It follows, therefore, that the concerns of the age seem fixed all along the normal lines for at least a century to come; that they will go on multiplying, and that discovery and expansion of knowledge will be incessant within these limits. It follows also that as in science, understood in its widest and most embracing sense, so in literature, the production will increase; that good books will multiply as the average of talent rises; but that the great sum of interest and real value does not stand towards appreciation, and it is questionable whether this outlook offers real consolation to the mind.

An inexpensive process for the extraction of radium so that it may be utilised for domestic purposes might be an immense convenience; the cure of cancer and consumption a great amelioration for a suffering section of humanity; the discovery of the bases of gold very interesting and possibly highly valuable, even if it upsets the currency; and since these few instances may be taken to stand for thousands, let it be asked: What next, Muse of Science, and what for the twenty-first century? Or, if nothing next, what then? So also, if Egypt permits her explorers to disinter still earlier dynasties; if other walled-up libraries lift up some corner of the veil which covers the mysteries of the East; if the remanents of an undreamed civilisation were found in Australasia; if another Gospel should be discovered; if the exact area of the circle no longer baffled mathematics; if some new motion might be distinguished in the solar system; if empirical psychology should establish some of the disputed points in mental philosophy; would it not still be true that "knowledge comes but wisdom lingers" and that the path of these particulars, these details, wonderful as they may be, is not the path which leads to the things that are universal, while it is those only in the last resource which lend value to life and can alone be added to the abiding heritage of man?

Now if this be so, the great question which arises is whether there is another way, for an answer to which, if indeed there be an answer possible, recourse must be had to the ground of those convictions mentioned previously, that man has other interests which are quite distinct from anything that is attained or attainable by the faculties of external observation. In the nature of things these convictions are not open to experimental demonstration by the way of physical science. They baffle experimental psychology in the same way that the ultimate nature of life baffles the biologist, but they exist as life exists, and they are older than the prophecies of Isaiah, the religious epics of India, or the Egyptian BOOK OF THE DEAD. They are precisely that element which constitutes the greatness of Plato in philosophy; of the fourth gospel, as it can be appraised by the literary sense; of Dante and Spenser in poetry; of St. Thomas in theology; of Jeremy Taylor in personal religion; of Francis Bacon at his highest, though essentially he was an experimental philosopher; and, despite the apparent jumble of this enumeration, of certain old books of knight-errantry and other mirrors of the romantic spirit. But if this element has found its expression thus diversely in literature, it is no less evident in Gothic architecture; in the early Italian masters; and in such "great tone poets" as Sebastian Bach.

The ground of the conviction must not be understood as religion in the conventional meaning of the word, and yet it can be defined only as the sense of the infinite. It is the deficiency of this sense which has taken greatness out of modern poetry and once at least reduced the modern novel to an involved study of character, of situation and of manners. It is the sense of this deficiency and the desire of this lost consciousness which have brought about the revival of romanticism in literature. It is the realisation of the truth that man does not live by bread alone and that for the same reason his mental nourishment does not or should not consist exclusively of facts; that he is not really better or worse for the discovery of a new star in the constellation *Lyra*, or for the household adaptation of radium; and that the prevention of cancer and consumption, though an enormous safeguard for his body, will not really console his heart.

But if the ground of this conviction, that there are better things possible than the providence of science can confer, is to be sought in the sense of the infinite, by the presence of which some men and women have been great in all ages and have left imperishable monuments, does it not seem to follow that there is a side of consciousness which calls for cultivation, and has been neglected amidst the rapid methods and specialisation of modern life ? Man in the last resource is that which he thinks ; he grows wicked by thinking evil, but if he thinks only that which is good, the good fills him entirely. And if amidst the multiplication around him of all those pressing yet lesser interests which make modern life so complex and so differentiated, he can learn how to detach himself occasionally and revert to the things which are simple and not differentiated ; if, in the crowded city, he can remember the great world ; if he can embrace the larger interests which are not of one age but of all time, will he not, amidst the full appreciation of all that science and research have effected in his temporal interest, and the full enjoyment of their utilitarian benefits, gain something also of that larger consciousness, that contact with things immeasurable, which gave us Plato and Dante ? There may be effected in this way a certain marriage between the interests which are universal and the interests which are particular, and seeing that thus early in the twentieth century the want of some such union is finding a voice everywhere, is written everywhere in our literature, our painting, our music, and finds a dumb expression even in our painful reproduction of Gothic architecture, it is not a rash forecast to dream that the twentieth century may accomplish it, and that art and thought and letters shall receive the gift of a new voice which they are certainly demanding.

These considerations might stand as irremovable prolegomena to any exposition of Mysticism. It should be remembered, by way of conclusion, that the investments to which I have referred are nearly all subject to forfeiture because the only inalienable title-deeds are those which we can take into eternity ; that the exhausted greatness of discovery is only in respect of the outside world, bis avocations in which have left man still on the threshold of his soul, as at the gates of an untraversed realm ; that the things which remain over to say embrace the unrealised secrets which are within ; that it is well to know earth and sea, because when we have exhausted these there remains that hidden cosmos wherein is the rest for the people of God ; that the disillusion of Alexander was owing to a limited horizon ; that the mystery of life becomes simple in the mystery of God ; that astrology is probably a vain science, but as a matter of experimental research it is not perhaps more vain than the conventional study of the stars, the general history of which tends to justify the criterion of Edward Young that " the undevout astronomer is mad " ; and that a theory of the stellar universe does not ultimately matter at all.

Now, here are paradoxes intentionally, but they make it possible to add what is intended in all seriousness, namely, that we have learned a great deal of externals and having thereby multiplied our solicitudes as well as our material conveniences and sureties, it is opportune at length, if indeed it be also practicable, to take another way. One poet has recognised in all Nature a disguised humanity and has said further : " All that interests a man is man." But we look for another who will dare to tell us that all which interests a man ought to be God, because outside the Divine there are ultimately no interests for humanity, if that which we brought into the world should have at any time its part again in God.

In its proper understanding the sense of the infinite is the sense of God in the universe and of God in the soul of man. For however few among us, is it not possible now that there should be a greater and holier spiritualism in the cultus of this sense ? Whither it can lead those who explore the world within them the great precursors of the mystic quest remain in their records to testify, and reflected from their experience we are aware intellectually already of that which can be known at first-hand in experiment made with our lives, that the " part again in God," of which I have just spoken, is not of the world hereafter and another mode of being but of the world that is here and now.

LIFE AND DOCTRINE

IT has been advanced in Anglican apologetics (1) that the Christian Doctrine of the Holy and Undivided Trinity is of practical value at the present day; (2) that it is of intellectual value also, thus creating a somewhat fantastic distinction—as if for the purpose of a schedule—for these two are at best but contrasted aspects of a status which is one at the root; and (3) that the doctrine is of such kind as to warrant a presumption of its truth. By the indication that it is worth while, I take it to be meant that the doctrine offers to those who accept it—in a living sense of this term—some experience in realisation, that is to say, some extension of the inward knowledge which rewards the life of religion, or the path of holiness in the Lord; and this is the proper, as it is indeed the only test of truth in doctrine. Thus, and in every way, from outward to inward the appeal always moves. Heaven—so far as we can approach it now—is an idea of location transcendentalised to the ineffable degree; but such location is within, though we may pass through many strange outward places of worlds before we reach our term in this order.

The vital quality of Trinitarian Doctrine—if any—rests on its inherent capacity for translation into our consciousness, so that it can help us to the attainment by realisation of fuller union with God. The Persons of the Divine Trinity must be the mode in which our consciousness as Christians confesses to the experience of God, supposing that we reach experience, and this because our faith in Him testifies by its hypothesis to the postulate that He does not deceive His children, above all that He does not betray them by false experiences. Here is the assumption, and out of this the question of fact arises, it being understood obviously that I have no concern with simple mental assent, with doctrine accepted *pro forma* or with belief too tepid for the pains of doubt or challenge. Moreover, I speak as a mystic and address those only who confess to this designation, at least by a disposition of the mind. In what respect therefore does it signify to us as mystics whether the unity of God subsists in a Trinity of Persons ? If we are Christian mystics in any valid sense of the term it must signify something, if only in the intellectual order, because it was not until Christ manifested in flesh that a Doctrine of the Trinity was explicated, while according to the Catholic teaching of all the Churches that which manifested was the Second Person of the Divine Triad. Here it will be of course understood that the simple intellectual conception, even in the grade of sincerity, is not that which signifies but only the inward realisation.

I have put forward a canon of criticism by which all doctrines must be judged, and this is their capacity for ministration to the needs of the soul, so that the soul can advance through experience of life in God and shall thus walk not merely by simple faith but by sight also, which is the fruition thereof. Out of this criterion there arises the further and keener question whether Trinitarian Doctrine responds for us individually to such a test. We shall arrive at some conclusion on this subject by a considera- tion of the Doctrine itself from the standpoint which has been thus indicated. But in the first place it is necessary rather than desirable to reflect for a little on its analogues in religious and theosophical systems which are other than Christian.

Now, the religions which are called pagan have indubitably some broad analogies of Trinitarian Doctrine, but ingenuity has increased—as by artifice—the closeness of such likeness and once at least tended to present it in false terms of identity. The development of the critical faculty on the side of its sanity has done much to reduce these exaggerations, and it is now admitted by general consent that in order to avoid confusion it is a wise plan to set them aside altogether. The only really important collateral fact is the way in which a similar doctrine unfolded in Jewry during the period of the greater exile—otherwise, that of the Christian centuries—concurrently with and yet indepen- dently of its development in Christendom. It is an amazing growth—by its complications, its involutions and the grotesque- ness in its mode of formulation—yet I regard the result, intellectually speaking, as a considerable light of constructed theosophical doctrine and, at whatever distance, the only formulation with which Christian theology can suffer a moment's comparison. Its major defect is that which is inherent in its conception, namely, that it is devoid of any correspondence with the manifested Christ. And yet it was held so sincerely in the past to admit of and even to involve such a correspondence that for generations the Christian students of Kabalism regarded the development of its sole and own implicits as the one form of propaganda which might be possible with success in Israel.

The implicits of Trinitarian Doctrine are in the New Testament and all that which may be held to lie behind it; those of Jewry are in the Secret Doctrine, of which the Kabalah in its written form—very large as it is—seems to be a formulation only in part. Whether there was in any sense a common source from which both drew lies far outside the measures of these few words on a great subject; but the intellectual life of Christendom during the growth of dogma moved in strange paths and issued from strange clouds of darkness. Whether also any root-matter of the Secret Doctrine was indigenous in Jewry as a consequence of the captivity in Babylon, or whether it was a derivation from things antecedent and subsequent, remains an open question after generations of discussion. I may hold an opinion on this subject which is reflected from the schools wherein I have been nourished theosophically, but in the present place this must be set aside also—not that it is extrinsic to the issues but, like the antecedents of Christianity, it opens gates into the infinite, while this is a brief excursus and not a treatise at large. It remains that both systems ended by producing something *sui generis*. As regards the analogies between them, it must be understood that Christian apologists who have undertaken to shew that the Kabalah contains specific Christian doctrine in the specific Christian sense have carried their enthusiasm beyond the horizon descried by that literature : they have done exactly what might be expected at their period and under their circumstances ; they have given the particular meaning to a general and fluidic sense.

The doctrine, for example, of the threefold Divine Nature is assuredly in Kabalism, but after the Christian mode it is not

there at all : it is there after the mode of Kabalism, and so only.
How great the distance which intervenes will be appreciated by
anyone who has acquaintance with the Sephirotic system, as
it is found first of all in the ancient BOOK OF FORMATION and
as it is developed in the Zoharic books, not to speak of rabbinical
theosophists in the sixteenth and seventeenth centuries and all
their wilderness of commentaries. The original Sephirotic
system was a doctrine of the emanation of the universe, or—if
this be putting it too strongly—of the manifestation of universal
things externally. It contains no suggestion of a Trinity ; the
explanation of everything is by the ten Numerations, of which
the first is the Spirit of God, explicated as the Divine Name in
the forming and constitution of things. At a later period the
Numerations or SEPHIROTH were divided into Four Worlds : the
World of Deity, the Angelic World, the World of Formation and
the World of Action, or that of manifested and material things.
In some distributions of the SEPHIROTH among these Worlds,
a Divine Triad is postulated in the World of Deity, being God
in the transcendence, from Whom issue the Father and the Mother
and these together correspond to the first three Numerations.
The notion of a Divine Son answers to six lower SEPHIROTH,
whose Spouse is the tenth Numeration, the Kingdom of this
world—understood in its assumption by the Kingdom which
is above. It is also the Church of Israel, and, according to the
precarious speculation of certain Christian commentators, it is
the Holy Spirit, in which manner they carry the Kabalistic
system a still greater distance from the Christian idea of the
Trinity. A certain general analogy inheres, deeply imbedded,
and this will emerge as we proceed. At the moment it remains
only to add that as all things are in the mind, but at first by
way of root or vestige, so I do not doubt that some who looked
for Messias and spoke of the Spirit of God had, far away in the
past, an implicit of the Trinity among them. It is only another
way of saying that in such case the experience of sanctity had
brought some in the Church of Israel a certain distance towards
apprehension of the Mystery in God.

Recurring to Christian Trinitarian Doctrine, a true Key to
the position of mystics will be found in these words of

St. Augustine : " We say Three Persons, not as being satisfied with this expression, but because we must use some expression." In other language, all doctrines which are of truth in symbolism are part of the path towards that term which Augustine recognised as the soul's rest in God ; but the path is not the term, and it does not yet appear what awaits us in fine, unless in a cloud and darkly, amidst all our realisation at its highest. For this reason the highest doctrines of the path issue in a mystery, and the words by which we express them are words that fail because they body forth in part but cannot contain their subject. Being Christian mystics, we recognise that Christ was manifested as the Son of God and communicates to us who are His followers the sonship of our own relation to the Divine. But if we are sons of God, there is beyond question the principle of Fatherhood in the Divine Nature, of which He is the witness Who came with the glad tidings and is called in orthodox terminology our Elder Brother. As Christian mystics we do not claim to know what fuller and deeper and more exalted mystery may lie behind the relation of Christ to the Divine, any more than it is possible in moments of highest attainment to conceive the depths and the riches of union which await the human soul in the experiences of its everlasting future. Beyond those abysses that we can fathom there are all the unplumbed deeps.

In the logic of its high symbolism there rests an implicit of Motherhood behind the doctrine of Fatherhood in God, and because of its realisation at this day among many persons disposed towards popular Mysticism there has come about a certain tacit change among them in their appreciation of the relations one to another of the Divine Persons. As the doctrine concerning the Son of God has created an analogy between the Sacred Triad and the human family, the logic of this analogy seems on the surface, or at first sight, to set aside the *Filioque* clause of the Nicene Creed, though it does not in any sense bring about a rapprochement to Greek orthodoxy on the subject. It suggests rather a procession of the Son from the Father and the Holy Spirit, understood as a feminine *Persona*. On this difficult question, symbolist as I am, it must be said in the sense of sincerity that analogies carried to an absolute degree tend to land us in confusion. In the present instance we get at the truer view by killing the analogy after it has served our purpose. To do this we must realise that within God, conceived as the Father, there is that which precedes *ex hypothesi* the state and relation of Fatherhood—I mean to say that there is Love. But in the Divine Nature, regarded in Itself and Its essence, there is no passage from subject to object, so that the Motherhood of God can be conceived only in the Fatherhood, and conversely. God the Father is therefore God the Mother, and the procession is God the Son, but as constituting a Duad only. The Sacred Triad is completed by the Holy Spirit, Who is the Bond of Ineffable Love between the Father and the Son, but still not passing from subject to object, for of the Three that give record in Heaven it is said that " these Three are One." The place of the Holy Spirit seems indicated therefore rightly by the clause of the Nicene Creed : *Qui ex Patre Filioque procedit*. But the Son is the Word of the Father, by Whom the universe is made—that is to say, the order of things wherein the Fatherhood is manifested through the Sonship, which order the Spirit or Bond of Love also embraces as the Comforter, and is perhaps to be declared more fully at the end of these times, or when God—through the Paraclete—shall be All in all on the manifest plane, awaiting that other more remote and indeed timeless condition, after the balancing of things, when the Son shall deliver up the Kingdom to the Father, and after the ineffable mode of cosmic being which is conceived as One in all there shall follow that super-ineffable state of all in One, and the worlds withdrawn therein. The words of man cannot shew forth that union.

Though somewhat deeply involved, the analogy in Kabalism to the Sacred Triad, thus conceived remotely, is delineated as proceeding from the Inaccessible God above the scheme of the SEPHIROTH, an unsearchable unity outside all numeration. The procession is that of MACROPROSOPUS, symbolised in the first SEPHIRA, but still unsearchable, from Whom proceed, however, ABBA and AIMA, the personified modes of Fatherhood and Mother- hood conceived in God and referred to the second and third SEPHIROTH—in all, one triad, below the unknowable transcension of AYIN-SOPH-AOUR. But from ABBA and AIMA there is begotten

ADAM KADMON, who is MICROPROSOPUS or Messias, and from Him comes forth the Bride, Who is Shekinah in manifestation, the *Gloria cohabitans*, the Divine Presence in the Church of Israel, the Title as such of its election and its Leader in fine out of exile. It will be seen that in the remote sacramentalism of the Supernal Triad there is adumbrated a kind of substituted Trinity, but the Messias has not been born on earth, so the analogy remains phantasmal.

In the Christian Doctrine of the Trinity the root-matter is the Fatherhood of God manifested through the Sonship of Christ, by which we are affiliated and enter into the realisation of our legitimacy, and this operates through consanguinity with Christ, by enlightenment of the Holy Spirit. I hold that such sacramentalism does respond to the test which was laid down at the beginning, that it may become a subject-matter of experience by which holy life can enter into holy knowledge, and that it contains a legal abstract of our titles. The Christ-Mystery was formulated on the external plane ; all symbolism requires this fulcrum, from which the great things can move the universe of thought ; but they become vital by translation into the sanctuary of our consciousness, whereby they are made part of our personal history. The historical Christ goes before us, rising from grade to grade in that consciousness and drawing all things after Him, as it is said : *Christus autem assistens pontifex futurorum bonorum . . . introivit semel in sancta, æterna redemptione inventa.* The gist is that He entered and went in ; He opened the Sanctuary, and we follow, a part of that great procession which has followed previously, through time and worlds immemorial, and which constitutes the Hidden Church.

I have spoken of the historical Christ and of Christ manifested as the Son of God, but it is not as one affirming the official formulation of Trinitarian doctrine. The Church dogma is a typical example of the symbols that are placed in our hands, to be understood as we can at our highest. So only is it possible to apply the honourable creeds of old and the records of inward experience to the living needs of the age. Those records offer their unvaried testimony that there is a way to the knowledge and this is the realisation of God, which is reached and maintained within. It follows that He is immanent in the soul, and we conceive Him also as abiding in the universe, or that cosmic order to which we belong and of which we form a part. So far as God is present therein, the universe in which He is immanent is as His vesture; so far as He dwells in us He has assumed flesh in our nature. Here is our possible and reasonable understanding respecting the dogma of God incarnate. It is adequate to cover the whole field of spiritual life in man, and as such any proposition of a special incarnation must be termed redundant, while one of an exclusive kind is at issue with the theory of immanence. The Christ-state is that of the Abiding Presence realised in a plenary sense, and the Presence is the Cosmic Christ, the immanent, indwelling and therefore knowable God, in the knowledge of Whom we can advance daily as we follow the mystic path. This is also the Second Person of the Holy and Undivided Trinity. The Father is the First Person, unknowable here and now, except through the Abiding Presence, and therefore God in the transcendence. The Holy Spirit or Third Person is the supernal ground of identity, the bond of union, the principle of love between them. There is no distinction between the Immanent and Transcendent God, save only in our human respect. The Cosmic Christ is the one Way of our attainment because He dwells within us. The realisation of His presence is by love, which is conceived and sustained in the soul by integration in the office of the Holy Spirit. Therein and thereby we ascend to the knowledge of God, or by the gift of love within us. The root of all is in a maxim of the Christ of Nazareth: "I and my Father are One." It is the definition of His status in the realised Abiding Presence. Because of this He is our Exemplar, the Captain of our salvation, our Leader into eternal life. He is the representative for us of the immanence, its guarantee and spokesman.

We are concerned in this way solely with a living, valid and practical question when we contemplate the doctrine of the Trinity. It is our ground of faith, giving entrance to a path of experience. The realisation of the immanence by Himself in Christ, or His state of oneness therewith, is our reasonable way of regarding the dogma that the Word was made flesh. When it is added that He dwelt among us, the higher and vital under-standing of this pregnant sentence is the affirmation of the Presence within ourselves, by which we are called to the Christ-hood as heirs and coheirs with Him.

Hereof is the practical and hereof the intellectual value of Trinitarian doctrine to those who follow the mystic path. The presumption of its truth rests on the basis of experience. And if we look into our own human nature, we find that there is a trinity within us. We are mind, desire and will, corresponding to the Great Mind, the Great Purpose and the all-embracing Love. We know also that this trinity must be brought into a state of unity for the mystical work in the soul.

A STUDY IN CONTRAST

THERE are many definitions of religion in its absolute consideration, but there is one of them which might include all as their
ultimate reduction. There are also many external or official
religions and one of them underlying all; there are numerous
churches, schools of tradition and doctrine, many differentiations
of sect existent in Christendom; but there is one Holy Assembly.
It so happens, and this perhaps fortunately, that the definition
herein referred to depends on no process in philology, though the
word which expresses it acknowledges indubitably a synonym
for which a claim of the kind was once made, and plausibly, but
it has now, I understand, been voided. The definition is not
therefore a novelty, which may help to make for its righteousness;
it is a variant rather; and because it is no longer considered
warrantable in scholarship to say that the word Religion signifies
Rebinding, I suggest alternatively—but far apart from philology—
that it means Reunion, which will express also the term desired
by the mystic and thus serve fitly as a preliminary to any consideration of his life.

Reunion involves the idea of something which has been set
loose, has broken away, or has come otherwise—after whatever
manner—to abide in a state of separation. In the case under
notice, this is the present estate of man's individual spirit, the call
of which is to return—the reunion of man's essential nature with
the Divine Nature being not so much our desirable end and
beatitude as the one thing needful. It is in all truth so needful
that it is only to avoid misconstruction that it is not described as
necessary and, in a sense, inevitable. Under all the politic
reservations, shall we not then say that our destiny is to get back
somehow to God—with our free will, if we can, but get back we
must? Shall we not acknowledge that, begin where one may in

the universe, all roads lead ultimately to God—that the path of
sin leads there, though it passes through perdition by the way?
Does not the spirit return to God which gave it? It scarcely
concerns us how or why the original separation took place. We
may have many worlds of experience to pass through before we
shall sound that silent deep of an immemorial past. It may be
true that no written Mysticism and no oral traditions of wise and
secret sodalities can ever expound that mystery, except by
offices of the letter and by such economies as Churches also use—
that is to say, by the channels of sacrament and symbol. But
the end of all Mysticism, as of all religion, is to attain that reunion. The possibility is not merely the fundamental doctrine
of what has been termed in a peculiar manner transcendental
religion; it can be said that it is the one doctrine—issued from
one experience. All else is a question of processes and of such
conditions as they involve. Though it is casting the plummet
of thought at once into the abyss of a great subject, it seems a
question of good counsel to say this, even from the beginning,
because it enables us to create a right and valuable distinction
between the mystic life and certain extrinsic things which have
passed too long as its coincidents and collaterals when they have
properly no part therein.

The mystic life may be described not inexactly as the soul's
advancement in the path of interior religion, and this, almost
indubitably, will occasion the question how far it is connected
with two subjects much more widely familiar, and defined by
those who accept them as occult or transcendental science and
occult philosophy. One answer is that the mystic life is concerned
indubitably with an experimental knowledge, because it is
concerned with experience, but this experience is within. The
path of that life is also a path of wisdom, and its region is entirely
in a world of transcendency. This nothwithstanding, it calls to
be distinguished expressly from what is understood officially by
putative " transcendental " sciences, namely, the investigation
of psychic phenomena and the pursuit of strange arts, as in like
manner from all those branches of philosophy—authentic or
otherwise—which are dedicated to the interpretation of the universe apart from that point at which the universe passes into man.

For the better exhibition of these questions I must have recourse to a consideration which is not less important because at first sight it has a certain aspect of artificiality. Seeing therefore that the mystic life, in respect of its nature and mode, is a pursuit of religion at the highest, it should be said from the beginning, having regard to all the issues, that there are certain conventional terms which, on the one hand, do not represent accurately the construction placed upon them along a given line, but this construction has been accepted so long and so generally that the defect in the application may be regarded as effaced partially. On the other hand, there are also conventional terms between which a distinction has come into existence, although it is not justified by their primary significance.

As regards the first class, the very general use of the term " occult movement " may be taken as an example. It is inexact after two manners : it involves at once too much and too little— too much, because it has served to represent a good deal that is not at all of the occult order ; and too little, because a slight change in the point of view would bring within the range of its meaning many things which nobody who now uses it would think of including therein. The doings of more than one great secret political organisation might, in the full sense of the words, require to be classed as part of an occult movement, though no one will need to be informed that the latter is not political ; while certain events which have occurred and are occurring in the open day, and have all along challenged the verdict of public opinion, cannot be included strictly under the denomination of occult, as they betray none of its external characteristics. I refer to the phenomena of animal magnetism, hypnotism, spiritualism, in a word, all that which is included by the field of psychical research. In respect of the second class, a very clear differentiation now exists between the terms " occult " and " mystic," and it is one also which it is necessary to recognise, though, fundamentally speaking, the two words are identical, differing only in the fact that the first is of Latin and the second of Greek origin.

By the occultist we have come to understand the disciple of one or all of the secret arts—the student, that is to say, of alchemy, astrology, the forms and methods of divination, and of the mysteries which used to be included under the generic description of magic. The mystic at the first attempt is perhaps more difficult to describe, except in the terminology of some particular school of thought. He has no concern as such with the study of any conventional secret sciences—real or supposed ; he does not work on materials or investigate forces which exist outside himself ; but he endeavours, by a certain habit of mind and the application of a defined rule of life, to re-establish correspondence with the Divine Nature from which, in his belief, he originated, and to which his return is only a question of time, or what is commonly understood as evolution. All normal or accepted connotations of this term are to be set aside, however, in the present high connection.

The distinction between the occultist and the mystic, however justly the representative of science at the present day might be disposed to scout the imputation, is therefore, loosely speaking, or at least from one point of view, the distinction between the man of science and the man of reflection. The statement, as we shall see, is not exhaustive, and it is not indeed descriptive. It was said in Victorian days by the late Edward Maitland, that the occultist is concerned with " transcendental physics, and is of the intellectual, belonging to science," while the mystic " deals with transcendental metaphysics, and is of the spiritual, belonging to religion." The distinction in the mind of its maker was intended to recall the doctrine of Plotinus, which recognises " the subsistence of another intellect, different from that which reasons and is denominated rational."

The proposition in any case is that there are phenomena of the transcendental, produced on the external plane, capable of verification and analysis, up to a certain point ; and, on the other, there is the transcendental life. " That which is without corresponds with that which is within," says the most famous Hermetic maxim ; indeed the comparison suggested is almost that of the circumference with the centre ; and if there is a secret of the soul expressed by the term Mysticism, the phenomena of the soul manifesting on the external plane must be regarded as important ; but these—by the hypothesis—are the domain of occultism. The importance must, of course, differ as the phe-

nomena fall into higher and lower classes ; the divinations of
geomancy may be frivolous, even for occultists, while the design
of ceremonial magic to establish communication with orders of
extra-mundane intelligence wears a momentous aspect, at least
on the surface ; but both are an exercise of seership, and this
gift, as a testimony to the soul and her powers, is trivial only in
its abuse. If the Kingdom of Heaven is within it is found in virtue
of seership. The soul sees, for the soul has inward eyes, opening
on an inward world, its own and its very self. In so far as the
occult subject calls for treatment in any aspect whatsoever, it
should be on this understanding only, granting from the beginning all needful reserves concerning the final insufficiency which
is drawn rigidly enough about such circles of research.

Assuming for the moment therefore a relationship subsisting
between occult practice and the divine life of the soul, it seems
worth while to contrast for a moment the work of the mystic with
that of the disciple of occult experiment, so as to realise as accurately as possible the points of correspondence and distinction
between Ruysbroeck, St. John of the Cross and Saint-Martin,
as types of the mystic school, and Arnoldus de Villanova or
Martines de Pasqually, as representing the school of occult
knowledge. The examples of such a contrast must naturally
be sought in the past, because, although there are secret arts
pursued at the present day, and by some ardently, they can be
scarcely said to have votaries like those who were of old. The
inquiry belongs largely to the past in respect also of the mystic,
for, to speak plainly, the saint is of the past, though sanctity is
still in the world. So far as concerns the life of activity on the
external side, there is little opportunity amidst mundane distrac-
tions for the whole-hearted labours of other centuries. The
desire of the house is indeed among us, but the zeal of it is scarcely
here, or not at least in the sense of the past.

The distinction in question is, however, more than that which
is made between the man of action and the man of reflection ;
and if we cease to speak loosely, it is more than that which
differentiates the man of science from the philosopher. There
are several examples of synthetic occult philosophers—among
them Cornelius Agrippa and Robert Fludd—who neither divined

F

nor evoked—who were not alchemists, astrologers or theurgists—but rather interpreters and harmonisers; and yet these men were not mystics in the proper sense of the term—though there are times when the Kentish theosophist seems almost on the mystic threshold. Nor is the distinction quite that which constitutes the essential difference between the saint and the specialist, though the occult student of the past was in many cases a specialist who was faithful to his particular branch. The activity and the strenuousness of the life were often greater with the mystic than in the case of the man who was dedicated to some particular division of occult knowledge, though alchemist and astrologer were both laborious men—men whose patience imbued them with something of the spirit which governs modern scientific research.

The ground of the contrast is in the purpose which actuated the two schools of experience. The crucible in which metals are transmuted, on the assumption of alchemy, is still a crucible and the converted metal is still a metal; so also the astrologer may trace the occult and imponderable influences of the stars, but the stars are material bodies. The practical work of the mystic concerned, on the contrary, the soul's union with God, for, to state it again, this and this only is the end of Mysticism. It is no study of psychic forces, nor, except incidentally, is it the story of the soul and her development, such as would be involved in the doctrine of reincarnation. It is essentially a religious experiment, and is the one ultimate and real experiment proposed by true religion. It is for this reason that in citing examples of mystics, I have chosen two men who were eminent for sanctity in the annals of the Christian Church, for we are concerned only with the West; while the third, though technically out of sympathy, essentially belonged to the Church. I must not shrink therefore from saying that the alternative name of the mystic is that of the saint, when both have attained the end of their experiment. There are also others terms by which we may describe the occultist, but they refer to the school of practice which he follows.

The life of the mystic was then in a peculiar sense the life of sanctity. It was not, of course, his exclusive vocation; if we could even for a moment accept the occult " sciences " at their own valuation, most of them exacted, and that not merely by implication, something more than the God-fearing, clean-living spirit, which is so desirable even in the ordinary business man. He who was in search of transmutation was counselled, in the first instance, to convert himself; the device on the wall of his laboratory was *Labora*, but also *Ora*. The astrologer, who calculated the influences of the stars on man, was taught that, in the last resource, there was a law of grace by which the stars were ruled. Even the conventional magician, he who called and thought that he controlled spirits, was supposed to know that the first condition of success in his curious art was to be superior to the weakness of those inconstant creatures whose imputed dwelling is amidst the flux of the elements.

I have said that, in most cases, the occult student was, after his manner, a specialist—he was devoted to his particular branch. Deep down in the heart of the alchemist there may have been frequently the belief that certain times and seasons were more favourable than others to his work; that the concealed materials which he thought of symbolically as the Sun and Moon, as Mercury, Venus or Mars, were not wholly independent of star and planet in the sky; and hence no doubt he knew enough of elementary astrology to avoid afflicted aspects and malign influences. But, outside this, the alchemist was not an astrologer, and to be wise in the lore of the stars was an ambition that was sufficient for one life, without meddling in the experiments of alchemy. On the other hand, the mystic, in common with all members of his community, having only one object in view, and one method of pursuing it—by the inward way—had nothing in the external to differentiate, and could not therefore specialise.

Again, occult arts are justified by their hypothesis as the transmission of a secret knowledge from the past, and the chief books which represent the several branches of this knowledge bear upon them the outward marks that they are among the modes of this transmission, without which it is certain that, even *ex hypothesi*, there could be no secret sciences. The occult student was therefore an initiate in the conventional sense of the term—he was taught, even in astrology. In the fluidic sense at least, there were schools of Kabalism, schools of alchemy schools of magic, in which the mystery of certain knowledge was imparted from adept to neophyte, from master to pupil. It is over this question of corporate union that we have yet another analogy and another distinction between the mystic and the occultist. The former, as we find him in the West, may be called an initiate in a sense, because he was trained in the rule of the Church and because he was indoctrinated by the teaching of a great experience attained at first hand ; but the historical traces of secret association for mystic objects during the Christian centuries are very slight, whereas the traces of occult association are sometimes rather strong. The Mysteries of pre-Christian times have been presented by certain writers as schools of mystic experience. The proposition is highly speculative, but Plato and Plotinus were assuredly mystics who were initiated in these schools and discovered a mystical significance in that which they heard and saw. Unfortunately, the nature of the experiment has come down to us, for the most part, in a fragmentary and veiled manner. But, outside exoteric writings, there are those who hold that it has been transmitted from the past and that it is possible to reconstruct it, at least intellectually and speculatively, for it is embedded in the symbolic modes of advancement practised by certain secret societies which now exist among us. The evidence is not only precarious but of an exceedingly complex nature and can scarcely be explained here. Nor is it necessary at the moment to my purpose, for Western Mysticism—as affirmed in my first study—is almost exclusively a gift of the Church to the West, and the experiment of Christian Mysticism, without any veils or evasions, is written at large in the literature of the Church. It may call to be re-expressed for our present requirements in less restricted language, and to be followed by other paths, but there is not really any need to go further. THE ASCENT OF MOUNT CARMEL, THE ADORNMENT OF THE SPIRITUAL MARRIAGE and THE CASTLE OF THE INWARD MAN, contain the root-matter of the whole subject, whatever imperfections may inhere in their modes of presentation. I have also found it well and exhaustively described in obscure little French books which might appear at first sight to be simply devotional manuals for the use of schools and seminaries. I have found it in books equally obscure which a few decades ago would have been termed Protestant. Through all there is the same independent unanimity of experience and purpose which the alchemists have claimed for their own literature, and I have no personal doubt that the true mystics of every age and country constitute an unincorporated fellowship communicating continually together in the higher consciousness. They do not differ essentially in the East or the West, in Plotinus or in Gratry.

In its elementary presentation, the life of the mystic consists primarily in the detachment of the will from its normal condition of immersion in material things and in its redirection towards the Goodwill which abides at the centre. This centre, according to the mystics, is everywhere, and is hence, in a certain sense, to be found in all ; but it is sought most readily, by loving contemplation, as at the centre of the man himself, and this is the quest and finding of the soul. If there is not an open door—an entrance to the closed palace—within us, we are never likely to find it without. The rest of the experiences are those of the life of sanctity, leading to such a ground of Divine Union as is possible to humanity in this life.

In the distinction—analogical, as already said—which I have here sought to establish, there lies the true way to study the lives of the mystics and to contrast those who graduated in schools of occult experiment. The object of that study, and of all commentary arising out of mystic lives, is to lead those, and there are thousands, who are so constituted as to desire the light of Mysticism, to an intellectual realisation of that light. The life of the mystic belongs to the divine degree, and it is not easy to think that it is attainable in the life of the world ; but some of its joys and consolations—as, indeed, its trials and searchings—are not outside our daily ways. Apart from all the heroisms, and in the outer courts only of the greater ecstasies, there are many who would set their face towards Jerusalem if their feet were put upon the way—and would thus " turn again home."

It remains to point out in conclusion that so far as there is an occult philosophy, its elements and summaries are accessible in Aureolus Paracelsus and in Agrippa, whom I have named already.

It is pseudo-eclectic or composite in character, deriving from classical sources and from crude Kabalism, chiefly on its artificial and corrupt side. It is not only reflective and composite but an undigested mass, innocent alike of any critical sense or of a definite term in view. It is like a bewrayed wind of the spirit, which is not the Spirit of God, blowing from all quarters and finding repose nowhere. It is therefore not a philosophy in the sense of an ordered system of thought. It is a *collectaneum* of reverie, without a rational beginning, middle term or end.

In so far as there are occult arts they fall into three main divisions. The first belongs generically to the realm of psychic practice and includes all that is covered by the technical name of magic. I have referred to it once in this essay under what I may call its benignant aspect—of course in a hypothetical sense. I am speaking now on the basis of its records and history. Considered as a system of divination, it sought to produce seership by automatic methods and was encompassed on every side by base and egregious superstition. As a supposed method for the direction of occult influences, it belongs to sorcery and was the exercise of abominable arts which failed mostly of their desired effect because they proceeded from a maniacal basis. There remained, however, the evil will of the operator, being that which in magic always works unfailingly, to poison his own wells. There is finally that which is distinguished more especially as ceremonial magic and is the supposititious art of invoking and controlling spirits—usually for frivolous, absurd or evil ends. It is the cultus of auto-hallucination, its records are those of mania, while every kind of barbarous vestige surviving from the savage past has been incorporated into its foundation.

The second and third divisions of occult arts are mentioned only to indicate that in the present connection we have no concern therewith. I refer to astrology and alchemy. Astrology is an empirical practice based on traditional methods which furnish substantial results in restrospective calculations of past events and the influences to which they were due, but so little respecting its real business in things to come that they can be accounted for by the so-called law of accidents. Who are the astrologers that have left us their tabulated records of future happenings and have been justified by subsequent events ? There is otherwise no antecedent reason in the nature of things to warrant the assumption that there is a veridic hypothesis at the root of astrological art. For the rest, it is only in virtue of popular ascription that it is classed among occult arts, since it works on formulæ that are known and available everywhere.

As regards alchemy, in so far as it was concerned with the transmutation of metals—attempted or achieved—it is no part of my concern here, a statement which would obtain also respecting a veridic practice of astrology, if such there were. But the records of Hermetic art are extant only in cryptic and unintelligible forms, about which any speculations are foolish, pending a Rosetta stone to unlock its hieroglyphs or a grammar of its unknown language. I have indicated here and there tentatively that some texts seem open to a mystical construction and cannot be explained otherwise. There is no doubt in my own mind that this is the case, but if the literature at large can be accounted for in this manner—which must be negatived almost certainly— the ground or canon of interpretation has not been found, so that under this aspect also the subject cannot at the present time be brought within our province.

It has been necessary to elaborate these successive points at a certain length, that we may have done henceforth and for ever with the modern theosophies, the new thoughts and theomagical systems which are seeking to marry occult practices to mystic ends, to trace the immemorial history of individual souls in astral records, to find God by developing the soul's powers in the phenomenal order and not by sanctifying grace abiding within the soul. The science of the soul is a science of active love directed to Divine things, in connection and in comparison with which all occult arts are vain and all their process void.

THE HIGHER ASPECT

THE spontaneous phenomena of the double, with which psychical research has made all the world familiar, have a legendary history which is older than any written chronicles, far older than Akkadian tablets or the Egyptian BOOK OF THE DEAD. If we may venture to define that which is implied philosophically in this curious subject, assuming what many serious persons at this day regard as experimental knowledge, safeguarded by all necessary precautions, it may be said that the phenomena in question are the sign-post of a natural possibility, from which, as from a starting-point, investigators both old and new have proceeded on their path of research into the mysteries of the unseen. The results, if genuine, offer an express contradiction to some of the most favoured conclusions of official science which have been brought over from the second half of the nineteenth century.

We hear little comparatively at the present day concerning those inferences which less than four decades ago had been almost elevated into principles and by which the limits of research were fixed. If this be the case, it is the indirect consequence of psychic investigations, working on the spirit of the time. Already the dogmatic budget of the Belfast Address reads with an antiquated accent, and may one day recall the physics of Robert Fludd. No one mentions now that Law of Continuity which in the interests of ordered reason forbade all interference with the known sequences of what was understood as Nature. We have come also to see that it was in virtue of some unstated quality of faith that philosophers could once affirm a positive agnosticism and so—as if once for all—make void the word in its meaning. Ruysbroeck, Jacob Böhme and Saint-Martin were forgotten for a moment when it was said that the noumenal world was beyond all experience of humanity. But again we remember Ruysbroeck and the long line of mystics, and we feel that the Divine part of man is not excluded utterly by the phenomenal from all communication of the Infinite. We must realise, however, that the history of this communication is not the history of the soul manifesting on the external plane, or of the research into those powers by which the soul is supposed to manifest. Having established this point in order to define the position, I am concerned here for a moment with the phenomenal side and with those portents which it uplifts like signals to the mind of the present age. The purpose is to determine their import for those on the mystical quest, in view of our findings respecting occult practices and their results—actual or putative—in the previous essay.

We are all of us aware that the natural religion of Paley has failed not less signally than the scientific non-religion of the agnostic. It was said on the threshold of the Christian centuries that "the world by wisdom knew not God," nor has it been advanced towards that knowledge by the "teleology of the watch." Nature, when she is taxed, does not respond to us with any testimony concerning an infinite benevolence. For her, the race is to the swift and the battle to the strong; but if fleetness and force are outwitted, it is because of superior cunning. There is no mercy in Nature; her law is *sauve qui peut*. She has assuredly her higher aspects, and from these we can gather consolation, encouragement, something of the illuminating message which we need to fill the soul and to satisfy its hunger; but Nature herself can offer us no warrant for distinguishing between her higher and her lower part, or for saying that the peace of a still sky shining over a still sea presents her more truly than does her law of "plunder and prey." And with a single great exception, not as yet disentangled, the alleged revelations do not help us, for they carry this self-same law of prey and plunder from the natural into the Divine order. These are common difficulties enough, and their recitation is by way of transcript; but if they lead us to a method of escape they are worth transcribing even for the thousandth time. We need a warrant for hearkening only to the "higher ministry of Nature" and for severing intellectual correspondence with her more coarse and sordid part ; to eliminate from our horizon the brute in her, as in our search after a higher life, we must seek to expel it from ourselves.

Now, the central doctrine of Christianity has been taken to be that God is Love, and that He Who is one with the Father appeared on earth to make known this Divine Fact of the universe in the face of all that shrieks against it in Nature. Few have understood this fact, from Dominic to Torquemada. Nevertheless, it was the one message which the world needed of old and still cries for ; it had no demonstration then and it has none now, except in the hidden region of our own nature.

But if psychic research, apart from all other and indeed higher evidences, can and does offer a demonstration of the existence of the soul and of its survival after death, man is at once placed in connection with another order of being than that with which he is at the present time environed, and it may be possible to take an entirely different view of the mixed and disconcerting lessons of the natural world. We are neither the beast nor its product ; we belong to the unseen future and perhaps even to eternity. Another light than that which reveals their misery falls on gutter and rookery, and it does not signify any longer, at least to such a degree, that there is plunder and prey in the woodland. All these things are transitory, and their lesser mysteries may be left to unravel themselves, if need be, in the light of that order to which we do not belong less truly because it is not as yet manifest. This is the rude and general consequence of the first indubitable demonstration of the soul operating outside its physical part, or of communication from disembodied humanities, which falls within the experience of an ordered reason. It is neither science nor philosophy ; it is not of religion on its surface or of religion in its mystic deeps ; but it may become the warrant of all. Its first philosophical consequence is that the noumenal world is within us, and from that consequence we may proceed to interpret to ourselves the nature and meaning of our present place in the phenomenal. We shall make in this way an initial step towards the only truly natural religion, which is sacramental and regards the visible universe, with Emerson, as an omen and a sign, or, with Saint-Martin, as a great parable which sooner or later will give place to a grand morality.

The research which has led us to the recognition of this natural religion may reveal to us also the deeper and higher order which is beyond it—being that which is signified by the omen and the morality behind the parable. It may lead us also to the respectful acknowledgment of a great and abiding mission within the official churches, because these are also sacramental. They may have their imperfections and their futilities ; they may mistake incessantly the type for the thing typified, and may offer the gross sense in place of the true spirit ; they might be scarcely official churches if they did not something of all these things. They may also have many shameful pages in their history, but they are still true churches, or assemblies of the faithful under the light and leading which comes from beyond the present sacramental dispensations : in other words, they are valid channels of grace.

But above and beyond these general considerations, there are others which are more important because they are more vital, and they are more vital because they are particular to each of us who can receive them into the life of his mind. From the facts of psychical research to the acknowledgment of the noumenal world, from the recognition of this world to the consciousness that it is abiding within us, and from such consciousness we may pass to a realisation of the great truth that all real knowledge is within us, and that outside all ministries of Nature, all postulated communications of grace through official institutions and churches, it is possible for the light and wisdom of the greater world to enter directly into our souls.

It is in this sense that outward things must be held finally insufficient, even as ethics are insufficient, but their office in both cases is like that of Virgil in the Divine Comedy ; they are wardens in the places of darkness and they leave us only at the heights.

But the fact that there are higher warrants for the convictions here mentioned, with greater and more signal justifications for the life which should follow therefrom, does not derogate from the importance attaching to the lower ranges of evidence. Through them indeed is the pathway for most minds, and so only that the soul enters, it does not very much signify by what means it passes into Houses of Peace.

The manifestation of the powers of the soul being, as already put forward, important under any circumstances, it seems advisable at this stage to say that more important still is the manifestation of its graces ; and here is another distinction between the things which are called occult, with all their derivatives and collaterals, and the things of the mystic life. If it may be doubted that the code of ethics has ever led man to his proper term—which is scarcely the office of ethics—it is more doubtful still whether the phenomena of the soul have done anything but awaken within people already predisposed a sense of their place in the universe. That such things are, however, the coincidents of the spiritual life at its earlier stages cannot be denied, and here is their value, on the understanding that the dwellers at the threshold should not be mistaken for the threshold itself and much less for the wardens of the life within. They are valuable, that is to say, because directly or indirectly they connect with the idea of the end and with the stages of progress thereto. That end being not merely hyperphysical but transcendent in the absolute degree, and supposing as it does the development of a transcendental faculty in man, it cannot be without interest and importance if in certain cases certain personalities can and do develop on the external plane those powers which, within recent years, we have come to term transcendental, though not, for the rest, exactly. It is at least relatively and externally interesting ; it is in some cases a sign and, if one may so say, a transitory warrant appealing to the logical understanding and bearing witness that the spiritual end is actual and not merely a conception of the mind which is, and has been, without any evidence in the external world. The spiritual end does not stand in need of this warrant to those who know it, for its evidences are in reality everywhere ; but such things are valuable as collateral and extrinsic testimonies, and it is not, as need hardly be said, without reason that the soul from time to time develops powers as well as graces. The powers to which reference is made, as apart from the graces, are by no means peculiar to alleged fraternities which are said to dispense Initiation, while the graces also are no exclusive and particular heritage. According to one hypothesis, the latter can be received more fully through contact with certain Instituted Mysteries and under the influence of their rule of life, while in respect of the former their process is carried further, and is also safeguarded by the accumulated knowledge of several generations. The simple fact of this claim calls to be noticed here because of its insistence among us and because it pretends to represent a transmission from that past of occult knowledge and practice which was considered in the last essay. But the important point in the present connection is that the psychic faculties of humanity have, from time to time, been manifested indifferently in all places, while the position of the subject in these our later days offers no unfruitful field for our consideration, whether we are in a position to approach it as students who are acquainted at first hand with the said Mysteries or simply as educated observers capable of comparing what is going on around us now with accumulated records of the past.

The history of modern supernaturalism—to make use of a decried term—and the world's history, both exhibit that the content of supposed secret association—if any—by no means exhausts the range of transcendental phenomena : that from all times, but in a marked and special manner during the last hundred years, such phenomena have occurred, and do now manifest outside putative circles of initiation—real or ascribed. Thus we have the phenomena of Animal Magnetism, of Hypnotism, of Spiritualism, of Thought Transference, our familiarity with which is due to no Initiation, while they have developed their several testimonies without any indebtedness to concealed modes of communication. They have also reproduced admittedly—and the point should be marked by emphasis—at least within certain measures, what has been termed by makers of hypothesis the reserved knowledge of occult sanctuaries. It is said to be only a small part, only the fringe of that knowledge, but telepathy, for example, or the power of impressing at a distance, offers results which are similar to the alleged exteriorisation of

the psychic body by means of processes which have been preserved for centuries—as their claim states—in secret associations
from all ken of the outward world.

After every allowance for the fact that the great secrets, the
really incommunicable experiences, will always be the great
secrets, made evident to inward faculties and not by outward
words, there is warrant, if it were necessary to dwell upon such
a point, not merely that modern occultists who possess or claim
Initiation are alive to the fact that their secret knowledge has in
part transpired but that the natural divulgation of more in the
course of rigorous research into psychic matters has become
inevitable. As noted elsewhere, the divulgation in question is
thought to have begun with Jacob Böhme, who, in virtue of
a particular faculty in an extraordinary degree of development,
would appear to have entered without personal Initiation those
realms of higher consciousness with which true Initiation is
concerned. In any case, it is from this possibility chiefly that
psychical research, so called, borrows for occultists an aspect of
importance, a fact which on its own part it would be indubitably
the last to recognise. Whether it has added or not to the existing
stock of knowledge, it has gained what it possesses independently,
and it is on the eve of further acquisitions. Physical science,
moreover, imbued with far other ambitions, is traversing a
parallel road which at any moment may abut on the same
track. We have therefore :—

I. Phenomena arising outside circles claiming Initiation,
that is, independently of transcendental knowledge transmitted
by the oral way.

II. Phenomena occurring *ex hypothesi* within circles of Initiation, and it was in the second half of the nineteenth century
that the claims preferred by the latter were put forth most
prominently ; though it must be remembered that old occult
books, as already noted, claim to transmit knowledge from still
earlier times.

Outside these two main divisions there is a third less important class, not falling under either of the preceding heads
but including special revelations and independent schools,

teaching with authority in virtue of some private credentials, but neither possessing nor pretending to a participation in any transmitted secret knowledge. They are not, as a rule, of consequence, but it might be unfair to say that they are unqualified delusion or imposture. A fourth class, which is so much the most important of all that it stands from all apart, belongs especially to Christian Mysticism. It has no conventional methods and derives at this day its peculiar inspiration from the literature and devotional practices of the centuries of the Christian Church. It is for the most part, though not entirely devoid of conscious or admitted connection with the phenomena called psychic. Its claims are those of interior experience ; its manifestations on the external plane are—comparatively speaking—rare, and may be termed the phenomena of sanctity. It is mentioned here only on account of these occasional and sporadic occurrences.

For the historian, as for the philosopher, there is, however, a connection subsisting between all divisions of the subject. As the spontaneous phenomena of the double, the history of which is older than any occult systems, are, as I have shewn, the sign-post of a natural possibility, from which, as from a starting-point, some old investigations may not inconceivably have proceeded on their path of exploration into the mysteries of the unseen, and as in this sense, therefore, the double may have given occult practices to the world, so the unaided researches of the modern mind have already in a certain measure delimited the supposed Sanctuaries of Initiation and have earned by the best of all titles a right to some of their hypothetical treasures. Again, as the mystic experience of the saint produces, by the testimony of his life, some external manifestations which are parallel to others occurring in certain psychic fields of investigation where there is no sign of sanctity, so it may be inferred that the adept, the spirit-medium and the contemplatives of the Catholic Church are all working with similar forces, with instruments more or less alike, and to an investigator having no preconceptions this fact gives fresh significance to research and fresh interest to its history. Nor does it tend to confuse the saint with the man of science, or the adept with the physical medium. Miracles—so-called—are an accident of sanctity and the voice of the saints has pronounced with some distinctness that they are also its weakness. Furthermore, there are many miracles which have an official connection with sanctity which are its burden and humiliation. The stigmatic is a signal witness to the pathological facts of transcendentalism but, I submit, is no witness at all to Divine pleasure in the devotion to the Five Wounds. And as on the one hand the Host which is defiled in the Black Mass of the Satanist proves nothing against the doctrine of the Eucharist, so the legends of the ensanguined bread and other devotional travesties can do nothing to confirm it.

It has been claimed that occult practices, or the knowledge of powers and processes apart from the philosophical end, can assist the seeker along the steep path of sanctity ; but no warrant for the statement is found in history, which testifies, on the contrary, with no uncertain voice, that the adepts of this knowledge were almost anything rather than saints, notwithstanding the audacious aphorism cited by Éliphas Lévi : *Vel sanctum invenit ; vel sanctum facit.* On the other hand, neither by Initiation nor method were the saints in any sense to be regarded as occult adepts, though, without Initiation, they were certainly advanced in the mysteries.

I am taking here a point of view which is, perhaps, scarcely more foreign to the ordinary observer of human affairs and interests than to the average occult student ; for there are, at the present day, large, flourishing and insistent schools of occult thought which seem to make no distinction between the noumenal and phenomenal world, engineered as they are by persons who have apparently no consciousness of that which is essential to Mysticism, while, of course, mere psychical research has little pretence of dealing with matters outside the tangible field of observation.

For the rest, and speaking for the moment simply from the evidential standpoint, there is just that kind of connection or bond of similarity traceable between what is known and proved in the external domain of psychical research and that which may be gleaned, surmised and inferred tentatively concerning alleged secrets of lesser occult sanctuaries from the hints, legends and half-revelations of old occult books, to warrant us historically in thinking that there may have been an experimental knowledge of some development in the past and of which only rumours have come down to us. There may be just that kind of broad analogy between all that we can glean, however vaguely, concerning it and the incipient processes which now prevail among us to make it barely tolerable if we regard the latter, with all their obvious limitations, as the first keys to a research which was carried further in the past and—in such case—may be renewed again by investigators working with purely scientific objects in the open day.

There should be no need to add that the hypothetical research would not be represented by the records of occult arts on which so severe a judgment has been pronounced in the immediately preceding study. According to the claims and suggestions put forward in more or less recent times, sometimes on behalf of Initiations, these records and the practices with which they are concerned are, *ex hypothesi*, like froth and scum on the surface of a deep lagoon. Behind the extant literature and the past practices in the public ways there lies something of a very different order. This possibility belongs to the problems—if any—of so-called Instituted Mysteries and the question of Initiation at large, but it must be reserved for our consideration in a later essay. Meanwhile, occultism, as it accounts for itself on the putative practical side in all the available annals, comes forward with great claims, like the seven sages of Boccalini, who debated by command of Apollo on the reformation of the world ; but it voids them all successively in proportion as it unfolds their nature. As the sages were reduced in the end to fixing the market-price of sprats and cabbages, so are these " sublime and terrible arts " brought down to the lees and gutters of philtres and love-potions, hands of glory, the science of bartering souls for the price of a hidden treasure and of tricking the foolish devil who entered into the compact. The protagonists of this subject are not Zanoni and Mejnour, nor even Saint Germain and Cagliostro, but Casanova and the common mountebank exploiting the country-side. Psychical Research, on the other hand, is the

G

exploration of an unknown world, apart from preconceived theory and apart from claims on knowledge. I have shewn something of what it has attained, and we shall enter now into a broader phase of the subject.

The present essay introduces only the matter of its chief concern, being the significance and practical consequence of that research and its findings from the standpoint of the mystic quest and term.

SPIRITISM AND THE MYSTIC QUEST

THE standpoint regarding our everlasting future from which mystics look is in notable contrast with that of some equally earnest thinkers in minor schools of spiritual thought. I speak of the present day and modern minds therein. I speak also of what is based on experience rather than on official belief in doctrinal sources of teaching, important as these are in the history of universal religion. Moreover, most mystics themselves have authority and history as their basis, in the sense that these have taught them the possibility of an experiment within their own nature. From such ground the mystic proceeds to the inward work itself, being the attempted realisation of an union—usually much qualified and yet expansible—between his knowing, self-knowing part and that universal mode of being called God. In virtue of whatever quality of correspondence between knower and known this realisation is possible, there is something on the knower's side which must pass away or be suspended for a time, in order to success in the experiment : he must turn aside from self-knowing who would attain knowledge in God ; he must realise pure being outside thought-processes. All that is commonly understood as meditation, contemplation, concentration must go utterly ; he is not dealing with a thing conceived intellectually, or following out a process in the mind. I am not proposing now to speak of the work itself, nor am I concerned at this moment even with its validity or with the veridic nature of that which may be reached therein. With the cloud of witnesses who stand behind my thesis, there is warrant, however, to conclude that I am dealing in no mere dreams and am justified in postulating attainment—provisionally at least and at least in certain cases— so that we may consider the position in which a mystic is left after such an experience. An *Apologia pro vitâ mystica*, much

83

larger than the *Apologia sua* of Newman, would arise from an answer in full, but I am concerned here with the standpoint from which any mystic who has reached or even approached the proposed term must regard the everlasting future and the part of his being therein. There is no need to say that immortality for him is found ; but it is set apart by a gulf from all the picture-heavens of old theologies, for even the Thomist doctrine of Beatific Vision is as far apart from the state mystic as subject is apart from object in a dualistic understanding of being. Not only do the past pantheons fold up their tents of dream but also old legends of the soul, its travels and metamorphoses, its trans-migrations, metempsychoses and incarnations. It is not that they have been put out of court as provisional hypotheses, but that the past has ceased to signify. So also as regards the future, there is a manner in which the end of things is known ; and, with the pictured heavens, Summer Lands and Blessed Vision, there goes also—once and for all—the human anxiety for reunion with those loved on earth. The experiment which is possible to one who fulfils its high conditions is impossible to no other of the human race on the same terms, and the law which secures it to one must be law for all—to-morrow if not to-day, in a year or an age to come. Does this make it clear why the mystic as such is never an occultist, is not a psychical researcher, and is not concerned with the question whether the dead return ? He may recognise in these explorations an accumulated body of discovered facts, out of which at the very least provisional hypotheses can be constructed. He will infer on his own part the existence of intermediate states between earthly life and Divine Union attained. Curiously enough, he will have the chief seer of modern Spiritism on his side. Though Andrew Jackson Davis had no means of construing rightly the Divine End of being, his concentric series of Summer Lands brings pilgrim souls gradually to a state of Deific Vision, after the manner of Thomists and of Dante—their spokesman in immortal verse.

Having looked on one aspect of the everlasting future, let us look also on that other, to which I have just alluded, being the standpoint of innumerable earnest persons, whose way of pro-gression towards certitude is through paths of psychical research or paths of Spiritism. We have to recognise that the two aspects do not exclude one another, though for want of mystical experience the psychic school knows little of the end of things. How earnest this school is may be learned from the lives and work of its chief apostles and exponents, from Gurney, Myers and James, each fully qualified to speak on the deep things of their subject and the vistas opening therefrom. To the reaction of their research on character James has testified eloquently in the case of his friends, while if ever a man died with his face towards the Higher Salem in these our modern days, that man was Frederic Myers. But there is a cloud of witnesses who belong to the same category, as regards not only the zeal of quest itself but all its high intent, though they stand in lower ranks. They have not cried out with Myers that they " must have God," but they are concerned vitally with the everlasting future and the place—if indeed any—of human souls therein. It is these who slowly, and how slowly, but yet, it may be, surely, are opening paths to knowledge of the unseen universe, untiring students as they are of the relations between telekinetic forces and better known modes of force, of the psychic relations termed telepathic, and of those classed broadly as spiritistic. Their consideration leads up to a conception of the immediate future spirit-world on the basis of the records, and hence comes my final point.

We have seen that the theological heaven has dissolved for the mystic ; so far as records go, it has dissolved also from the life beyond the grave of Spiritism and its adjuncts. We are *vis à vis* with a *post mortem* state which is " simply this life with all its healthy interests expanded and relieved of many limitations and pains." So testify those who are in the forefront of the movement at this day, and so said A. J. Davis, " the Poughkeepsie seer." For them it is a place of progress, a place of satisfied longings. The question of validity is again beyond my province, but these things granted provisionally on the warrant of the records, their message to me as a mystic is in their delineation of a training state, leading up to our end in God, as an infinite fulness of being. We may miss that end in life, but we do not fail in fine ; we may gain in part here, but there we shall win through utterly ; we may arrive here intellectually, not essentially, but there with very life in all-embracing experience. It comes about in this manner that there is possible a real peace in understanding between convinced exponents of psychical or spiritistic research and followers of the inward path.

But the kind of eirenicon which it is sought to establish thus must insist, if it is to mean anything in the sovereign reason of things, on the complete independence of the two quests. For the mystic is concerned with the last end of being and not with the immediate next beyond, whether or not he may pass through it on his way. As in God there is no death except to all reaction on the lesser self, there is no problem of personal immortality which the mystic is set to solve. But this is the first great urge which prompts all explorations " through the grave and gate of death." And the second is part of the first, being whether communion with souls in the near hereafter is a truth of the two worlds, whether those worlds are married so far together that prayer helps in both ; whether death itself is progress and souls advance therein—in a word, the question of reunion. I have indicated already that by the very nature of his profession and its sacred pursuit in life these questions are answered for him on other considerations and evidence than those of psychical research. For him the only term of aspiration, the only term of thought was expressed long ago by St. Monica, as rendered by Matthew Arnold : " Life in God and union there." For him the communion hereafter of soul with soul is therefore in God and so only—again whether or not there are objective meetings to come in the " hither hereafter." He knows on other warrants than those of modern Spiritism, and outside all the range of its phenomena, that when it was said of old : " Bear ye one another's burdens," the message was to pray for the dead ; but that which is understood by prayer comes scarcely within the range of official conventions. He knows also at his best that every soul goes on, in the life which is now and all the life that follows, until the term is reached.

To say all this is to illustrate after another manner that the science of the mystics answers the recurring questions which impel psychical research in the sense that such research desires with its whole heart. But there is another side of the subject, and a word must be said thereon, because I as a mystic have affirmed a science of Mysticism, while psychic explorations are followed in a dark borderland, and though the grade of certitude has been reached on certain facts there is no science of the quest. During the ages of Latin Christianity the desire of the living for the dead was only of peace for the soul; no one tolerated the idea of seeing them, no one sought to communicate with them. It was known that they were blessed, assuming that they died in the Lord; it was believed that "Masses on the earth" would aid them "at the throne of the Most Highest." The *Paradiso* of Dante represents the highest water-mark of some far-off idea of re-union, but it was so sublimated that it gave no reflection to the sympathies and sorrows that must have reigned in the lower world of thought and life. That this is all changed is assuredly an indication that something which has been implied always in human consciousness has become manifest, and marks a stage in the development of the soul. Theologically, it has been recognised from the beginning, so far as Christianity is concerned—as our creeds shew; but the communion to which our faith is pledged thereby was not of that kind which either sought or would have suffered the idea of individual communication. To speak plainly, and under due correction in respect of sporadic differences, this has been, both as regards the assumed facts and the expressed aspiration, a growth of the last century or two, and if it is not, in its later development, the work of modern Spiritism, it has at least grown largely out of the phenomena which are familiar under that name, regarded as evidences testifying to the desires of the human heart, which at their period had become far more strenuous. Unfortunately, the history of communication with "the world of spirits" under this auspice has not produced certitude that its experimental research has ever dealt really with departed intelligence, though it has created certain occasional strong presumptions. Unfortunately also, it has given us, on any assumption, no real knowledge of man's estate in the universe after his passage through physical life. The revelations continue, but ever as before they minister to each circle of investigation according to the belief of that circle. The pathological facts are very curious, as strong witnesses of our undeveloped potencies, but over all the records there is written in other respects a great note of interrogation.

The hypothesis of the immediate next hereafter, expressed in terms that I have quoted, has proved winning to many thousands and irresistible by its mere simplicity : it is like another gospel of so-called natural law ruling in both worlds. But as to the " messages " themselves, of all kinds and through all channels, it can be said only that of those who have gone up into the mountain of the Lord there is no authentic voice that has come down. In place of them, within the sphere of modern Spiritism, there is a cloud of witnesses, and there has been through all its years an inchoate clamour. From Davis and his " Harmonial Philosophy " to the latest automatic writings, it is like Babel saying that it has taken form and that it possesses a real programme.

If, however, the hypothesis of Spiritism has a real ground in fact—and I tend to think that it has, as will appear in the next paper—it must be recognised that we are exploring only the threshold of an illimitable field of being and that we know next to nothing at present as to the proper conditions of research. If it may be allowable to make such a comparison between things greater and lesser, we are very much in the position of early scholars like Athanasius Kircher who collected vast materials respecting ŒDIPUS ÆGYPTIACUS generations prior to the discovery of the Rosetta stone. Their time was by no means wasted and there is value still in the materials which their zeal collected, but they wanted the key to knowledge. We also are in search of a better medium for the communication which so many investigators believe to have been established crudely, and it does not seem likely to be attained until colleges of psychic training replace the present haphazard methods of experiment with instruments which come into our hands by mere chance. There is no field of research which calls more loudly for endowment or is more likely to repay it better. We have to look therefore most probably to the next or some later generation before it can be said that we have crossed the threshold and are making real advances in the field which lies beyond.

It must be understood in conclusion as to this part that

psychical research for the mystic is and can be regarded only as affording a possible preliminary ground of faith situated in the external order. It is to be believed that it may hold a high office therein, and I am assured that as its investigations proceed, especially along the lines just indicated, it is destined to find titles for religion which it is no longer possible to seek either in mere records of the past or in official doctrines that presuppose a teaching power communicated on Divine Warrants to Churches which are at issue with each other on all matters of development, if not at their roots.

OFFICIAL CHURCHES AND SPIRITISM

WE are almost weary of hearing that common sense is, comparatively speaking at least, rather a rare quality, but it should be
understood perhaps of that sense in one of its superior degrees.
I mention the point to introduce a conclusion which I have
reached on my own part about the analogous region of common
place, having found that some of its examples call for continued
repetition because few persons have any realisation about them.
It is, of course, a commonplace to say that the realm of religious
doctrine can only go counter to the world of things as they are
—the domain of actual fact—at its own peril, or that Christian
Theology, as an established science of dogma, has been much
too well planned to fall into very obvious pitfalls of this kind.
In the doctrine of a Trinity in Unity there may be grave difficulties, but it does not contradict mathematics, as it belongs
to another order, and—*cæteris paribus*—so also of the rest. They
stand or fall in their relation to intellectual truth and by the
hypotheses of the scheme of revelation, not by a supposititious
place in the world of external facts. If these patent, yet often
unnoticed, considerations are granted, we see at once that the
question of relation between Christianity and Spiritism is grave
for both sides, because the warrants of both are in the unseen,
by way of revelation therefrom. In so far as Spiritism is a philosophy—which it claims to be—it stands or falls by its relation
to intellectual truth ; in so far as it is a revelation of life from
the unseen it is of necessity a challenge to other systems which
are held to have emanated from the same source. In one sense
it is the most important of all challenges because, in place of news
from the invisible world and gospel-tidings coming through
divinely elected channels, it is offered on all sides, is placed in
the hands of all, and directly or indirectly the supposed source

of revelation can be tapped by anyone who follows the proper lines of communication.

Now, this is a ground on which the Churches as official spokesmen of Christianity have every title to be concerned in respect of Spiritism. There are people in the past who have set out quite sincerely to explain its identity with primitive faith and practice during the first Christian centuries. Save only as an index of intention, their findings are without value. There are people who believe themselves in communication under the ægis of Spiritism with friends and kinsfolk now on the other side, as also with guides and instructors, yet they are living members of one Church or another, even regular and devout communicants. But what—if any—is the light which "spirit intercourse" casts upon the field of Christian doctrine and its peculiar quality of faith in a future of being? The answer is that there could be no two schemes more completely independent of each other. In the orthodox sense there is neither heaven nor hell; there is no entrance into a supernatural mode of being; there is no vision of God; there are no tidings of Christ, unless—and then rarely—as a teacher of olden times who, with many that are like Him, is now in some high sphere. The official scheme of redemption has passed utterly away. In place of it, the world beyond is a reflection or reproduction in psychic terms of that world in which we live. If such testimony be true, the whole body of Christian theology belongs to the region of intellectual conventions, and when we pass into disembodied life it falls away, as fell the cloak and scallop-shell of old from the pilgrim who reached his bourne.

This is a clear issue, but it tends to get lost or clouded for those who are tacking on Spiritism to their Christian faith, like a new clause added to one of the creeds. It should serve some purpose therefore to establish that this issue constitutes the vital case of the Churches, at the value of their proper standpoint and on the warrant of their respective claims, against Spiritism in all its forms. By all its hypotheses and on all the basis of its evidence, the world opened up by intercourse with disembodied spirits knows nothing of so-called Christian evidences, and is implicitly an undesigned witness against them. On the other hand, the case of the Churches against Spiritism is that of the custodians of a rigidly defined faith against a sphere of experience in which that faith has become of no effect.

There is a sense in which as a mystic I stand apart from both schools, and can look upon them therefore independently, more especially as regards their reaction upon each other at the present time. I am entirely certain that the fact of their co-existence is the most important fact of this age, and if I did not bear my witness when a need arises I should be guilty of disservice to my own standpoint as well as to the two interests which are here contrasted. It should be realised that the subject has extended greatly during comparatively recent years. To cite only specific examples, we have on one side the three epoch-making volumes of the American Society for Psychical Research concerning the case of Doris Fischer, and on another the records of such investigations as those of Sir Oliver Lodge and Dr. W. T. Crawford. It has been suggested that Spiritualism is like a tidal wave which ebbs and flows, and this is true as a point of fact, but I believe that we stand on the threshold of more ordered experiment, with its almost inevitable consequence of improved and surer methods. It has long since reached that stage when to set it aside on *a priori* considerations can signify only a most inadequate realisation of the things that are at stake. So also it should be impossible any longer to speak of Spiritism as rushing in " with its false and fatal comfort," presumably interrupting the words of Divine consolation which are uttered by the Churches. The question at issue is precisely whether the comfort is false and whether its results are fatal. On what grounds soever I have challenged and must still challenge the validity of most messages they are not of this order, nor do I find that the wardens of official religion communicate anything except as an echo from the past. About the dangers which loom in certain quarters of research there is indeed no question, but the voices of warning must sound a clearer note if they are to call for hearing.

There is no question that " table-turning " must be set aside as evidence of any intelligence outside that of the medium or circle, until we know better concerning our own inward nature. There is no question that most, if not all, automatic writing must be set aside in like manner, and for the same reason. But for what the speculation may signify to those who can receive it, I feel that we stand perhaps on the threshold of things unrealised, that the day may come when a consecrated and ordained " automatist," assisted by a dedicated circle—in the plenary sense of these expressions—will obtain records from " dissociated personality " or from " the other side," and that they will carry an authentic note. If there are deeps unsounded beneath our average humanity there are also heights above. The prophets spoke of old in virtue of a power within them, and there is nothing to tell us that it was only for once and for all. We need them no less at this day than did that crooked generation of the past which was called Israel, and it is the kind of need which is an open door of opportunity for the only kind of help. Meanwhile, as I have intimated, there is danger from the other side, and it is of all that which tends to befall the unsanctified. I am quite sure that Catherine of Siena was what we term a medium, but her protection was that Catherine of Siena was a saint. Even so we are not at an end of the problems for—outside the Latin Church—no one can say that her Guide was That which He called Himself, the Christ of Nazareth, though **His** intention to help the Church of the period may not ha**ve tak**en place without high authority beyond the normal bar.

As regards the fact of communications on the part of disembodied intelligence, the evidences have extended since 1906, when in a work of that period I felt that it might be admitted provisionally. Whether in the nature of things an absolute demonstration may be obtainable is another question, but I do not see that we have reached it. Meanwhile it is not the messages of Spiritism which signify, save indeed in respect of a single conclusion that they tend to justify, and to which I shall advert at the end. It is the phenomena which really matter : I mean, of course, those which take place under circumstances that are beyond challenge and above all certain amazing records in Germany just prior to the war, and more recently in Paris. They shew that there is yet untrodden ground in psychology and physiology, that here also we stand on the threshold of discovery —in things that are psychic, things of mind and things of the body also. Beyond and above these is " the holy spirit of man," where lies another ground, untrodden by the great majority of men. Some of its vistas opened to Greek philosophers, to Christian and Vedic saints. I have to say in conclusion as to this part that outside the closely woven circle of Roman doctrine a significant change has passed over Christian eschatology. The idea of redemptive processes beyond the gate of death is replacing within the Churches those old theological dogmas of heaven and hell : I believe it to be a reflection from Spiritism and from the peculiar congeries of hypothesis and intimation connoted thereby.

Between Spiritism and the mystic quest there is no issue whatever, except in so far as the quest remains in official wedlock with the dogmatic side of Christianity, on which it throws no light and from which it receives none. The way of the mystic is the way of Christ, the path is He, because the life is His and so is the truth thereof, but the magnificent Christology of the Church belongs to the logical understanding, which is not the mind of the quest. There is nothing, as I have explained elsewhere, in the experiences of Divine Union, on the faith of all its annals, or in those which lead up thereto, that has the least complexion of doctrine. We may hold firmly in our hearts that the Precious Blood of Christ cleanses from all sin ; that its outpouring opens the door of salvation to every believing soul ; that Jesus of Nazareth was born of the Blessed Virgin by the intervention of the Holy Spirit and not from human intercourse ; that in literal fact and not in sacred symbolism He is seated in His risen body at the right hand of God the Father Almighty ; or alternatively we may regard all these dogmas as the body sacramental of high Christian Theosophy, and the Christ of Palestine as the Great Captain of our redemption because He travelled before us the path which leads to the union, and because the efficacious sacrament of His life on earth is an epitome of those veridic states and stages which—again on the faith of the records—are attained successively by the soul on the way of its return to God.

In so far as terminology is concerned, the quest itself may be either the quest of Christ or of God on the path of Christ : its reality is not altered by a variation of words or names. In

the glorious old language, the Vision which is He was inter-
changeably the Vision of Christ or God, except in so far as the
golden tongue of symbolism postulated at times that it was a
dilucid contemplation of the Trinity in Unity. And the Union
which is beyond the Vision is one only, amidst all its sacramentalism of language. It is a collateral purpose of this volume to
make it plain that the LAMPS OF WESTERN MYSTICISM are not
lights on dogma. There is a consecrated place in the mind where
the Lamps of the Schools of old are reserved and shine, and a
light among lights therein is he who is hailed as their Angel,
St. Thomas Aquinas. But it is a sanctuary of the rational mind, a
world of thought assuming the forms of logic, and it is not therein
that the soul attains its term. We know, for the rest, exactly
what Ruysbroeck subscribed to as a contemplative of the Roman
Church, and the body of orthodox teaching maintained in the
Carmel of Avila by St. John of the Cross. But the witness which
they bore in the heights was not on these subjects. It is the
main purpose of this volume to remove from the way of the quest
such hindrances as can be taken lawfully out of the way, and
it is in this sense that it appeals to men and women of the spirit
who in the midst of an age remaking are looking for God to
guide.

It must not be supposed that Mysticism thus presented, in
a state of liberation from the liberal side of dogma, has entered
also into a state of harmonious correspondence with philosophical
Spiritism, if this can be said to exist. The consciousness of the
mystic term has never—so far as I can trace—dawned upon the
mind of this subject. I have shewn that by the nature of things
Spiritism is at issue with doctrinal Christianity because it offers
on the faith of communications received by its hypothesis from
the other side of being a scheme of the life hereafter in which the
doctrine has no place. On the other hand, Mysticism lies as
regards the issue beyond all doctrinal regions and has nothing
to depose thereon. The one is concerned, as I have said, with
the " hither hereafter " and the other with the last end. It seems
to follow quite clearly that there is no living relation between
them. At the same time the spheres and planes of Spiritism are
thinkable propositions in connection with the mystic quest and

its prolongation beyond this life, while the conventions of hell and purgatory are certainly not.

This is how the case stands, and in conclusion on both sides, he who doubts whether there is a soul in man may stand to gain something from the paths of Psychical Research, but he who is on the quest of God has nothing to learn from Spiritism. The purpose of this study has been to shew such a seeker in what direction he may save his time and pains.

THE PATH OF THE MYSTERIES

IT has been intimated in a previous essay that certain Instituted Mysteries, affirmed to exist among us and heard of by report or otherwise from time to time, are custodians—*ex hypothesi*—of hidden knowledge concerning the soul and its destiny. They come before us for the most part in the guise of occult Orders which can and will impart to their initiates the whole curriculum of that science which lies behind the common claims and pretences of magic and its collateral arts. Egypt and its Mysteries are behind them, Greece and its holy Eleusis, the immemorial East and all its starry dark. Their popular and inspired evangelist might be said to be Éliphas Lévi, for he testified to the manner born concerning that for which they stand, but he darkened counsel by renouncing their cause and going back on his chief pleadings. There have been other witnesses whom it would serve no purpose to enumerate, and behind them are their unknown superiors who—like those of the Strict Observance in German Freemasonry of the eighteenth century—cannot be brought into the light. Along paths like these I have journeyed in the old days and have suffered such Initiations, in case they should lead thither where I was called to go. I have dwelt among those who travelled in the spirit vision, who rose in the planes, who communicated together in the astral, who read the astral records, who worked with Tatwas and with Talismans, who divined and evoked, according to alleged traditional methods which could not—so was it thought or said—be found in books. Within the limits of personal opportunity, I speak of that which I know, and the truth is not in these things or in those who sought them. It came about therefore that a few in those shadowed Temples said one unto another : " It is well ; but let us have done." They remembered a little space which has been given us to redeem the time, that we may see with our own eyes the things that we have desired. And these are not of that order. It is for this reason that herein and in other writings I have pronounced separation for ever between the occult and mystic. The magic which is behind magic in associations of this kind is neither better nor worse than that which appears on the surface in records that are known to all: it belongs to the abyss of folly when it is not of hell's abyss.

As regards other so-called occult Sanctuaries in the past, it is within the possibility of things—as already seen—that there may have been early workers with other motives and a very different kind of zeal. There is no real evidence of any kind, but there are certain serious claims and legitimate, if tentative, inferences to be drawn from them in old books, including those of Paracelsus. They suggest at their own valuation that the secret annals of the past, were it possible to get behind them, would have something to offer at this day which might represent a further stage than has been reached by psychical research. It is not possible at present to carry the question further, and meanwhile we have no reason to pause over the pretence of modern claims or dreams about past adventure, whether in mediæval days or " before the Olympiads, in the dew of the early dawn and dusk of time." The mystic quest is one thing and Occult Initiations are another.

But these considerations open the whole problem of the Instituted Mysteries and, seeing that there are other Mysteries than those of magic, the further question arises whether any of the Secret Rites can help people who have entered, or at least desire to enter, upon that path which we know to be of all most secret because it is followed within.

Seeing that in the last resource the mystic experiment is concerned with the reduction and not the multiplication of mental images, it must appear antecedently doubtful whether persons who are fitted by their natural gifts or by the inward disposition of their minds for such an undertaking are in need of sacramental aids, like those of initiatory processes. It is certain at least that in advanced stages the path emerges from all extrinsic offices, including the need of books, which are also sacramental aids. Yet we find that the great mystics were often earnest readers, that they abode always under the ægis of Church symbolism, and that the place which they frequented most was that Sanctuary wherein is the Altar of God. Moreover, they founded Orders or lived under the rule of Sodalities, and all of them without exception drew their original inspiration from that branch of the Secret Tradition in Christian Times which began with pseudo-Dionysius and was transmitted in a Latin vesture to subsequent ages by the mediation of John the Scot. But the Path of the Mysteries is the Path of a Secret Tradition, of a work in symbolism, and it belongs to the life of the Sanctuary. In reality therefore it is antecedently possible that it may have a valid claim on recognition at the beginning of the mystical life, if not subsequently. It stands in a category apart, and yet it may be comparable to the aids which come from books. It may help in the sense that a spade helps the soil, though it may not be a principle of fertility : in other words, I believe that Rites like books are great creators of opportunity, even if nothing beyond. I believe also that for the prepared mind there is much to be gained by the study of mystic symbolism, in which we find everywhere a disguised humanity. It is a catholic illustration of the truth that there is but one vase and one matter, as there is only one proper study and only one subject which has ever really engrossed the mind of all true men. It is therefore the positive and absolute subject, and under all outward illusion, and beneath all external phenomena, the Absolute is to be found within. Here in this material age, amidst the modern interests, it seems nearly impossible to speak of these high pursuits, as I have undertaken to do. They sound somewhat fantastic, as if a man should set forth to find Avalon in the West Country or the Enchanted City of Hud. It is, however, with the antithesis of such an enterprise that we are really concerned here. Those who believe that they can get nearer to wisdom by varying their position on the map are pursuing a distracted quest. Silesia and Nuremberg, Rome, Egypt and Lhassa are no nearer to wisdom than London. The wise man therefore travels only in his youth, because Egypt is also within.

On the hypothesis that there are Sacred Rites which belong

to the life of the Sanctuary and communicate in sacramental forms a deep intimation concerning the path of the soul and the end of being in God, there is every warrant for raising at this stage of our studies the question of the Instituted Mysteries, whatever their multiplicity and however remote are some from the term in view. At one or another time most people have come across something concerning them—some book which hints at their existence, some person who might have belonged to them. Speculation must have arisen as to the knowledge possessed and the objects proposed to themselves by such Hidden Fraternities; and, all material preoccupations notwithstanding, there are many who desire to learn—if this be possible—something concerning the Religious Mystery, as apart from the occult society.

It is a difficult subject to approach from an external standpoint, but it involves nothing which will exceed the comprehension even of ordinary minds if they will put themselves for a moment in the position of any one among the thousands of individuals who, in the past or present, have set before themselves, as their chief end in life, the attainment of an assured knowledge concerning the soul, its nature, origin and destination. It is claimed that such knowledge has been imparted in the past, and is still communicated in the present, by Great Religious Orders to their initiates. History preserves the memorials of certain institutions which are by the hypothesis of this kind, but some among them failed to perform what they promised, and there were others which pursued paths of experiment that have been regarded as dangerous rightly, though outside the occult arts.

Whether any of them attained the true end of religion, as it is understood in these studies, whether that end is in any real sense possible of enaction in the Mysteries, are questions which must be determined according to individual belief and predilection. To some who have passed in their experience beyond those regions which are open to the ordinary mind, there will be no need to say that a man's soul is not so wholly set apart in isolation from his outward self that he cannot enter into its sanctuary and learn something as to whence it came and whither it can direct its course, even if he is not actually and consciously following the Path of the union. Moreover, within very definite limits he can impart the purport of his attainment, in which sense Initiation is antecedently a conceivable thing. It is from this standpoint I approach the subject in hand, being the nature of the teaching imparted by Initiation and the limits which must be assigned thereto.

Let us remember in the first place that the great gifts are possible only to those prepared to receive them, and the fact that most people are unfitted for the truth is sufficiently exhibited by the further fact that they are without it. No one waits in vain for the spark from heaven to fall, for the spiritual mysteries of the whole stellar universe are ever ready to descend into the soul, if the soul be capable of bearing that light which they will enkindle within it. The way is always open ; there is always a method of ascent and descent between superiors and inferiors ; there is an instrument, a ladder of the soul : in a word, the soul has a *scala cœli*. Again therefore it is within the sphere of possibility that keepers of the great vigils in strange and secret places may have transmitted one to another in succession from age to age the expanding knowledge of their research.

If we take in succession the chief initiating Orders which have within the historical period existed in various countries of the world, and if we attempt to summarise shortly the claims on record concerning them, it will be found that, in spite of their variations, they have in reality—or at least by the hypothesis concerning them—taught but one doctrine, and, in the midst of enormous diversities in matters of Rite and Ceremony, there has still prevailed among all one governing instruction, even as there is one end. The parables differ, but the morality is invariably the same. From Grade to Grade the Candidate is led symbolically from an old into a new life. The Mysteries of Greece have been described as an introduction to a new existence ruled by reason and virtue, and to both these terms something much deeper and fuller than the conventional significance is attached by those who have expounded the Mysteries with first-hand knowledge concerning them in their day and generation. I speak of Plato and the Successors. With this notion of a new life there is also connected unfailingly the corresponding idea of a return. In other words, the new life is really an old life restored to the initiate, who recovers, symbolically at least, that state of perfection and purity which he is supposed to have enjoyed originally as a spiritual being, prior to what Greek Mysticism regarded as the descent into generation. From this it is clear that the doctrine of all its Mysteries includes that of pre-existence, but not operating in the form of reincarnation, and usually apart indeed from specific teaching as to any mode of the metempsychosis.

Those who are acquainted with some at least of the several Orders which at the present day continue to dispense Initiation, will know that this doctrine still prevails among them; the statement is true not only of avowedly mystical Fraternities, but is made also at its value of others that are better known and far more widely diffused, though in the latter cases the teaching in question cannot be on the surface of the Rituals, while many members of such bodies may pass through all Grades and Advancements without being aware of the real nature and the concealed significance of the particular community which they have entered.

At this point let us shortly define Initiation as it appeals to the minds of those who have entered into the life thereof: it is the selective and inherited intelligence of ages acting on the chaos of processes, including those of official religions, by which man has been offered a means of returning whence he came. In the course of that selection two chief lines of development have, I think, arisen. In the first class, the picture which is presented to the Postulant in the successive Grades of his progress is the operation of that universal law by which he was brought originally into natural life, and by which, under the providence of a peculiar guidance, he is taught how he must reascend and, in fine, return whence he came. The condition of the Postulant's illumination is one in which the will has been directed to an act of obedience, and this stipulation corresponds symbolically to that imputed position of the Candidate for participation in the lights of the mortal world, when he comes down, *ex hypothesi* also by a voluntary act, to put on mortality and assume its law of obedience. The undertaking to keep the law opens the door of the Sanctuary; the symbolical procedure therein exhibits the kind of life which insures the true leading, being actually the process of return; while the last pageant is that of the return accomplished, the state and place of its attainment. For the Mysteries are unlike the romances; these, for the most part, stop short at the marriage day, but those foreshadow that great knowledge by which the Candidate may rise to an experience within the real Order, namely, that of the " pure land lying in a pure sky " and the indissoluble life therein.

I have mentioned the variety of symbolism and the variety of ceremonial in connection with the various Orders and Fraternities which have existed for the purposes of Initiation throughout the ages, and I have said that, amidst these varieties, as regards all those that are important, the object has been one only. Amidst the cloud of diversities, and in conjunction with the recognised unity of object, there has been also a similarity of form which separately considered would be exceedingly curious. The Grades of Initiation are, of course, tabulated after many fashions, but in those of the second and last class to which I shall refer they are mostly reducible to three, with a fourth following very often, to outward appearance, as a species of supplement, while, as a matter of fact, this fourth Grade is frequently the key of the whole. There is, in the first place, what may be termed, perhaps a little conventionally, the Degree of Birth, which is followed by a Degree of Life; the Third Degree is, after one or another manner, a type of Death; and, finally, there is its sequel, typifying all that which may be supposed to follow from the experience of resurrection. It may and, in one important case within my knowledge, does imply actually something beyond in the hiddenness, the nature of which is left to those who can discover it and so perhaps attain a title of further advancement.

Let us take in the next place these schemes of Initiation, thus unfolded briefly, and consider in which of two ways they call to be regarded. Are they simply a sacramental experience that enacts in Ceremonial Pageant a traditional teaching which answers to dogmatic invention? Or alternatively can Initiation enable a Candidate to pass, actually and psychologically, through the degrees of that experience which he undergoes dramatically in the presentation of the Mystery ? An answer to this question is complicated in several respects, and although in the final consideration there emerges but one view, we have to remember at this day that there are memorable survivals from the past which continue to present the spectacle, while the Candidate, if he looked for that spectacle to be followed by any realisation on his own part, would be regarded as distracted. In a word, the Hierophant, by whom he is supposed to be restored to light and to pass through the new birth, would be sometimes the last person in the world, and indeed in almost every case, to understand what was meant if transcendental knowledge were expected to follow therefrom. I do not at the moment particularise this section of the initiating Fraternities, because some of them are too well known and too widely diffused to make such a reference necessary. On the other hand, those who can read between the lines of that which the old writers have told us regarding Greek Mysteries in the days of their purity, know well enough that, by the hypothesis of Platonic and Neo-platonic philosophy, a real knowledge was communicated to the Epopt, and that he did come forth from the initiating temples as one who had participated in a sacrament which was not of this world.

Unfortunately, with the lapse of the centuries, these Mysteries, without being invariably profaned, seem to have passed into the position which some Secret Fraternities that I have mentioned occupy at the present day. There came a time when the deeper teaching of the Mysteries was lost apparently and when that which was substituted for it was little short of profanation. Whether, however, that secret had truly perished is a question which cannot be determined by simple scholarship. It can be ascertained only by the experience of those who, in modern days, have contrived to make contact with very secret Orders which still exist and perpetuate ostensibly, at least in part, the traditions which have come down from antiquity, though historically they may have no claim thereon. Now it is needless to add that not one among such persons would feel themselves in a position to give more than an affirmative response. I mean to say that they cannot produce evidence on the subject in the open light, while otherwise they can testify only to the particular reaction of that which is transmitted on themselves.

At what stage of their best and highest the sacramentalism of the external Pageant gave place *ex hypothesi* in the Ancient Mysteries to the inward experience, following either the entrancement of the Adept or his exaltation in the light and revelation of pure mind, does not appear in the memorials. The essential point which calls for notice is, however, that at some epoch thereof Rite and Ceremonial passed away, outwardly at least—according to the testimony of later Greek philosophy—and that which followed is what must be termed the Secret of the Sanctuaries—a secret which, though obscured, has not been lost to the world.

The terminology in which the transcendental experience has been described here must not be regarded as adequate in respect of that experience. We are dealing with things which in their essence are of necessity inexpressible, and the only language which can be used concerning them is a sacramental or mystery language. Moreover, neither intellectually nor spiritually at the present day can the soul rest satisfied with a delineation of the nature of its progress in the words of Greek theosophy, however that theosophy is exalted. If, on the other hand, we are going to translate the experience into the terms of Christian mystical theology, and make use for example of the wonderful words of St. Thomas when discoursing of the Beatific Vision, we shall still be far from the attainment of commensurate language ; but in this respect we must adopt the words of Pasqually, and must needs be content with what we have.

There is one other point : Those who are unversed in the literature, to say nothing of the first-hand experience, of the mystical life will think not unnaturally that the identity of the subject is lost in contact with the universal, but that which passes away for the time being of the experience is the reaction of the knowing part on the outward self. The kind of suspension, moreover, is without prejudice to subsequent recollection of the state, though its mode is ineffable and escapes therefore all attempted formulation in the verbal forms of the mind. The misapprehension which I have noted is due precisely to this essential deficiency of language in the attempt to describe the absolute conditions of transcendence. We shall get much nearer to the truth by saying that normal consciousness is merged into higher consciousness in the Absolute, that—in the words of Scripture—we know all things in God and are united with all in Him. The self-knowing part within us is embraced by the experience so that we know in our own reality, even as we are known, or—to put it in the language of philosophy—we are self-realised by a direct act of the mind and not as now only by reflection.

It remains to be said on this part of my subject that the voice of Greek philosophy represents the reaction of the Mysteries on the mind of Greek philosophers and not its reaction on the great crowd of Initiates. For them the Secret of the Sanctuary was that which they saw and heard, but for Plotinus and Proclus it was that which the Mysteries communicated in the stillness of mind within, and it did not differ materially—save only in mode of presentation—from the idea of the mystic term as it is set forth in these studies. My inference from all the evidence is that the pageant of the Mysteries remained a pageant, that so far as there was anything outside dramatic presentation it was given by the way of discourse only, and that at no time did communication take place except through such sacramental forms. They presented the symbol and doctrine, and it was for Initiate and Epopt to incorporate them—if they could—into the higher life of mind.

Some modern Initiations reproduce elements of those old Mysteries in which Divine Life was communicated figuratively to the soul. They contain in their Rites and their symbols the marks and seals of this similitude, and aspirants who have passed through them will be aware that, under various veils and with various modifications, they communicate analogical lessons. It is conceivable therefore that those among them which are, comparatively speaking, of yesterday might be no less efficient than those of the furthest past. The initiate of the present age stands at the apex of a triangle from which the lines recede into the past; historically he can follow them a little way, but they are soon lost in obscurity. Possibly at a later stage of his progress some attainment of the purely interior experiences which are shadowed forth by Rite and symbol may place him in another relation with the early Mysteries, as these were understood by the experience of the Greek schools.

Our considerations so far may be called general in their application, but if we descend to things particular we must be prepared to find that several instituted systems of symbolism, however discriminated, are insufficient, some signs have ceased to signify, certain modes of representation are exceedingly vain and trivial. Many of the Initiations must be held to have missed their way, while if others had devoted the same earnest application to higher quests which they have given to lesser paths they might have attained the proper end of their existence. We cannot attach, for example, any living consequence to Mysteries founded on mythologies, the dispensations, if any, of which have passed away, or to systems of ceremonial designed to inculcate principles which are of universal recognition already and are obvious or elementary in their nature, or which can be taught as well or better by an obvious and direct method.

It is not surprising therefore that many thoughtful persons who are members of various associations which inculcate civil conventions in symbolism, or, in other words, the obvious by the not obvious, should confess, secretly or otherwise, to a consciousness of their insufficiency. When describing this insufficiency recourse has been had to no special terminology of the Secret Orders, and the charge of insufficiency may apply least where it may be supposed to obtain most, while the associations to which it would apply are too numerous to warrant the selection of one only for criticism at this particular stage. Secret Societies existing for ends which are specifically permissible are numerous at this day, and, though independent of each other, they can be classed in definite groups. Some which appear at first sight as merely cosmopolitan or practical, indicate in their symbols, their successive ceremonies and their legends that they are in a better position to convey other subjects of instruction. The sacramental edifice in these cases seems to be like the " columns left apart of a temple once complete," but obviously in the mind of things and not in any historical sense.

It is an excellent and incontrovertible truth that the content is less than the container, but a story illustrating this elementary fact of natural actuality belongs to the region of *trivia;* the admitted social conventions are also excellent and incontestable, but they do not lend themselves to symbolism; and if we find in the symbolism of some among the Secret Orders much which is unexplainable by elementary knowledge or by the common maxims of jurisprudence, we have the right to look further than that knowledge or those maxims; and any student of the subject will be justified frequently at once by the haunting sense that throughout the impressive Rituals there are certain elements which are not modern, there are certain affiliations and allusions which take us back through all the Christian centuries, as if to Eleusis and Egypt. The mystery surrounding such elements frequently constitutes in these days the only secrets attainable in a particular Order, except, indeed, the rise and origin of its corporate union, but this is another aspect of the same mystery. It is therefore true to say that the real secret is not taught in these Sanctuaries or Assemblies of Adepts, or in any manner communicated to initiates, but is discovered, if it is indeed discovered, by the recipient for himself, and that this being so the adepts in modern orders are exceedingly few, being those who are admitted to the adyta, though the Postulants at the threshold are innumerable.

It is known that some kind of Initiation is to be found in almost every country of the world; like the tradition of rebirth, it exists in the wilds of Africa, as it does among the old civilisations of India and the furthest East; while the fact that it is possible to write with knowledge upon the subject at this time and in the present place would be evidence that Initiations exist also at this day in the Western World, were it not otherwise a thing of universal acquaintance. Let us glance at the root-procedure which is common to several examples now at work among us, but I shall speak only of those which in view of certain teachings and professed objects are claiming to lead their Fellowships to some valid term of being. Whether or not it may prove to have been discerned rightly is another question and one respecting which I am not pretending to offer any guarantee, other than may be implied by statements already put forward, and I tend to think that these have been guarded adequately.

The threshold of Initiation is crossed as a rule by the aspirant in virtue of the possession of certain secret words which are imparted to him for this purpose. These words are, at first sight, simply conventional, and of themselves they convey nothing, but a consideration of their secret intention will take us a step further towards the understanding of the purpose of Initiation. That which is in this manner imparted to the Candidate stands for the Word of Life ; it is an awakening of the soul's consciousness within the material man, and this consciousness is the first participation of the human in the Divine Nature. It is that consciousness which, by the hypothesis, was lost to man at the Fall, and the restoration of which is man's first necessity, if he is ever to attain his end. Peace has departed from the Sanctuaries and light out of the Holy Places, the Sacred Cities remain unfinished, and the Holy of Holies can be erected only in the heart because this consciousness, this Word of Life, has become lost or obscured.

When by means of the conventional word the Candidate is at length admitted into the secret presence, we know that he looks to be restored in light, but he finds himself encompassed only by various signs and symbols which are also in a sense conventional. Within certain limits they vary with the nature of the Fellowship, but there are signs and emblems common to all Fraternities. The Candidate meets invariably with a figurative mode of ascent, as if some spiritual mountain rooted on earth but with its height ascending into heaven, signifying not only the just man whose body is in this world while his soul is in the world to come, but also the line of transcension by which the kingdom of earth is taken up into a kingdom that is not of this world, being the place of the King in his beauty. He will find also the secret stars of the microcosm and the macrocosm—otherwise, the Pentagram and Hexagram. The employment of these figures is universal in symbolism, and the explanation of their meaning occupies an important place in its literature. They are, indeed, the most widely diffused of all secret emblems. In the present place there can be no attempt to give an account of the Pentagram through the ages or to deal adequately with its sacramental value. In Indian symbolism it is said to represent the conjunction of Brahma and Siva, and thus even in the far East it was a sign of equilibrium, which is a palmary meaning appointed to it by writers in the West. A Pythagorean origin has been sometimes ascribed to it, and it may have been derived by Pythagoras from Oriental sources, but historical evidence is wanting to countenance its connection with his name. It has been described as the badge of the Jewish nation, and it connects among Kabalists with the Holy Place, the Sanctuary of Initiation, which connects also with the microcosm. It has been found engraven upon Jewish tombs in Roman catacombs. It was one of the Templar emblems, and has been thought to be identical with the mysterious symbol prescribed in the Diagramma of the Ophites for presentation by the ascending soul to the genius of each succeeding sphere, so as to obtain an unimpeded passage to the supernal light. Lastly, this same symbol has been discovered among prehistoric remains in the New World. The Pentagram has externally five acute and internally five obtuse angles, and therefore consists of an outer and inner pentangle. To the inner pentangle great mysteries are ascribed by Cornelius Agrippa. The period of its introduction into Western symbolism is a matter of dispute ; by some it is regarded as an early and by others as a late emblem. While in its conventional or elementary aspects it is a symbol of health and physical equilibrium, in a deeper sense it represents Man in his entirety and the domination of the spirit, signified by the uppermost point. Reversed for the purpose of Black Magic, it represents the contrary of these ideas, namely, the demon and the materialisation of spirit.

The symbol of the Hexagram, unlike that of the Pentagram, is especially Jewish, though it may not have originated in Israel, and it is met with frequently in Kabalistic parchment talismans and manuscripts of the Middle Ages. It has, of course, been naturalised on most Christian soils, and has been derived from Jewry into Islam. Though known generally as the Seal of Solomon, it has been termed also the Shield of David, which for the Kabalist signifies the Covenant, by a graceful but exotic analogy. It is not entirely unknown to India ; it is found on some Gnostic gems, and, like the five-pointed star, is met with occasionally in old books of alchemy, though neither emblem can be regarded accurately as characteristic of the Hermetic department of cryptic literature. The Hexagram signifies in symbolism the circulation of life from heaven to earth and from earth to heaven, and therefore illustrates the correspondence between things above and below.

Through the several Grades of his advancement, under the obedience of all the Rites, the Candidate passes symbolically through experiences recalling those which were once assumed to restore within him the consciousness of the soul, and the process of such restoration is almost invariably represented as a passage from death to life. Some of the Mysteries deal only with emblematic death, wherein the Candidate is practically left, and we must turn to others for the life which follows therefrom. In plainer words, it is almost idle at the present day to look to any single manifest Order or Fraternity for the complete experience of the Adept, and it would be only by the codification of many Rituals now in use among these sodalities in the Western World that we should present, if that were possible, the entire scheme of extant Initiation.

It comes about therefore that those which are best known and most in public view are dismembered, and the catholic sense of their message is therefore clouded. But those who miss the meaning on this account may be told for their consolation that the equivalents and almost the synonyms may be found outside the circles of Initiation, in books which are used daily by many thousands of persons who are altogether unaware of their significance. For example, the secret history of every Initiation has been written once and for all time in the Gospels, where it can be found by any prepared student much more ready to his hand than in the BOOK OF THE DEAD, in the remains of the Greek Mysteries, or in what can be gathered from the sacred myths of India or even of Christian Rosy Cross. But it exists in these also for those who can interpret their symbolism, while it follows from scattered intimations already given that the same subject is treated after another manner with great beauty and significance in the Rites of certain hidden societies which now exist in the

West, which are not included by the short tabulation here offered, and which do not differ materially as regards their intention from those Greater Mysteries of the past that claimed to communicate to their adepts that which at all times has been understood by the word illumination.

I am too well aware that the measure of the fulness of this doctrine is even for its preliminary realisation by the logical understanding outside the possibility of many, and I speak therefore only to a small assembly of the elect, and of those who are capable of election, not doubting that the larger concourse which remain in the letter of the symbols, as in the porch of the spiritual temple, are also in the grace of the symbols and are partakers, according to their capacity, in a certain light and leading which shall befit them, by an age-long process of the Initiation which we understand as life, for the greater ends beyond.

Those who are conscious of the call, and have been or are about to be affiliated with any of the Secret Orders, must be prepared of course to discover for themselves, and at their own personal cost, that which has been outlined here. They will be met by many difficulties which at first sight may seem insuperable. It must be remembered that Secret Societies have no history in the strict sense of the term; they do not hand down literature or collect archives. In those which are of recent constitution, to say nothing of others, it is no less than astonishing how the circumstances of their first incorporation, and the incidents of their early years, pass into doubt and obscurity; therefore the historical sequence is the first thing which will be found wanting. And, secondly, as already indicated, the whole experiment is comprised but seldom in any single Order. From the sacramental standpoint they are not in themselves perfect and complete ceremonies, as their technical description is sometimes made to affirm. They are more often as they stand a story without an end or alternatively without a true beginning; they presuppose a further or antecedent action elsewhere, just as the Greater Mysteries of antiquity were to be inferred from the Lesser Mysteries or as the novice postulated the knight. Thirdly, the action of the symbolic drama may be said, in a certain sense, to move in a dream, and the state of inhibition or somnambulism, which is a proper and sacramental description of our material life, is the most which is exhibited even in the last resource to the Candidate, who retires often with the simulacrum only of his desired object. He possesses the keys of death in place of the keys of life ; he has participated at most in a light which is like that of the Lamp of the Sanctuary placed behind the altar and not restored to the temple. I need not say to that higher class of students for whom I am really writing, that the lesson of all the Mysteries is that man does not easily escape from the sacraments and that he does not elude his shadow by reversing his position in the sunlight. Such persons will be in a position to remember that the second sense is immanent in the letter of the word, and that, as Paracelsus said, " He who eats but a crust of bread is communicating in the elements of all the starry heavens." But I think also that by following this line of contemplation they will see dimly through all these aids to reflection that, although the original scheme of human experience, according to the Secret Tradition, became void by an event which appears under the parable of the Fall of man, and was subsequently replaced by another and lower form of experience, there is a narrow path leading back to the original estate, and that human knowledge is not absolutely cut off from the source of life. In other words there is a way through the soul's legends, past all her sorrows and aspirations, past all her sacraments and elementary education of the material world, into a Divine Alliance.

Speaking for the moment simply from the standpoint of the diverse associations, one word of encouragement can be added ; that which we may fail to find in any measure of completeness among the several manifest Fraternities can be sought, not indeed fully and completely, but still with much greater success in more hidden Brotherhoods. For there exist certain Orders which are probably, though not without breaks and omissions, descendants of anterior societies, and these in turn have derived from the Adepts of the Rosy Cross or other dispensers of Initiation about the period of the Renaissance, even as these in their turn may have drawn something from older mystic groups. Those who preserve and work them may not understand always the whole

I

of their significance; they may have tampered even with the traditional doctrine which they have pledged themselves to transmit intact; but the scheme of Initiation is contained in these almost unknown degrees, the very names of which in some cases have not transpired. Withdrawn as it may be frequently from the outer sense of their Rituals, they do in the last analysis direct our minds to that great experience which is granted to man alone in the contemplation of the highest unity.

I believe that those who can enter into the considerations of this thesis may agree that they have expelled that sense of insufficiency which was mentioned at an earlier point. They will be reminded also of at least one experience which occurs in the course of Initiation; I refer to the consciousness that, in entering almost any one of the various Brotherhoods, the Candidate has been incorporated by a vital organism, and has entered into a living house. I am not speaking of the spiritual consanguinity which should and does frequently subsist between those who are brothers in the spirit, but of the enfolding power of the spirit itself as of a great and abiding presence, in some great and holy House of the Lord and Man. For myself and for the school which I represent, it is a sense of the presence which leads man from house to house of Initiation, through many symbolic deaths, through many byways of the underworld, that he may at length be exalted truly beyond the sacramental orders.

I have abstained from naming modern associations and, as far as possible, from all direct reference. I am acquainted with several persons whose opinions on these subjects would be entitled to respect, and by whom it is questioned seriously whether there is anything in the Mysteries which might not be put forth in the open day, because secrets of this kind in the last resource always protect themselves. That this is true within wide limits I am resolutely assured. At the same time, from the circumstances under which they are imparted, I am not less convinced that they will always remain secrets, and in these pages I at least have done nothing to unveil them. There are moreover other points of view from which reticence is entirely necessary, and it is not a convention which issues from an arbitrary pledge. If this were the only protection afforded to the Mysteries they would have been betrayed long ago, but at a certain stage the initiate knows why a discretion has been imposed upon him, and during all which precedes that stage, half-secrets and preliminary instructions are alone within his reach.

So far as this essay is concerned it deals with the fundamental basis and the true purposes of Initiation, and this general groundwork together with its particular applications, are not secrets : they are the common possession of all mystical philosophy. The method of attainment is known to the whole world ; it has been followed with all kinds of variations by many thousands of people in every age and country ; and in its elementary aspect it is an exercise of that faculty without which even the commonest success in daily life is impossible.

To sum up : the Sanctuary of Initiation, symbolised externally in the Temples of all the Brotherhoods, is actually and mystically within man himself, and the most catholic and natural outward symbol of that Sanctuary is the physical body of man. It is this which man enters at birth to undergo the initiatory experience of terrestrial life ; it is through this, as through the gates of a temple, that he must pass again for the higher experience of which the highest Mysteries are but a philosophical economy. Among the difficulties which encompass the early stages of mystical experience, within and without the secret circles, is the co-ordination of the outward life in respect thereof, and in the divagations of all schools indifferently as to the induction of suitable conditions. The existing Initiations which contain in their Rituals, their symbolism and by the hints which we can derive from their history, the process in one or another of its phases, but now in a petrified condition, are many, but the living Initiations are few, and it is usually only through the first that the student can, with good fortune, work his way into the second. Even then the work will rest almost entirely within his own hands, and the chances are, in the majority of cases, that he will obtain merely an intellectual knowledge. The certainty which such intelligence conveys and the horizon which it opens are, however, in themselves an exceeding great reward.

It seems part of the unsearchable dispensation which is peculiar to secret associations of this kind that they are subject to periods of suspension and temporal abeyance which are liable to be identified with paralysis and even with death. Those, however, which belong to the valid Mysteries are not destined to perish, and there comes a time when the process of transmutation or of resurrection is found to be at work among them : their hour of sleep has passed. After the great and fervid period of the eighteenth century, when almost every country of Europe was for the time being a centre of manifold Initiations, there followed an universal epoch of inhibition, when all Rites seemed to pass under the obedience of an interdict, when all Adepti—as they were called hence—could scarcely find their inheritors, or the successions proved inoperative, and when the fact of such Mysteries would appear to have been remembered as if only in a troubled dream. The interdict was prolonged and heavy in certain cases, but it was destined at length to be withdrawn in respect of things that mattered, and the benefactions of another day of grace were poured upon expectant hearts which had watched through the dark hours.

It should be realised that the Spiritual Orders to which I have referred as subsisting in hidden places—if indeed they are several and not one only at the highest—must not be regarded as in more than very distant analogy with manifest Secret Brotherhoods, emblematic and so forth, which are public facts of the present time, though in so far as there is or may be anything of reality in the latter, it is in the spiritual group or groups, and there only, that members of the external bodies will reach the higher meaning and end of their own Sodalities.

I have given a brief account of the more open and available Initiations, but it must be confessed that it has been written of necessity from this deeper standpoint. He who is acquainted with both can do no otherwise. It must be said further that I have raised the whole question concerning a Path in the Mysteries, and whether it can aid those who are disciples of the mystic life, as one who is aware that there are things which matter therein and that it is possible to find these, if they are sought in the right direction. When I say that they matter, the meaning is that it is in respect of this consecrated life. It follows that there are means of mystic grace in certain Secret Orders, though it is not to be affirmed that they are exclusive thereunto, as if the kind of life could not be followed otherwise. But there is a further qualification which belongs to this exotic subject, because all souls are not called by the voice of Ritual and not unto all does symbolism speak a language. I hold no warrant to advise them that they must either hear or learn.

In my own case I have followed too many paths of this kind not to know their value, though I know also their limits. The symbolism, the ceremonial pageants and all the sacraments of the Mysteries are firstly that which those who administer as *servi servorum Dei* can make them for others by maintaining the life of the spirit in themselves and in those. This is why one undiscerning Master or Hierophant is a hindrance in the Rite which he administers. But secondly they are that which those to whom the communication is offered can make of them to themselves within them, and this is why an undiscerning Candidate or Member is no better for the purpose of the Mysteries than an idol of the Gentiles, being without purpose on his own part. Of such are the limits of Initiations and their Holy Brotherhoods, drawn about them by the nature of things. But when a living Candidate, by means of Rite and Ceremony, is brought within a living circle of knowledge communicated in symbols he finds that there is life in the symbols and a voice which speaks to the voice of the life within him.

As regards the Greater Initiations, within all their environments and behind all their vestures there is the concealed mystery which is the heart of all. Of this I can say only that it is the symbolism, the adumbration, the sacrament of the Great Work and that this is the communication with the Divine of the soul and spirit of man in a high state of awareness. Here is also the hope and aim for which they are incorporated and to this end they draw those who are prepared within the Holy Places and Houses of their Sodalities.

As regards the historical side in respect of such associations, I shall never minimise its interest or indeed its importance within the proper lines. Experience has taught me, however, that the history of symbolism is one thing but its life is another, and though the first may cast light on the second it cannot impart it, while it is very seldom indeed that it happens to illustrate the life, even on the external side. I had studied certain departments of symbolism along all available lines, but it contributed nothing to my knowledge in respect of meaning and term till I left the paths of documentary research for reflection at first hand on the typology itself. The understanding of this constitutes a better and more valid title in a given association than if it could trace its descent from a so-called time-immemorial without a break in the pedigree, provided only that it makes no false representations in respect of antiquity and historical continuity. To sum up on this part of the subject, for those who understand symbolism and its peculiar modes of presentation in Ritual, the evidence of history to both is of value in its own degree, but it is not vital and it lends at best only an accessory light. I have been a visitor in my time at many Houses of Initiation which claimed and possessed antiquity, having indeed all its seals and some of its vestiges, but I did not find that their Members had or pretended to have any corresponding understanding as to the content of their own treasures. There were cases indeed where spiritual life was lower, the sense of reverence less and even the common capacity for Ritual appreciably less than I have met with in humbler quarters.

It follows that archives are good, but archives are not life; the associations of the past are good, but the past is dead, unless we have in ourselves the power and grace by which it can be made to live. So also we may communicate to others the Mysteries of Ritual, and it may be the greatest Ritual which God has ever put into the heart of Epopt to conceive; but if we are an arrested, clouded or poisoned channel we shall arrest and cloud or poison the import of that which we confer: if we are dead, we shall convey death rather than life. There may be in rare cases such a tincture of grace and holy spirit from God in this or in that recipient that he can transmute on his own part; but the Candidate, speaking generally, is in search of life, and if we have not this to offer he will go starving. The Offices of a once Holy Order may become thus anathema in the heart. They will be even as those lesser Houses of Initiation to which I have referred, buried in their own ruins or in the dust of the past. Even if that dust be consecrated in a certain sense, it will not serve to hallow them, and a cloud of darkness will quench the lights of the Sanctuary.

The sign of life is in the symbolism; the life itself is in the grace behind the symbolism. What is the grace of symbolism? An answer to this question involves a distinction between that which is according to Nature and that which is of the instituted kind. The grace behind Nature is in respect of Divine Immanence, and we know that it flows in through all channels; it stands at the door and knocks; it is with us all days, even to our consummation in this world. It is qualified and limited only by the power of receptivity in us who are placed in Nature. Symbolism of this kind is a vehicle of light and grace, but that which it communicates depends upon the state of our own psychic vehicles. It may be said that the centre of its grace is everywhere and the circumference nowhere. It has been a leader of many into salvation.

But if we take the symbolism of Ritual, this is of the instituted order, and the grace which it conveys to the soul is that of the meaning which lies behind the symbols. All that is understood as revelation consecrates this doctrine, and all that is termed religion is based thereon. In its last and uttermost reduction it is that which arises out of the formulated appeal of the soul to God. The warrants of Ritual and Ceremonial Observance are in the hallowings of aspiration and in the high meanings and holy purpose of those who have created them. If they have the eye of consciousness open and fixed on God, it follows by all the hypotheses that God is with them and in them. He is ever on the side of those who are on the side of Him. The consecration may be deepened by intelligent and venerating use, but it is present from the beginning of the symbolism; or the grace which abides therein may become like the Sleeping Beauty and be unawakened for a hundred years. But it is there under its proper veils, and ever will the Prince of the Priesthood, when he comes at his due day, be able to restore it in fulness by the touch of the clean hand, by the sound of the living voice and the kiss of worship.

But there can be no automatic workings. Everything depends upon the recipient, and yet it cannot be denied that—as in the great Rites of the great religions which are also, or may be, channels of Divine Grace—some who enter to scoff may remain to pray. Everything depends upon those who administer the Rituals, and yet—as we have seen—it cannot be denied that a Rite itself may communicate electrically to the Recipient who is prepared properly. It is in this sense only that we can defend the old hypothesis concerning the efficiency of sacraments and its independence of unworthiness in the priests. It is given to all and each as they shall administer and receive. The Hidden House of the Lord, like the outward Church of the Redeemer, can become a den of thieves or a place of traffic in idle and unholy wares. It can be made as a House of death and formalism instead of a Holy Temple, because those who minister and those who dwell therein have murdered the hallows in their hearts.

But again the grace may be awakened in the Name of Him Who is to come, Whom we look to be born in the heart. So also the grace may be promoted, till about and within the symbols and the high pageant of Ritual that inward sense of dedication which is one of " Holiness to the Lord " shall be declared, as if in characters of fire, and the Divine White Brilliance shall be seen in its descending, not only with the psychic eye but with the open eye of absolute being and as a reflection of the vision which is He. This is what has been called in one of the secret places that " point at which faith passes into experience," and we are not merely within sight of the Promised Land but on the banks of Jordan ; we are not merely by the river of milk and honey but in the Holy City ; and we are not in Salem only but in the Temple also, with a hand on that veil of palms and pome-granates through which we shall be called to enter the Holy of Holies.

From this point of view the living headship of every Sacred Order speaks to the body thereof and the body responds to the headship, for the life of the one depends on that of the other. There is a solidarity, a concurrence, an interchange ; they are not apart from one another, and each is to each essential, keeping the sacred things green in memory, so that the *ficus religiosus* of the Hidden Orders may bear the same manner of fruit as the Tree of Life for the healing of the nations.

Be it remembered always, however, that neither Ceremonies nor strange elaborations of symbolism can communicate to anyone more than he possesses already. All things are implied in the mind. The poet is born and not made, but the congenital possession of his faculty is without prejudice to the dependent fact that he needs great making in development before he can assume the perfect function of his art. So also in the case of the mystic : the faculties for attainment and possession of all truth and grace are within ; but at the beginning they are implied in the mind, and the work of the Secret Orders which are dedicated to the mystic end is to raise them into the region of realisation, into the realm of consciousness. But the things of grace in these regions of institution are conveyed always through a vehicle, and the correspondence of this with that which it is designed to impart is adequate only according to the measures of symbolism. By the hypothesis of the Eucharist, within the domain of ecclesiastical doctrine, the Bread and Wine impart something to the communicant which is infinite in comparison with the simple external pretexts ; but the analogy is that the Food of Souls is like unto that of the body, while the reality on the material side is that Bread and Wine are not only our physical nutriment but are the root-matter and perfect representatives thereof. Herein is the perfection of symbolism. So also in the cryptonomy of alchemical literature there is a rigorous analogy created between the mysteries of the soul and those of metallic transmutation, while in one of its departments—about which all of us have heard at least in these days—the deep things of spiritual knowledge are held to be veiled in occult chemical nomenclature. But in such case the validity of this instituted analogy rested in the knowledge or belief shared by both branches that alchemy in its literal understanding was true in the domain of chemistry and that there is something in the life of the soul which corresponds to the hypothetical growth and evolution of metals. In fine, as there is a covenant on the part of the Secret Orders that their sacraments should be received worthily, so is it implied or expressed that these sacraments do in some manner shew forth the things signified, being a mystery of grace behind the outward forms, in the communication of which—as it is said in another

Ritual—" the eyes see and the heart desires the eternal object of research."

And now, in drawing to a conclusion, let it be said to those who can discern between the inevitable imperfection of every written statement on a subject of this kind a living heart of truth which constitutes sincerity therein, that the force which has led human civilisations onward from their immemorial beginnings has been always a secret power working behind the thrones, kingdoms, political systems and religious institutions of the world, and that this force has abode always, because it can abide only, in Sanctuaries of Initiation. It may not be working less surely, because it is not ostensible, in this modern age than it was at Thebes and Eleusis. In the Sacred Scriptures acknowledged by the Western World we find the first reference thereto even at the inception, when God is said to have walked with Adam in the cool of the evening ; while, so far as those Scriptures are concerned, we find the last reference in the last chapter of the Book of Revelations, in the description of the Mystic City. As from Egypt the Book of the Dead, and from India the wonderful literature which is contained in the sacred books of the East, so also from Hidden Sanctuaries Christianity came into the world ; while, lastly, those who can understand in their full extent the references which are here made, will acknowledge with me that in the time which is to come, and perhaps, at no distant date, another manifestation of that Word, which under its various forms and with its multitudinous variations constitutes the Word of Life, is destined also to issue forth from the secret places.

From this point of view it may be said truly that the material of the Mysteries is about us. The Higher Initiation recalls us to a sense of our true place in the cosmos, so that we may recognise ultimately that for us at least the whole universe is within, even as a landscape is within a looking-glass. It is only in so far as the external order is within us that we participate therein, and that it subsists for us. So far as it is independent of ourselves it is no concern of ours : it exists only in proportion as it is known. The purpose to which I have referred is accomplished partially in the Mysteries by means of a legend, which, variously presented, but always under deep veils, is, in fact, the soul's legend, the legend of our life. Another end of Initiation is to shew that outside the communication of physical life there is all that imparted to man which we understand by Divine Grace. There is no reason to suppose that such Grace is something that is outside the universe, even in the imperfect manner that we are now accustomed to look at it, and to understand it normally ; if the idea is to correspond with the term, then the universe must of necessity contain all things, but human consciousness is only awakened partially to the various cosmic orders or to the infinite varieties in the ministrations of any single order. It is in this sense that the instituted sacraments can be regarded as entirely natural and even as higher Nature, and it is in this sense also that it is possible, as one German poet has said, to bear uninterruptedly the consciousness of the whole of humanity within us. In other words, the reflection, so to speak, of the individual glass of vision becomes merged in that of the universal glass of vision, common to the whole race ; and this reflection, in certain stages of consciousness, is so full that it would seem to represent all things.

I have now reached the extreme limits of this inquiry. I have endeavoured to put its points temperately, but Truth is apprehensible with difficulty, and I cannot hope that I have succeeded entirely, at least in respect of clearness. After every will has been exercised to give expression to such conceptions as I have sought to convey, they remain from their nature obscure as regards their essence. The great secrets are ever the great secrets, and mystery issues into mystery. We can realise enough, however, to be aware that, although certain experiences are essentially incommunicable, they are within the horizon of the soul, and that it is possible to say something concerning them after a sacramental manner. It is possible also for those, and they remain in the great majority, who are not likely to participate in such experiences during their material life, to attain an intellectual conception of them in the normal consciousness, if it be only sufficient to realise that the mystics have conceived a great philosophy which is large enough for heaven and earth. Such things, however, being matters of experience, are to some extent outside the region which is covered by faith, and there is, indeed, not much opportunity among the great things for the mere zealot or believer.

My last words shall be not indeed my own but those of a profound writer who has been recognised insufficiently because of several peculiar difficulties in his terminology, meaning for the ordinary mind. I say therefore with him that " the absolute eludes consciousness "—if not in the last resource, at least as it subsists normally—" but the good fills it entirely. We have only to love it, and the truth of Pascal's sentence is realised : God known of the heart." The love of goodness is the first experience of the natural man, and all spiritual advancement is an extension of the soul's journey through its great distance. It is the end and the rest. Within that idea of goodness—which is love itself—at need, even as realised in the lower mind, most of us must perhaps be content to restrict the limits of our advancement for the moment of this life. Perhaps, after all, it is not so difficult to be good. Perhaps in the process of becoming, thus intimated, we shall find that our term in goodness itself is that which lies before us, in virtue of a reasonable covenant, at which term we shall have grown into love itself—God, world without end.

PART II

LAMPS OF LIFE

OF CROWNED MASTERS

JOHN RUSKIN acknowledged Seven Lamps of Christian Architecture : very sacred and wonderful things he wrote under this title concerning shrines of the Western World, built to the glory of God in the Highest. The lesser lights of homes and temples and palaces are like the sands of the sea and beautiful as the names of God. So also there are Lamps of Western, which is Christian Mysticism, and they are collected together as my subject in this volume. They are Lamps of Quest, shining lights that lead in the Quest—pointing to true paths, warning away from others—and on these I have been contemplating in the first part. They are Lamps of Life in sanctity, and with these I am concerned now. But in fine there are Lamps on Heights, and thereof is the part to follow, in which it will be sought to abide on the Carmel and Patmos of the great and real subjects, seeking for lights of attainment so far as the mind can reach. There are many great personal Lamps of Christian Mysticism, but I should affirm that they are twelve at least in the highest, rather than seven—twelve signs of grace and glory in a zodiac of the Holy Spirit, with that Sun of the soul and all the worlds of being Which is Christ Mystical in the centre. But again there are lesser personal Lamps of Western Mysticism, and yet are they refulgent beacons, shining over altitudes of the written word, and thereby are we led to the deep meanings of the unspoken word within. Between the greater and lesser the path towards the higher attainment can be missed as little in the clouded hours of the soul as it can in the summer solstice ; while for those who can see in the heart there may seem at times scarcely one undisclosed secret concerning the life which is hidden with Christ in God.

I do not know whether it is needful in the present place to

enumerate those twelve apostles of the Presence who have walked uplifted in the light of high experience beyond "the walk of faith." The personalities in a long line of illumination are passing before me as I write, and I see now that any numbering is arbitrary, or that it speaks with eloquence only of special predilection. It will do better justice to the cloud of witnesses to say rather that I must classify only as the innumerable lights of first magnitude have appealed by their shining to myself. For others there may be another succession of Crowned Masters which I should be the last to challenge or reduce. To me the Divine White Brilliance is streaming more especially from above and within such talismanic names as these: Dionysius, the Unknown Superior and first who spoke in Christ, having all the experience and authority of the Greek schools behind him; his successor and translator, the great John of Scotland, who gave him to the Latin-writing world of the Christian West; St. Bernard, whose lamp is jewelled with starry light in those moments when he did uncover it, but they were rare indeed; St. Thomas Aquinas, when he forgot his special quality of angelhood and gave that to the soul which could not belong to the schools; Eckehart, the Great Master, like an Elias whom God takes; Ruysbroeck, and we are beginning to realise a little at this day what sea of God he searched; it may be, Hugh of St. Victor, but his lamp for the most part is under his monk's robe; his successor and pupil certainly, that Richard of the same chapel; the English author of THE CLOUD, who carries a solar glory; St. Bonaventura, in whom are far-off reflections of Hermetic theosophy, but he is uplifted above them as on wings of seraphim; St. John of the Cross, a traveller in the valley of darkness, which is that of the soul in its night-time, and yet another traveller who toiled at times as if with weary feet on the steep ascent of Mount Carmel but at others was borne on wings, so that he stood at length on the summit, and the Sun of Beauty, which is Justice and is called Righteousness, shone at the zenith on that uplifted platform of the soul. If you ask me now concerning my twelfth Lamp, for the time being at least, it shall remain an undeclared quality of efficacious grace; it is not the great Chancellor Gerson, who did not understand Ruysbroeck and who condemned John Huss. There shall be no one integrated in the line or linked up in the golden chain of the Christ-tradition, according to my numbering, who has caused or suffered the persecution of others—whether for "justice" sake or for something called right thinking in the matter of official doctrine. But this does not mean that I have any part in Huss or his business. Moreover, there is no woman-mystic who shall stand as a Regnant Lady among my Twelve Crowned Masters, though I have loved them all from the beginning—onward from the twelfth century and the blessed name of St. Hildegarde.

All this reminds me that as there are sheep which are not of a single fold so are there lights of Christian Mysticism which are called false in the institutes of orthodox theology. There is much clatter on this subject: let us turn aside the quicker, but with veneration for the kind of lamp which was lifted by Eckehart, who is one of them. For the rest, they are not in my chain. But the Master knows where his lamps are hung in the wilderness, and so do those who have seen in the light of their shining. That of Molinos, obscured in an Inquisition's dungeon at Rome, is worth all Vatican lights put up through the long years of his suffering, though it does not happen to have shewn me far on my pilgrim way—a question of no consequence—and not for one moment shall the great personality of that politic prelate Bossuet be interposed to obscure Fénelon.

I am but standing for a brief space in contemplation of a great host of witnesses, who are stars in a heaven of soul; if I dwell on one or another it is without prejudice to their co-heirs and peers who have entered with them the eternity which is in God. John Ruysbroeck, admirable and divine doctor, shines among my greater names and is of such quality that he can be put for a moment in apposition with Santa Teresa, the "undaunted daughter of desire," though she is not of my greater list. There is something in Ruysbroeck which we can find elsewhere only in occasional flashes and with great rareness. He is on the side of white light—calm and clear and steady, notwithstanding some valuations which have classed and appreciated him otherwise. St. Teresa is on the side of fire. As Ruysbroeck draws very little from authorities outside Scripture itself, so he seems to speak

K

and write with no enchaining sense of an external and official rule, to which he must defer for ever. He is humility and submission and obedience, as if such virtues had taken flesh beneath his monastic gown; but they are things implied or presupposed: they are not, so to speak, enforced and much less paraded. His characteristic is rather that of liberty in attainment: but I am telling of him at his best and highest. On the other hand, a characteristic in chief of St. Teresa is so much in the opposite scale that if in ways so divine as those which were trodden by her it can be said that the student-soul grows tired, then her iterations of submission are wearisome. She has written her life with her own consecrated hands, but she is afraid that her nuns will not be permitted to see it, so she pens immediately thereafter the WAY OF PERFECTION, and is no more certain of its fate. Her directors, her advisers, her censors, her ecclesiastical enemies at need are men of learning and sanctity—real or imputed— whom she does not tire of praising. Their names spell nothing to me, and of explicit intention I may never learn concerning them; but one is haunted by a rebellious conviction that not one of them was worthy in attainment to loose a latchet of her shoe. When, however, she rises out of clouds like these, and out of corresponding darkness of a terrible time in Spain, you begin to see after what manner her way of perfection emerges into the high light. It was written for her cloistered sisterhood in a convent of St. Joseph, but in the great issues of its end there is a school in which we can all be nuns, whether we are male or female, in virginity, espousals or widowhood; whether we are men on 'change—perchance as some and many of my readers— or a writer, like me, of essays and books without end, in which I have forgotten for a moment if the grace of God and His union are not mentioned on every page. It does not matter if some or most must read her at this day from another standpoint than that which is her own exactly, and so retell her thesis, as if in their own language, by putting it in practice—if indeed they can and do—after a different manner. The same need arises and the same case obtains with all the witnesses. We may come notwithstanding to be as those who, having received divine favours, do "desire to be where they will no longer taste

of them by sips." It is remarkable how much her WAY OF
PERFECTION contains for any and all the followers of inward
life, including those who are outside the Latin communion.
But I must avoid misconstruction here; it is for beginners with
a good intent rather than for those who are advanced; it is
hindered somewhat by the saints' continual self-depreciation,
and it is not perhaps to be signalled as throughout a great spiritual
work, though it rises greatly towards the end. It is what the
old writers would have called "exceeding profitable" for many
who stand at the gate of the life of God in the soul.

Of the Admirable Ruysbroeck it was said by Dionysius the
Carthusian: (1) that he was the Divine Doctor and (2) that he
had no teacher but the Holy Ghost. And Surius, who translated
Ruysbroeck into flowing Latin of the schools, bore witness that
his every word was a work of salvation: it was God alone Who
spoke, said Surius. We owe a great debt to Maeterlinck, who
first translated Ruysbroeck's greatest memorial of experience,
THE ADVANCEMENT OF THE SPIRITUAL MARRIAGE, out of its
rugged original Flemish into the glorious French which is his.
It has been put into English also, but whether from the French
or Flemish I have found time to forget. It is available therefore
to postulants of the beautiful house and the mystic temple, and
they will realise that their reward is with them. Others have
translated other tracts from Surius or from the French of Ernest
Hello, who depended on this source and was a mystic of his own
day—being somewhere midwise or later in the nineteenth century.
So have we records of Ruysbroeck after many modes of reflection,
even through successive alembics of three languages. Between
one and another the English reader shall hear therein most true
witness concerning holy and unsearchable life; of integration
in the abyss of Divinity, by contemplation of a royal road, which
is that of most perfect resemblance and most blissful union;
of the possession of our own essence in the deeps of our own being;
of the individual spirit's enjoyment of God in that depth of very
ownness; of the liberty of the naked spirit which is above reason;
and further concerning that liberty, when the simple inward
eye beholds, in the Divine Light, whatever God is; of the knowledge therein, which is without mode or form; of the state that

is beyond this state and is a free ascent up infinite heights of God, in a naked love; but yet further concerning the state of love, wherein the spirit is united to God above reason and virtue, beyond all forms and images. There is no more catholic testimony than this anywhere in the world of records, even if I have found in Eckehart some points of individual light which can be clustered into great galaxies, as of light beyond the light. Shall I add after such a summary that if any English reader should wish to know of the man himself there is or was a little book called A MEDIÆVAL MYSTIC, and they can learn enough therein, though I have forgotten long since who wrote it. No doubt it came chiefly from Surius and his preface to the OPERA OMNIA, which went through several editions in the days when we mystics both read and wrote Latin.

There are shining names in English Christian Mysticism, of which a word may be uttered in passing, as the eye in contemplation moves from star to star of different magnitudes; but in that which can be said of them at their highest they do not emerge at the highest except in a single case. That Unknown Lamp who is author of THE CLOUD OF UNKNOWING stands at the apex of our mystic literature, and there is a distance almost immeasurable between his light and the beautiful beacons set up by Richard Rolle of Hampole or Julian of Norwich. Both are in the annals of attainment and the Blessed Richard's FORM OF PERFECT LIVING has many memorable utterances—as for example, regarding some vanities of the ascetic way, the middle path therein and the ascent to the Spouse. It is also truth of very truth that He Who is Ordainer of all things suffers not that our sleep be without reward to us, if we "dress our life to his will." This is the sense in which it is said divinely that "He giveth His beloved sleep." That sleep is love: give us therefore the sweetness in heart of the love without end, that we may sleep in Him.

I have spoken of holy messengers who stand forth as first among peers innumerable, and to some of them I shall recur at length, so that here is a preliminary visitation or a numbering taken in short. It is also a marrow of their message. Now, in that which follows I am concerned in most cases with the message and with the way in which it can appeal to some of us here and now, not with lives of the mystics. About these there is nothing to be said that will be new in respect of fact, while sources of fuller information than would be possible under any circumstances in a place like this are available on every side, from that vast collection which is called ACTA SANCTORUM to the latest individual monographs. There are also questions of scholarship which are outside my field in view, as for example, the approximate date of pseudo-Dionysian tracts. There are questions in fine belonging to theological issues, such as the official condemnation of individual mystical teachings : these will concern us only if the latter appear to arise out of first-hand experience. The true Lamps are many but the light is one at its source, through long centuries of testimony ; and after the canon of sanctity may be said to have closed there came a period when certain candles and tapers were held up in the darkness : they assure us that there were still travellers on the path of quest, and they are of moment from this point of view ; but the records of attainment had ceased.

THE DIONYSIAN HERITAGE

I HAVE called Dionysius an Unknown Master, and such indeed he is, standing at a parting of the ways in the early Christian centuries, with the theosophies of all the world behind him at their meeting-point in Alexandria, the Mysteries also behind him, as if from their Greek font at Eleusis to those of Mithras, reflecting vaguely from the East. There are some who mark an epoch and other some the tide of whose influence passes down a succession of centuries : of this second class is Dionysius. He is not the Areopagite who is mentioned once in Acts xvii. 34, of whom it is said that he cleaved to St. Paul and believed when others mocked him about the resurrection of the dead ; but he passes under his name. To all intents and purposes he would be not less unknown than he is, were it possible to identify the two. The writings by which he is represented are subsequent to Plotinus and are regarded generally by scholarship as belonging to the fifth century. Their authenticity, from the standpoint of their apostolic claim, has been definitely abandoned, even in Roman Catholic criticism. For my present purpose the question of date and authorship is not of the least consequence.

Whatsoever his personality and period, he whom we know as Dionysius stands at the fountain-head of Christian Mysticism and is himself its fount, and he reflects the School of Alexandria re-expressed in the light of Christ. It has been affirmed that the body-general of mystical doctrine throughout the Middle Ages drew from that of Dionysius ; that scholasticism derived from his writings its general plan and the scientific solution of the questions which it examined ; and that his influence was perpetuated after the Reformation among Spanish mystics, especially in the memorials of Peter of Alcantara, St. John of the Cross and St. Teresa. These are extreme statements which would require to be qualified a little if I were engaged on a critical study, but they are true in the broad sense. On the assumption, moreover, that the first "mystical divine" wrote his "body of Divinity" from what is called the spring of experience and not only as a doctrinal excursus, it is obvious that it could not be otherwise, seeing that those who came after him wrote also from first-hand knowledge of inward states of being.

The influence of Dionysian texts is said to have been illustrated early by the fact that they were not unknown to St. Augustine, but this—if it happens to be true—is a sporadic example, and it was not until they were translated into Latin at the instance of Charles the Bald in the ninth century by Johannes Erigena, otherwise John the Scot, that they became widely familiar and of high authority in Europe. According to Cousin, the first result was that Mysticism began to assume a systematic character. St. Bernard, Hugh of St. Victor, Richard of St. Victor and St. Bonaventura are mentioned in this connection. Others say that the philosophy of Erigena had its source in the works of Dionysius and that from the writings of Erigena there issued the philosophy of the Middle Ages. It is again an extreme statement, but again it counts for something in the historical evidence of the influence. We know also that St. Anselm at the end of the eleventh century adopted the Dionysian doctrine of the DIVINE NAMES and the CELESTIAL HIERARCHY and that St. Thomas Aquinas wrote a commentary on the former text.

So far on the external side of the subject, but what in fact was this mystical Divinity which took such possession of Christian minds throughout the centuries that he who was its author became the recognised master of Mysticism? It falls for our purpose under two heads, of which the first is the nature of God and the second the way of His attainment. In respect of both it must be understood that Dionysius, though philosophically and mystically he is a faithful mirror of Proclus, is regarded doctrinally as an orthodox Christian, having the *imprimatur* and *nihil obstat* of the Latin Church set upon all his teachings. For him the Holy Trinity subsisted in unity and the "superessential Jesus" was the Second Person thereof. I find no call to go further, unfolding his teaching on the sacraments, on the Celestial

Hierarchy which is above and the Ecclesiastical Hierarchy which is below : there may be a true sense in which these things were the materials of a developed orthodoxy to come.

The longer texts touch but the fringe of the subject which is that of our real concern, and if only these had come down to us the Christian mystics who followed would have remained within the witness of their own attainment and would not have looked to Dionysius. On the authority of THE CELESTIAL HIERARCHY, THE ECCLESIASTICAL HIERARCHY and THE DIVINE NAMES, they would have heard (1) that the Venerated Goodness communicates its lights to men and remakes them to the likeness of His Sovereign Perfection ; (2) that while there is a sense in which inanimate things participate in God, it is granted only to reasonable beings that they shall share in His wisdom ; (3) that the end of the Ecclesiastical Hierarchy is to assimilate man to God ; (4) that there is a mystery of Divine Regeneration ; (5) that Christ associates us fraternally to His Divinity ; (6) that God is of infinite perfection, incomprehensible intelligence and supereminent unity ; (7) that He is above all goodness and all Divinity, and yet has created them ; (8) that He is not to be regarded as reason, power, understanding, life or essence, because He surpasses all, while at the same time He is in all things, as the plenitude of being ; (9) that all things speak of Him and none adequately ; (10) that all reveal Him, but nothing of all manifests ; (11) that He is absolutely incomprehensible ; (12) that creatures are made divine in His Divinity and attain unity in His oneness.

To teaching of this kind we may apply any denomination that we choose in the normal order of excellence ; but it is not of the kind that marks epochs or rules through centuries to come. There is, however, outside those texts a minute tract on MYSTICAL THEOLOGY which is the Dionysian pearl of great price, and there are certain extant letters which are its undesigned supplements. Before analysing its intimations, let us glance at what is said in the first chapter or section of THE DIVINE NAMES in the following summary form : (1) Touching the supreme and mysterious nature of God, it is permissible to utter and think that only which has been revealed in Holy Scripture. (2) No creatures can know that which He is, by reason of the absolute superiority of His proper essence. (3) He is an abyss which cannot be sounded, for there is no path leading to His infinite deeps. (4) This is not because the Sovereign Goodness would exclude any being from participation with Him. (5) On the contrary He dispenses to all things the benefit of His sacred splendours according to their capacity. (6) Moreover, He draws pious understandings to His contemplation, communion and likeness. (7) They are those who without hesitation and without fickleness advance in the light which God vouchsafes and pursue their flight with discretion, fidelity and courage. (8) Obedient to these holy laws, we may approach the Divine Secret—which surpasses all understanding—with religious respect, and honour that which is ineffable by humble silence. (9) The kind of approach is, however, by looking towards those splendours which are transmitted by Holy Scripture. (10) By the grace of its supernatural instruction we are prepared to receive that light according to our capacity and to praise the Principle of all Illumination, as it has manifested itself in the sacred writings. (11) The offices of this Principle are those belonging to the essence and life of all things, which recalls and resuscitates those who are in a state of separation therefrom, so that they are rooted in goodness. (12) In fine, it is this Principle which animates and sustains those who aspire to perfection.

It will be seen that these intimations of Divinity are apart from any doctrine of union conceived as attainable in experience here on earth. On the contrary, a little later on the text formulates the position of every Christian soul in this respect and also the eternal prospect which extends in faith before it. (1) Things divine are manifested here below by the mediation of symbols and aided by these we can attain spiritual realities up to a certain point. (2) By suspending all activities of the understanding, we may contemplate the splendour of God, so far as this is permitted ; but it cannot be seen perfectly because it is above all things, is absolutely unknown and surpasses those limits which can be reached by the essence and power of all creatures combined, angelic natures included. (3) The whole domain of knowledge has being for its object and ends where this ends, whence it follows that He Who surpasses all being in like manner eludes all knowledge. So far as regards the soul in its earthly career; but (4) when our human nature shall have become incorruptible and immortal, when Christ shall have admitted us to a participation of His glorious felicity we shall dwell eternally with the Lord. (5) We shall be called to the chaste contemplation of His sacred humanity; we shall be inundated by the floods of His light, like the disciples in the mystery of the Transfiguration. (6) He will pour His intelligible brightness on our souls, and they will be intoxicated by the radiance of this wondrous sun, amidst the sweetness of inconceivable union. (7) In a word, we shall be like unto the angels and sons of God, being children of the Resurrection.

In all worship and humility, it follows that the end of everlasting being is a substituted Beatific Vision, the glorified humanity of Jesus of Nazareth in place of the depth of the riches of knowledge attained in the contemplation of the Eternal Father of Lights, as offered by Thomist Theology. And we who are in search of the union have resolved long since that it is not attained in vision, because the state of the union is beyond the world of images.

Let us turn, however, from this region of radiant shadows to the tract on MYSTICAL DIVINITY, which is written to Timothy, meaning—as we have found—in the hypothesis of the literary pretence that Timothy whom St. Paul addressed as his own son and well beloved in the faith, wishing him grace and peace. It will be seen that we are entering into another sphere of thought. The text opens with a prayer for direction to that " highest top of mystical oracles " where the unchangeable mysteries of Divinity abide in hiddenness, the place of secret teaching, of sacred silence and the dark of dark. The instruction to Timothy is that it is reached by forsaking all sensible and intelligible things, all mental operations, and by elevation to a state of " conjunction and union with Him Who is above all essence and knowledge." The manner of this attainment is by separation from all things, " being freed and loosed from all things," the self above else included. Thus unclothed and liberated, the promise to Timothy is that he shall be " brought back to the super-essential beam of the Divine Darkness."

This is the first intimation and promise concerning an attainable state of Divine Union, and it will be observed that it is not relegated to the hereafter of disembodied life but belongs to the living present and is that which here and now can be done, so to speak, with our might, by "most intent study," though such study is distinct from activity of the mind. It is like the Zoharic science of "the secret doctrine," which at the root is an essay in deep experience and not a debate about it or a "great argument" concerning the Law and the Covenant, its inward meaning and the grace thereof.

There is, however, a second intimation, according to which he who is liberated from "things that are seen and things that see" shall be "swallowed up in the truly mystical cloud, or mist of unknowing," where all manner of scientific apprehensions are shut out. In other words it is said that the soul is in Him Who is "utterly inattingible and invisible"; that the soul is all His Who is beyond all things; that it belongs not now to itself or to ought else; that it is united after the best manner to Him Who is "wholly unknown"; that the manner of this union is by the utter cessation of knowledge; while the fruition thereof is that the soul, in and because of this unknowing, knows "above any mind or understanding." The ascent into this state of seeing and knowing "that which is above all sight and knowledge" is otherwise said to be performed by taking away all things, so that, "without any veil, we may know that Unknown which is (1) all things that are, or (2) is covered under all things that are known. After this manner we attain "that superessential darkness which is hidden by all the light that is in things that are."

It will be seen that Dionysius uses a strange language, mixing the symbols of darkness with those of light, and tending to describe God in the hiddenness by the way of negation rather than affirmation, though it is said at the end of all that "He Who is perfect, complete, only, and yet the singular cause of all, is above position or affirmation" and is likewise "far above all negations." I have discussed the use and validity of such language in another place and there is no need to consider it here. The revelation of the tract on Mystical Theology is indicated at the beginning as a secret thing to be kept secretly and not even to be heard of by those who are "not entered or initiated into our Mysteries." By the hypothesis at least therefore, the pseudonymous Dionysius wrote *coram populo* in his larger works but for one of a secret circle in his marrow of hidden theology. It is described as containing "Divine Institutions concerning things mystical" and as "above" those who "are still detained and holden in the things that are," but much more above those who are "yet more strangers," meaning idolaters and makers of images.

There seems no question whatever that out of THE CELESTIAL HIERARCHY there was developed the theological Heaven and that THE ECCLESIASTICAL HIERARCHY helped to establish the official Church of Christ. The statements may appear extreme, but the meaning is that these texts were promulgated in the Western World in the ninth century with all the force of the apostolic age to which they were referred behind them, and though, seeing that they belong to the fifth century, they embody the forms, ideas and beliefs of Christendom as then current, they were beyond appeal so far as their content is concerned, while all that they implied but did not develop was material for an evolution to come. The tract on DIVINE NAMES had also its influence within and without theology. But the point with which I am concerned is that none of these texts belongs to mystical doctrine, and when it is affirmed therefore that John the Scot gave mystical theosophy to Christian Europe by translating Dionysius, the meaning is that he gave the little book of DIVINE INSTITUTIONS addressed to Timothy and comprised in a few pages. By the supposition of claim and name it told all who aspired to the heights of sanctity that the Way of Divine Union had been taught by a disciple whom St. Paul converted at Athens and that its attainment was possible here and now. It was not the shewing of a vision, as we find it in THE DIVINE NAMES, but an experience beyond the world of images, or outside all distinctions which obtain between subject and object. There are references in the tract itself to the Trinity in Unity and the name of Jesus appears once therein ; but so far as the mystical path is concerned it is a quest after God in the hiddenness, outside all Persons and all attributions. Respecting the term, it is in God only and simply. All questions of Christian doctrine have passed away, with the other symbols and images.

It must be added that to all intents and purposes it is a quest followed in the mind, up to that point when thought is reduced to a vestige. It is most especially and completely outside the region of " discourse." The possibility of speech grows less and less as the path of ascent rises, and words are voided at the summit. When the mode of the mind is beyond all expression that state is attained which is called union with the Unspeakable. The meaning is that neither in the aftermath of such an experience nor at any time subsequently can it be represented by the forms of thought, for it is obvious that into the state itself the idea of its delineation could in no wise enter. As some of us know a first hand that there is an awareness of pure being in a mode of the mind which is above thought-processes and that it is of necessity incommunicable, we can accept the testimony of Dionysius as to the fact of the state. But it does not always connote a realisation of Divine Union, and it is to be inferred therefore that he carried it further than has been done in those cases to which I am now alluding.

When I say that the record is of a quest followed in the mind, I am indicating in very imperfect words that it is to be distinguished from a quest of love, that it is quite unlike the record of St. John of the Cross in his BOOK OF THE LIVING FLAME. The word love is never used in the Dionysian tract. We can infer that it is presupposed and may point out that the text is more especially concerned with attainment rather than conditions. But, explain it how we will, it remains that the word is absent and that for any consideration thereon we must have recourse to THE DIVINE NAMES, when it speaks for once in the fourth chapter of the deified soul casting itself " in a kind of headlong course and by the mystery of an inconceivable union into the splendours of inaccessible light." There are references to the love of God for all that His power produces, to the counsel of PROVERBS iv. 6, which tells us to love wisdom, and to Divine Love nourished in the soul of man. It is said that such love transports beyond themselves those who are possessed thereby and that a true lover is lost in God. The statement as expressed here seems definite and therefore final; but in the original it is weakened by an explanatory and apologetic content which excuses the use of such a term on the ground that it is met with in Scripture. But, however qualified, it is there, and the text in question is therefore in a different position to that of the shorter tract from the mystical standpoint.

It is in this connection that Dionysius cites his master Hierotheos and some of his HYMNS OF LOVE, which speak of its "incomprehensible and infinitely superior Cause," towards which "aspires unanimously the love of all beings, by reason of their proper nature." They speak also of the classes into which love is divided for the purpose of separating that which belongs to earth from that which is heavenly in its nature, including with the latter what is called the "sacred hierarchy" of angelic love and the love of pure intelligence. The source of all is affirmed to shine far above and beyond them in the Eternal Being. The HYMNS tell us in fine of "a simple, spontaneous force which establishes union and harmony between all that is, from the Sovereign Goodness to the last of created things, and thence returns by the same way to its starting-point, fulfilling by, within and upon itself its invariable revolution and turning thus in a perpetual circle."

The context of Dionysius implies that this force also is love, but the harmony or union seems to subsist in the state of distinction and belongs therefore to the mode of sympathetic attraction or to that which the Areopagite proceeds to indicate immediately when he says that the angels are plunged unceasingly in the love of Supreme Goodness. It is, however, the subject's love for its object, and this is not the mystic term. It follows that so far there is little to detain us in Hierotheos; but the Areopagite affirms that this "illustrious master" must have derived his divinity (1) from pious theologians, (2) from learned investigation of Scripture, or (3) was a recipient of special inspiration, as one who not only learned but experienced Divine Things and was fashioned by instruction of the heart in that mystical union and faith which are never imbibed from the teaching of man. But it happens that Dionysius cites to illustrate his panegyric the doctrine of Hierotheos on the Divinity of the Lord Jesus : it is high and luminous theology, exceedingly important for its period, but it does not belong to our subject.

There is, however, another witness who, even as the author of the Hierarchies assumed the style and title of the Areopagite, passes under the name of Hierotheos but tends to be referred by scholarship to the beginning of the sixth century. It is an unsettled question and is unimportant to the present purpose. By whomsoever written, there is extant a Syriac MS. which is called THE BOOK OF THE HIDDEN MYSTERIES OF THE HOUSE OF GOD. It has never been printed but was once described by Mr. A. C. Frothingham in a pamphlet belonging to the year 1886. The mystical term is defined as that real and plenary union with the Universal Essence by which the mind embraces all within itself. But the path which leads up to this union is a confused pageant of psychic experiences, and it is scarcely possible to regard it as presenting in symbolism the plan of our redemption and the veridic scale of our ascent. Its pictorial scheme reminds us of one yet more elaborate which connects in later days with the name of Saint-Martin, whose NEW MAN offers, amidst great differences, recurring analogies with Hierotheos, though there is no need to add that THE BOOK OF THE HIDDEN MYSTERIES could never have come into his hands or have been read by him if it had.

To conclude therefore respecting the tract of Dionysius, it directs those who would devote themselves to that " deep contemplation " which is understood as the path of the mystic to " lay aside the services and operations of the understanding, all that is material and intellectual, the things which are, those also which are not, and by a supernatural flight upward to unite themselves, as intimately as possible with Him Who is exalted above all essence," by a " sincere, spontaneous and total abandonment of ourselves and all things." It is described otherwise as plunging into " that darkness wherein He dwells Who reigns over the universe." But this darkness is like the central heart of an overwhelming light, while the process of unknowing which sets aside every intellectual activity and all understanding does not lead to privation but to Divine Knowledge after a transcendent mode : it is otherwise an " absolute and felicitous ignorance " which " constitutes precisely the science of Him Who surpasses all the objects of human science."

Behind these attempts to express the inexpressible by the aid of paradox and a play upon the alternatives of contradiction there emerges an issue which is in reality clear and simple—the distinction, that is to say, between the limitations of objective knowledge and the mystic state in which the Divine Object becomes known within the subject, or in other words, when God is realised in the heart. Now, whether in the East or the West, no mystic has borne testimony to any other root-fact than this of which Dionysius is the witness. He realised also and shewed that the path unto such end is a path of love, but his testimony on this essential condition of the quest is not, as we have seen, quite adequate thereto. That the state beyond the images can yet be a state of love does not appear in the texts, nor do they tell us clearly that it is love which cleanses and love alone that sanctifies. It calls to be added that the path of Dionysius is not an ascetic path in the sense of the later memorials, that is to say, in the bodily sense, though his plenary doctrine of detachment belongs obviously to austerity in mind. Apart from this there is no mystic life, and it is prolonged through all the days till that time comes when love alone is regnant.

THE EVERLASTING GOSPEL

I HAVE referred in an earlier essay to a modern " gospel of interpretation," as it was called in Victorian days. It has long since
become of no effect in the sense of its formulation at that period ;
but the " illuminations," for example, of Anna Bonus Kingsford,
some time subsequently issued in a separate form but originally
unfolded in respect of their principles by her kinsman Edward
Maitland in a book called THE PERFECT WAY, are not without
moment as memorials, because they offer a typical example of
modern endeavours to interpret old doctrines and texts in a
new manner which might bear fruit as a message to the age
that saw their production. The primary value of such unfolded
meanings is always to the person by or through whom they come,
but occasionally they earn recognition within a considerable
circle. The Kingsford " illuminations " appealed to many in
their day, but that day passed and another came in succession
with other inward needs. I have intimated already that so far
as the mystic quest is concerned there is no living aid to be
drawn from attempted reconstructions of hidden significance in
ancient books, while the one canon of criticism by which it is
possible to test their value, being that of the likelihood of things,
has always pronounced against them. There is nothing more
antecedently improbable than the notion that any modern
afflatus should penetrate successfully that which may have been
hidden in the mind of him who wrote the APOCALYPSE or the
PROPHECY under the name of Daniel. There is nothing more
reckless than the results produced from their seering by later
seers and nothing more final on values than the diametrical
opposition of findings by different persons working on the same
texts. The old inspired books must be left to textual scholars
who proceed by the way of research, not by that of inspiration

L

or second sight, and who are concerned with times and peoples and history, not with inner meanings, real or supposed.

The Victorian principle of interpretation was of course a modern application of an exceedingly old business. I have mentioned Gregory the Great, who belongs to the sixth century, and his second sense of Scripture, but there is a long succession through the ages. It may be described—a little roughly—as an art of allegorising upon ancient writings, and when it takes place under an orthodox ægis the art is without prejudice to the historicity side of the stories. When St. John outran St. Peter and came first to the Holy Sepulchre on the morning of Easter, their action had for Pope Gregory an allegorical significance, but they were there and they ran literally. In some other cases the historicity element dissolves, and the ancient texts—whatever they happen to be—appear as parabolic writings. The " gospel of interpretation " had no axe to grind about the external sense of the New Testament. It is in much the same position as were those in their day who explained that Christ is crucified annually in the starry heavens. Both systems read the texts and gave the independent meanings, and if they were at issue as to all things else they were at one on the fact that any question of an historical Jesus was beyond their province.

I have endeavoured to shew that this kind of thing, even if it worked on a defined principle and produced one result, instead of having no fixed law and begetting a multitude of meanings all in conflict, is foreign to the mystic quest and as the poles asunder from any mystic term. But if this be so there is another concern of interpretation which is still further afield, if this be possible : it is that which is exercised in connection with the fulfilment of prophecy. There should be little need to establish these distinctions, but there is no subject to compare with Mysticism for the utter confusion which still prevails about it, not so much among persons who make no claim on knowledge but rather those who are busy on the fringe of things and possess a congenital faculty for misreading everything. Nor is it confined to these, in view of such a brilliant and informed writer as Emile Gebhardt whose L'ITALIE MYSTIQUE is a consistent application of the term to cases where it does not belong. It is out of this position that there arises some need for a clearance of issues in respect of Joachim of Flora and his Everlasting Gospel. The period is the twelfth century, and Joachim was of Calabria and in monastic life a Cistercian. His gospel is not to be understood in the sense of a new revelation of the written kind, as a concordance or harmony between the Old and the New Testament, though he wrote a work of this order, or as an exposition of the Christian sacred books, though he sought to explain the APOCALYPSE. It was an expected final Dispensation, being that of the Holy Spirit, as foretold, *ex hypothesi*, by the Seer of Patmos (xiv. 6) : " And I saw another angel fly in the midst of heaven, having the everlasting gospel to preach unto them that dwell on the earth."

This is the kind of exegesis, and although it may be assumed that we know already where we are, it is worth while to glance a little further into the thesis that we may estimate the titles of Joachim to be classed among mystics as they are understood in these pages, or in the sense that this qualification is applied to Eckehart and Ruysbroeck. Let us see in the first place the best that can be said of the prophet, and as to this it is beyond challenge that he bore all titles of sanctity, that he was dedicated, called and chosen from his earliest years, as if he were naturborn to the life of inward prayer and the life of contemplation, as the mystic path was termed in those days. Could he have chosen his own course it would have been one of deeper solitudes than were known to Ruysbroeck in a Flemish hermitage, but the monastic vocation in his case meant years of activity, for he felt drawn into paths of reform, and moreover he had the preacher's gift. Above all he read after his own manner the darkling signs of the times and there was also a mission herein. It came about that his days were divided, but ever the solitude called, opening its spacious ways to graces and lights of the highest, and he fled to its refuge when such liberation was possible and even built the monastery connected with his name, that of Flora, on Alpine heights.

It is said of him that in the celebration of Mass, and especially at the Divine Words of Institution, his face was transfigured and that the glory of an angel covered it ; that his demeanour was of one who belongs to this world no more ; that his preaching was like unto the message of an apocalyptic herald, or of him who carried the book of the Everlasting Gospel ; that he lived in a perpetual vision ; that he held converse in his raptures with Christ, even as if face to face ; that beneath the text of Scripture he read the hidden secrets of God. This is on the one side, but seeing that Joachim was more than the spirit of the Prayer of Ecstasy and the Prayer of Union in a macerated body of flesh there is also the other side, and it tells us of work done amidst horrors of plague and famine, of the poor for whom he stripped himself, almost to the skin, of his first work as a porter in his first Cistercian convent, of his long farings all over Italy, visiting monastic houses for the extirpation of laxity and abuse, of the dying whom he warmed on his bosom, and in fine, of those who flocked to him from all parts, seeking for spiritual help of every kind and degree.

I have given a complete picture, as with a few strokes of the pen, and very perfect it must be termed, according to its high measure. But there was another kind of contemplation which he followed through long years, or indeed from beginning to end. It was the study of Holy Scripture, and out of it there came his three genuine books, amidst a mass of false attributions which were pious frauds of another day and generation. The CON-CORDANCE, the COMMENTARY and the PSALTERY—I have referred already to two—are called great, and they were pregnant assuredly with consequence. They are described also as the records of his hopes and his anguish. I am only concerned with them for a recitation of the bare facts which emerge from their theses : (1) that he saw in his capacity as a prophet—*Divinus Vates* and *Magnus Propheta* are the titles ascribed to him by his editors— the end everywhere of the order as it then was ; (2) that he looked for the immediate coming of Antichrist and the overthrow of Christendom in the first half of the thirteenth century ; (3) that the destruction of the Church in particular would be so complete as to render it impossible for anyone then alive to call openly on the Name of the Lord ; (4) that after these things the last trumpet would sound the fulfilment of all mysteries in the Old and New Testaments ; (5) that a day of peace and truth would follow these events and encompass the whole earth. It is evident from the closing words of the CONCORDANTIA that Joachim was prepared for the "last day" to find him still in the land of the living—so near did it loom in his mind.

What was this time of peace and truth which was to heal the wounds of the world? It can be read about in Renan's NOUVELLES ÉTUDES D'HISTOIRE RELIGIEUSE and in the work of Gebhardt which I have mentioned : there is no need to go further in the absence of a special purpose, for the course of history drew a great sponge over the prophet's pictured dream. Christianity was to be born again, a new body animated by a new Spirit, and then it would be the Reign of the Spirit, the Third Person of the Blessed Trinity. John the Scot before him had conceived three epochs—the Priesthood of the Old Testament, the Priesthood of the New and the Priesthood of the life to come. Joachim and his contemporary Amaury of Chartres called them the Dispensation of God the Father, of God the Son and of God the Holy Ghost. For the Calabrian prophet, the third kingdom and its reign was that of the Everlasting Gospel, the Gospel of the Kingdom and the Spiritual Gospel of Christ. It would be also a reign of contemplation, and the Church therein would be one of hermit-monks, who in some manner to us inconceivable would so fill the world with power and grace of the Spirit that there would be no longer Jew or heathen, Greek or Roman orthodoxy, but one fold, in the care of one hierarchic caste of perfect shepherds.

The prophet was taken into the shelter of the Everlasting Arms in 1202, and the promised advent of Antichrist was illustrated by the Albigensian Crusade, the sacking of Constantinople and the proscription of the Knights Templar. Joachim of Flora offers a singular instance of a man of heroic sanctity who was yet a false prophet, who misread equally the signs of the times and the hypothetical second sense of Holy Scripture. The lesson to us and the sole purpose of this brief monograph is the necessity of distinguishing the vain pursuit of interpreting prophecy from the business and life of the mystic. Having regard to the dedications of Joachim, it looks plausible on the surface to infer that he was set heart and soul upon the mystic quest and term, but his idea of the contemplative life is not that of the great mystics who were really on the path of the union. If, however, it could be shewn that I am in error on this point, the fact would only signify that he was diverted from the true path by the textual researches to which it is evident that he devoted the major if not the whole time that could be wrung from his strenuous activities on the external side.

THE MESSAGE OF ECKEHART

" I AFFIRM," says Meister Eckehart, " that had the Virgin not first borne God spiritually He would never have been born from her in bodily fashion." Herein is no new doctrine, as we can learn from St. Basil and the BREVIARY in those pregnant words : " Mary conceived in her heart before she conceived in her body," and so also in all ages of the Christian world, by virtue of another quality of election, have elect souls conceived their Christ within them, and He has become flesh in their own life, albeit as a " Man of sorrows and acquainted with infirmity." It seems therefore that we might take the affirmation of Eckehart as, within its own measures, a concentrated centre of high theology from which to develop a thesis that this simple far-searching master of experience was orthodox by spirit and intention, if there were times when his verbal formulæ create a reasonable doubt. I am concerned with no such undertaking, but when his theology is charged with pantheism and not by those who approach it from a Church standpoint but rather by makers of criticism who are disposed to regard his alleged leaning towards heresy as one of his titles, it is necessary to protest for the truth's sake. When Eckehart affirms that in the deep states of mystical union " there is no distinction left in the soul's consciousness between itself and God, though God still regards it as a creature," it is certain that this statement is theologically and otherwise at the poles asunder from pantheism. Furthermore, philosophical pantheism, or that which Vatican encyclicals denominate " the identification of the universe with God," is set aside expressly in the Sermons, which postulate the real distinction between God and the world, though affirming that their state is inseparable, the ground being that only distinct elements can interpenetrate each other. It sounds crude enough as metaphysics, but it affirms the immanence of God in creation, which is not only unchallenged by the Church but passes as orthodox doctrine.

The truth is that the real greatness of Christian mystics—when they are speaking, I mean, from outside the deep centre of experience—manifests most frequently not in their moments of possible divergence from any hall-marked theology, but in their faculty of presenting its teaching irradiated by the light of understanding which comes from having dwelt at the centre. When Eckehart says that the soul needs no human preaching or instruction if the Kingdom of Heaven has manifested already therein, he is not seeking to make void the office of the Church but is establishing the pregnant fact that it has fulfilled its work successfully in respect of the individual soul. When he says that it is impossible to turn from sin by one's own power he is not denying the existence of free will in man, but is implying the indispensable character of Divine Grace communicated *ex hypothesi* through the authorised channels of which the Church is guardian. When he says—after the manner of Dionysius—that God is unknowable in His essence, he is not preaching a modern agnostic philosophy, because no one knew better and spoke more clearly of God in His manifestation, of the soul's intimate relation to God, or concerning the Kingdom of Heaven and the nearness thereof, while presumably for the Church itself God is knowable only in so far as He has revealed Himself.

The root-matter of Eckehart's teaching is the capacity of the soul for receiving God in fulness. It is He Whom the soul conceives, He Whom the soul bears, He Whom the soul brings forth in consciousness; but God must be the Father of the soul before the soul can become in this profound symbolical and mystical sense the Mother of God. It is because of this faculty that the soul " may arrive at such an intimate union that God draws it ultimately altogether to Himself." This is the rest of the soul in God, the repose of all things being in their proper place. It is the marriage and that which lies beyond the last pictured sacrament of the Blessed Vision. We must recognise here the ineffable state which is characterised far away and imperfectly by the word absorption, as the last consequence of the vision and the union. The saints-mystic who are canonised in the Church Roll of Sanctity and the saints-heretic whose propositions have been condemned by the Church recognise it in the same manner if not precisely in the same terms. The Sermons of Eckehart are full of fruit like this, ripened in the sun of experience. It seems to me also that he himself is full of the wisdom reflected from that Word which St. John says was made flesh and in that reflection he is full of grace and truth.

But if this is on the side of panegyric holding authentic titles, it must be understood also that Eckehart has other aspects. He belongs so much to the faculty of debate on the great subjects that one is disposed at times to question whether his attainment was not more especially in the processes of the rational mind. His characteristics include a singular subtlety, combined with artifice, though the latter has no part in convention. He is almost always unexpected, but so far as argumentation is concerned he does not produce conviction. In his highest moments of vision, when the resourceful active mind seems to suspend for a moment its startling course of thought, one feels that his wings have folded over highest peaks, but these moments are comparatively speaking rare. His acute mental endowments are more than those of Ruysbroeck, but he knew little of the Flemish mystic's heights and deeps of stillness. So he offers most often an admirable mental exercise on the sublime themes and quick innumerable flashes of shining light, but we enter seldom with him into the repose of knowledge. On the ascetic side of the mystic path he is scarcely less inhibiting than are others about his own epoch or most of those who came after, but his peculiar mentality had the gift of presenting it with even less force of appeal on the basis of its proper implications. The little book which was written for her who is called his Strasburg daughter, Sister Katrei, offers a typical example of his defects and merits alike. It may be true in a sense that almost any peg will serve at need on which to hang a thesis about the perfect life and the way to God ; but there was never such an ill-starred choice as in this tract, and yet there are great insights here and there in its course.

Perhaps also—I know not—it is of moment on the personal side, as if the Confessor who had instructed the Sister were

Meister Eckehart himself, depicted as one who had attained in the mind but lacked "actual experience," who had lived in "spiritual light" and yet was "unfamiliar with divinity," while she whom he had exhorted and put in the true way had, stayed about by his aids to reflection, won entrance into the great reality. There came indeed a day when he announced to his brethren— they crying "Glory be to God"—that he had confessed one who knew and loved beyond any that he had ever met. There were two stages in her progress: (1) when she testified that her soul ascended freely but made no stay, and (2) when in the extravagance of rapture she calls upon him to rejoice with her because "I am God"—that is to say, beholding God within her and being "confirmed in the naked Godhead, wherein is neither form nor image."

The initial course of instruction which opened a path to God for the Strasburg Daughter offers the following amazing commentary of interpretation on the miracle of loaves and fishes: (1) The first loaf signifies the research concerning that which we have been always in God and that which we now are, even in Him; (2) the second belongs to the scrutiny of our life in time; (3) the third loaf is to be understood as representing the mercy of God, while (4) the fourth is His justice, and (5) the fifth answers to true faith; but (6) the first fish shews forth the notion of will and the second its fulfilment, understood as (7) the will to subjection, or paralysis of the will to sin, and (8) achievement of the virtues, or "virtue carried to that pitch whereat it becomes unconscious" and henceforth "is our very being." As I have intimated, the beads of this kind of rosary can be hung upon any string; but on the hypothesis that the miracle is matter of fact and not of sacred myth it would be intolerable to suggest that it carried these meanings for Him by Whom it was performed or those who were fed thereby; while on the hypothesis that it is myth it is not less insufferable to affirm that it was interpreted thus to the mind of him or those who invented it. In other words, the reading lies definitely outside all region of similitude and is to be classed as such with the not less amazing symbolical commentaries of Gregory the Great. There is no doubt that the work of interpretation was done with complete inward sincerity in both cases: the attributed meanings could be made to work somehow and were made accordingly; the question of internal likelihood did not intervene to protest; it was outside the spirit of the age.

The Jesuit Poulain affirms in DES GRÂCES D'ORAISON that the Church has never reckoned Eckehart among her orthodox mystics and adds significantly " or even amongst mystics." It is likely enough if it suited a season's purpose or does not represent the personal views of an exceedingly biassed writer. So also the Church did not reckon Galileo among authentic astronomers. *E pur si muove.* The only question at issue respecting Eckehart is his status in the mystical hierarchy and whether he is to be placed above Ruysbroeck, Tauler, Suso and all the later peers. He knew that there is a mode of the soul into which no image enters, neither activity nor understanding, and that its middle stillness is that into which God comes and where He unites with the soul apart from form or similitude. His counsel is to dwell in this state as the ground and essence of truly inward being, for he who is established therein cannot be separated from God. He shall " apprehend him without image, without semblance and without means." It is said otherwise that the soul is all things, because the soul is God's Kingdom and—presumably in the attained mode of union—the Kingdom is also God, meaning in the sense of an image. But this image for Eckehart lies in the powers of the soul united at the summit of her activity, in which activity she gazes into the Divine Nature and conceives also her own as superessentially in God. She lives and moves and has her being in Him by virtue of her prototypical image in the Divine Understanding, which for Eckehart is " the Person of the Son." But there is as if a door in this image through which the soul can pass upward and into a more transcendent prototype abiding in the Father " before He brought forth the Word." Herein is another door which must be opened and gone through to reach " the summit of Divine Union," wherein—as though after many mystical deaths and resurrections—she arises finally into the life of the Godhead.

It is not difficult to see behind these obscure devices of successively superseded prototypes an attempt to body forth the ineffable experience of deeper and deeper states attained in the union, or that which is called "the work of the inner man," understood as "knowing and loving." The path otherwise for Eckehart is only and always a path of love, or "so to live that our whole life is love." He quotes Dionysius as saying that "it is the nature of love to change a man into that which he loves," and this is the key, I think, of all the German mystic's doctrine of the soul in its stages of God-becoming. It must have sounded badly enough to the adviser of Pope John XXII—that great trader in indulgences, himself charged with heresy—who condemned certain propositions of Eckehart, but it resolves itself into the simple, intelligible and realistic issue that love is absorbed in its object and engulfed therein.

It would seem that the unknown master who is called Dionysius was a great witness for Eckehart. He cites him again as his authority for a simple maxim concerning the Blessed Vision outside the union, but perhaps, if I interpret rightly, on the threshold thereof: "To be separated from God is hell, and the sight of God's countenance is heaven." But he drew more deeply when he did not quote so openly, and a memorable instance is found in his sermon on the self-communication of God. There he speaks of the Godhead, as it were, behind the Trinity, flowing from the eternal height or depth, filling the Father with joy and the Son with wisdom, the Father and the Son flowing into the Holy Spirit and filling Him with goodwill. Hereof is the unknowable Deity, and of this abyssmal Godhead the Father is affirmed to be a revelation, meaning, that is to say, to our own human or other created consciousness. But the Divine Son is the Eternal Father's image or countenance, and the Eternal Spirit is the love ineffable which subsists and intercommunicates between them. It follows that the Divine Trinity is the mode in which the hidden Godhead communicates to man the knowledge of Itself; but behind this self-expression there remains the essential and unexpressed nature which subsists outside all communication, in the great darkness and for ever behind the veil.

There is no question that the contribution of Eckehart to the mystic subject is of great importance within its own measures and period; there is no question also that his message is pregnant with significance to the deeper issues of the soul at this day, in part on account of its strong individual character, but for the rest and above all because of its catholic identity with the witness of all mystical experience in every age and land, so that it is the voice of the East testifying as well as a Western voice. As regards the West, it seems to me the most resonant of all the voices, and is that which goes most directly to the root of the whole matter. In a word, it is the voice of a faithful soul which, seeing clearly, knew no fear or hesitation, whether or not we may be able to accept the message without reserve in every one of its aspects, including all their consequences.

Eckehart is one of the great apostles of Divine Realisation in the human heart and life, for it is in the sense of this vital term that we must understand all the symbolism which speaks of the soul conceiving God, of God being born in the soul. He Who is everywhere, without change or shadow of vicissitude, is never absent ; but He is conceived within us when we begin to apprehend His presence ; He is born within us when the sense of it rises like a sun over our field of consciousness ; He abides in us and we in Him when our realisation concerning Him is like a sun poised in the zenith. Of the deep experience of this state Eckehart is speaking when he testifies concerning the soul in " modeless unity " and when he says that " the naked essence of the soul finds the naked, formless essence of the Divine Unity . . . reposing in itself."

The question is not whether this is easy or hard to understand, when contemplated as a state of being by those who as yet have not entered therein. The great fact posed for our consideration is that there was a German Church-Master of the fourteenth century who knew of this state, whether in mind or heart or soul, or in an unity of this trinity. It follows that there is a great experiment possible in mystic life and that some have attained it. It is to be hoped therefore that the writings of Meister Eckehart will become at last available in English : they are known now only by a few detached sermons and a few extracts.

RUYSBROECK'S JOURNEY IN THE DIVINE DISTANCE

LET it be said in these opening words that he who is known to us as Jan van Ruysbroeck was born in 1293 at the village in contiguity to Brussels from which he draws his name ; that he was ordained priest in 1317 ; that he worked as a secular in Brussels for six-and-twenty years ; that thereafter he retired to the forest of Soignes, at no great distance, and abode in the Hermitage of Groenendael ; that his fame and sanctity drew many to this quiet retreat ; that an informal community arose which ultimately embraced the Rule of Canons Regular of St. Augustine, with Ruysbroeck as first Prior ; that he died at Groenendael in 1381, being in his eighty-eighth year.

The intellectual environment of him who is called the Admirable and Divine Doctor was that of the Church at his period, and there is no question that he held to all its doctrines in the plenary sense of the letter without reserve of any kind. I mention this, not as a matter for surprise, not as unusual among mystics, and not as if I or others might have looked for better things, but simply to define the position in view of all that he attained. There are luminous distinctions in his writings respecting the unity of nature and Trinity of Persons in the Godhead, on Jesus Christ as the begotten Son of the Eternal Father, on the excellence and dignity of the Blessed Virgin as the immaculate Mother of God, and so forward through all the golden chain of official doctrine. He expounds also the orthodox Church teaching on the everlasting punishment of the wicked, though he interprets their state of torment rather in a spiritual than in the gross material sense, and he is as convinced as any Council that unbaptised infants are deprived of God for ever on account of original sin, though—unlike some Church findings—he denies that they are punished otherwise. It is idle to look towards the mystics in search of liberal theology or the slightest alleviation of its hardest and most formal side. The desire after mitigated doctrine belongs to the modern spirit.

There will be no need to add after this that he lived in perfect conformity with his spiritual superiors and that he regarded St. Peter not only as Prince of the Apostles, but of the whole world. The affirmation illustrates sufficiently how he stood in respect of the primacy, then seated at Avignon in the Apostolic Chair. At the end of his APOLOGIA, which treats of high contemplation and of the union between the Lover and Beloved, in further exposition of profound intimations on these subjects in two previous writings, he submits himself unconditionally to the judgment of the Catholic Church, in the faith of which he is resolved to live and die.

Now, this is he who was led by the Spirit into such great heights and over a sea so wide that after the manner of symbolism I have called these few words an account of Ruysbroeck's Journey in the Divine Distance. The kind of path which he followed was named contemplation in his own language, which is to be understood as growth in love. He performed a great pilgrimage of life in love, and when he is concerned only with its proper business it seems to me that we encounter the real Ruysbroeck, a spirit on an empyrean flight, and the reign of official doctrine lies for the time being far away in the lower regions of the mind. He may be back among official teachings a few pages later, but we have looked meanwhile with him into the infinite deeps of Being and into the immensity of the soul of man.

He has told us, it may be, in vivid words incredible and fantastic things about the last day, the coming of Christ to judgment, the world's purgation by fire, the resurrection of the dead in material bodies and the casting of the damned into Tartarean pits. We have as much use for such pictures as for a notable treatise of our childhood on HELL OPENED TO CHRISTIANS; but a little patience takes us a few steps forward, and in very truth a change comes over " the spirit of the dream." We are examining the triple fruits of " superessential contemplative life," which are (1) light ineffable, and we are made one therewith ; (2) love incomprehensible, possessing the whole kingdom of the soul ; and (3) the fruition of these, wherein we are immersed and absorbed as in that which exceeds all limit and are cleaving essentially to God in supreme altitude of mind, yet looking for greater transformation, as from brightness to further brightness, from the created light to that which is eternal. Ruysbroeck affirms that this state, being that of the Kingdom, the Kingdom within of God's lovers, is in reality beyond grace and beyond all glory of light. It is the condition of those who above the rational mind are " introverted into the superessential unity." It is that unity as to which it is said elsewhere that God is in the soul and the soul in God, that it is at once vivid and fruitful, a mutual and inseparable indwelling, ever renewed in love.

But in an interval between the testimonies Ruysbroeck remembers the heresies and explains therefore that the soul which is one with God is united by love but not in nature or essence. Were it worth while to pursue the subject, the question would arise whether a real distinction is established in this manner ; but a little later on he denies in express terms that which he has affirmed freely and frequently. The MIRROR OF ETERNAL SALVA- TION says expressly in the version of Surius : *unum non esse cum Deo*, but afterwards : *unum effici non possunt*, referring to us as creatures. It is obvious that the explicits of formal doctrine are reacting on the writer's logical mind and that he who, among other activities, opposed some heresies of his period was called to consider for a moment his own position. All this is interesting enough as a side-light but is not of our concern otherwise, for we have only to act on our previous counsel and proceed onward to be with him once more, not in a doctrinal debate but among the memorials of his experience. We shall find our created essence compared to a vast and deserted solitude, but a time comes when God dwells therein, and moreover beyond this wilderness there is that which Ruysbroeck calls *superessentia nostra*, and this is *essentia Dei*, into which we can reach by love. He tells us also that we can become beatitude itself in the life of God if only we can die in love to ourselves. Here is the state of union, love in love and life in very life : a feud about words is idle.

When the Kabalist affirms that God and His Name are One

he defines the abiding presence of the Divine Word in man, for it is man who formulates the Name and conceives it in his heart. When the Christian revelation affirms that God is love it defines a state of unity between man and God, for there is love also in us, wherein is the ground of union between us and the Divine Nature. To go further, it is only by virtue of the love within us that we conceive love in God, we being the mouth of inspiration through which all gospels come. God has spoken to us many times through the world and the ages, but He has spoken only through ourselves. In high theology we may testify that it is the Spirit of God, and blessed be His Holy Spirit, but It moves and speaks from within us. There is no other witnessing than that which heart and mind make unto mind and heart, unless it be the silence of Nature ; but we are its interpreters and from our own deeps of being we lend a voice thereto.

And so it comes about that when Ruysbroeck has great things to tell us of love between God and the soul, it is not so much like deep unto deep uttering voice but as one great voice of all, and if the disciples of love are open and prepared in their hearts, then *gemitum ingentem pelagi . . . audiunt omnes.* When the heart opens thus, it is sometimes in the great stillness as if God Himself were listening. Alternatively a stage comes when we hear not Ruysbroeck or any other mystic, but the *ingens gemitus* only, and this becomes *vox magna Divinitatis pelagi.* He has told us that when the Lover and the Beloved are conjoined and united in the same wardenship of love, then is love perfect ; but this is like an overture or preface to the Great Mystery, as he also knows and rings many changes in consequence about various grades of love, till at last its infinite prospect unveils suddenly before him and we hear of that last state of the one and only subject, than which nothing more glorious or sublime can be obtained through time or eternity. In the attempt to give expression concerning it he takes refuge in Dionysian symbolism, because it is above cognition and above science, an abyssal infinity of unknowing in which the soul is plunged, an immeasurable beatitude in which we are all one, and That is one also Which is in itself beatitude. All blessed spirits are dissolved and self-lost therein, or in supersubstantial essence, as in an unknown darkness. So does the state elude the

M

words which seek to comprise it, but it is the voice of one who has known it in some part of mind and soul.

Now, it seems certain that love in its essence or true nature is one only thing, and nothwithstanding its misdirection in our present estate, if God is love then, as I have said, there is a root of unity between Him and us, and there must be a way by which it is uncovered. But this is the way of the mystics. Here is the subject in which Ruysbroeck made his exploration. I have called it his Journey in the Divine Distance, because when the ground of identity is reached we proceed from another direction than that of external life, and there opens before us the illimitable world of realisation in the Life Divine. I have quoted it often before, I must quote it once again : the intent of Ruysbroeck was *in vastissimum Divinitatis pelagus navigare*, which is at once a word in symbolism and a delineation of living experience. We can describe it as we like to ourselves—for example, as experience in the superconscious region of our nature. It matters not. Ruysbroeck shall distinguish as he likes between union and oneness when he is speaking as a Doctor of Theology and not as *Doctor Admirabilis*. Again, it matters not. Experience in the state denominated may connote theism or pantheism. It is neither here nor there. I say in my humility that God is enough. Whatever is outside this I give over to the schools. They have debated it through all the centuries, and the debate goes on. I never heard that anyone was wiser or better on account of it. I think personally that God is All in all—yesterday, to-day and for ever—remembering also how the Christ of Nazareth said that He was one with the Father and how He promised the same kind of union to those who followed Him—or at least He prayed for it. In any case, God is love, and a thousand mystical experiences tell us of the soul of man, that it can become love.

It would seem that there is no form of verbal symbolism which is at once more profound and more full of pitfalls than is that which describes (1) the union between Christ and His Church in terms of the bond in wedlock between Bridegroom and Bride ; (2) the union between Christ and every individual soul in the sacramentalism of earthly espousals ; and (3) that Divine Union which is the catholic term of mystical life as the mystic marriage *par excellence*. St. Catherine of Siena has been called in a particular manner the Mystic Bride, a title which, whether it is correct or not, is authorised according to the mind of that Church which keeps the records of her experience and those of its analogies without number. It is valuable also to myself for the purposes of this brief consideration, seeing that by an accident of things it provides an opportunity to offer certain reflections which may not be wanting on the side of practical interest—be it said, as a clearance of issues—on the general subject.

Catherine Benincasa, who was born in 1347 and died in 1380, had two outstanding experiences, one of which was the marriage in question and the other her reception of the stigmata. Both furnish points of difference from recurring instances well known to students who are versed in the annals of grace and election under the Christian ægis. Of the second I shall not speak, partly because it was an episode of purely inward experience of the psychic order, unlike that of St. Francis of Assisi among many others, and for the rest because in my own view at its value it bears little if any relation to the mystic subject. As regards the espousals, it is necessary to make a distinction before reflecting on the case in point, and for this purpose I must be permitted to vary the tabulation which, following leading authorities, I have made in my opening words. The consensus of sacred experience, as found in the records, distinguishes two mystic marriages, one of which is celebrated in this life, while the other may be begun here but is completed only hereafter. To make use of accepted terminology, the first is an union of our psychical and spiritual part in a state of consciousness irradiated by the light and grace of the Christ-life. This description must be understood, however, as approximate to the truth rather than truth exact : it would require a considerable thesis to justify a less simple but more precise form of expression. The second is an ineffable union between the spirit of man and God : it is the only real and indissoluble mystic marriage.

That of St. Catherine belongs to neither class ; it was a matter of psychic vision, and it took place in the early part, almost as if at the beginning of her advancement in spiritual life. The boon which it secured to her was the presence of a teacher at need, of a Guide in the likeness of Christ Who said that he was the Eternal Truth. He came to confirm her in the faith to which she belonged, and for her better assurance He appeared in the vestments and carrying the other insignia of that sovereign pontiff at Rome who was for Catherine—in express terminology—the Christ on earth. He was this no less when—in virtue of those warrants which she held direct from One Whom she hailed as her Divine Master—she was offering him religious and even moral instruction ; when she was denouncing his worldly policy ; when she was recommending his retirement from the papacy because his hesitation and delay imperilled the cause which she championed. He was this no less when he or his successor used her as a tool of his statecraft and closed the public side of her mission in comparative failure.

Let us look, however, somewhat more closely into this question of the marriage, that we may realise later on its utter distinction from the mystic marriage as understood by St. John of the Cross, remembering also that many persons of spiritual dispositions at this day may have quickening sympathies with a nature like that of St. Catherine, yet nothing of the mystical consciousness, so that the distinction with which I am concerned will be almost outside their categories. It will be necessary to proceed therefore with no little care in order to insure clearness. At the beginning there will be no difficulty in understanding the particular set of sentiments and preconceived notions which led the saint in her girlhood to resolve on a celibate life. The root of it has been described accurately as a state of rebellion " against the notion of her personality being butchered to make a sultan bridegroom's holiday " and may recall as such some of its Victorian correspondences apart from all sanctity or even its pretence. The feeling went back far into Catherine's life, for at the age of six years, getting to know in some reflected and unrealised way that there was a bride of Heaven and also a bride on earth, she had prayed to the Blessed Virgin that her Divine Son might be the Spouse of her soul and had promised on her own part that she would receive none but Him.

The experience of her spiritual bridal took place at the close of a certain time of carnival. In answer to her prayers, fastings and other austerities, the Lord Christ appeared to her and said that because of her denials and macerations—but not explicitly, be it observed, because she had renounced and disdained earthly marriage—He had determined to espouse her soul to Him in faith. The ceremony which followed was one of great pomp, performed amidst a concourse of the blessed, including Mary the Mother of God, St. John of Patmos and David the psalmist-king, as if the Old and New Covenants must both bear witness. A ring set as with earthly gems was placed on the maid's finger by the Bridegroom, with these pregnant words : " Behold I have espoused thee to Me, thy Maker and Saviour, in faith, which shall continue in thee from this time forward, evermore unchanged, until the time shall come for a blissful consummation in the joys of Heaven." The ceremony ended at this point and the whole pageant dissolved, including the ring of espousals, so far as external eyes and the sight of others were concerned ; but it is on record that the Mystic Bride beheld the precious emblem always on her hand, though it was only discerned spiritually.

It would serve little purpose to examine alternative hypotheses concerning the nature of this experience, which is taken at its face value by the Church Catholic and Latin, which would be termed pathological by official medical psychology at the stage in which we are, hallucination pure and simple by him whom we term in our derision the man in the street, and a psychic vision by several thousand persons who know or have heard that there are things called psychic happenings. There is no question of course that it belongs to the last class, but to speak of it in such terms, as if we were encompassed on all sides by its correspondences and analogues, is to confound all the issues. Since the date of the Rochester Knockings there are records behind us of seventy-five years of trance, vision, rapture, clairvoyance, communication from a postulated other side, but of this kind and order there is not one instance anywhere. It follows in the logic of the subject that the experience of St. Catherine of Siena does not fall into place among modern psychic happenings and that to which it belongs is the psychology of sanctity. The sooner that we elect to recognise that this is a class of experience by itself the better we shall order our minds for the criticism of psychical research.

Having established this point in the cause of rational thought, it remains to add one of those saving commonplaces which have a habit of eluding acute people when debating a difficult subject : it is and can be only in virtue of the same faculties that the psychic sees and hears and speaks in the workings of common mediumship and in the image-making experiences of dedicated and saintly life, just as the common bond between Dante's PARADISE and Blacklock's PRINCE ARTHUR is that both are products of mind. The difference between them is of quality and direction. The two orders of experience are important to one another because they vouch for one another. The holy men and women of old are credible and unimpeachable as witnesses to the fact of their psychic experience by all that we know of their lives and the great works of their minds, in which manner they make other psychic experience antecedently credible, while the phenomena of this order amidst which we live bear witness in turn to the credibility of earlier and higher experience.

I register therefore my personal conviction that the psychic records of St. Catherine were true and real after their own kind, more especially as—all things considered—she was one of the sanest saints on earth. She appears to have distinguished roughly those among her many psychic happenings which were merely the formulated images of her own thoughts. The pageant of her espousals belonged to another order. But that what was veridic in her experience was veridic also in the sense of her personal belief is a very different question. It seems certain that the face value sets an impossible premium thereupon.

We have to remember that, as I have intimated, her Guide, her Teacher, her Friend was thenceforward always with her. With her He paced the cell, with her He recited the psalms, and at a later stage—in answer to her prayer that He would create a clean heart within her—He removed it altogether and two days later substituted His own in its place. We pass after this manner into the region of openly symbolic vision and it is a key to that which had preceded it. There is a wide field of pictorial representation which belongs to this order and it has been studied by psychical research but without reaching a satisfactory canon of criticism. We know only that the mind is a great maker of images, that in certain states it presents them objectively to itself, that such states are frequently those of disease and hence belong to pathology, but that this explanation by no means covers them all, and that those which are not included are not improbably the larger part, as they are certainly the more ordered and thus the more important. We are all of us acquainted with people of normal sanity—men and women indifferently—for whom experiences of this kind are as a part of daily life. Whether the objective presentation operates automatically from within the mind or is an impression from without, that is to say, from other minds on another plane of being, we do not know. The latter alternative is the explanation of Spiritism and is obviously that also of the Catholic Church, which recognises, however, the intervention of Divine and angelic mind in the body-general of sanctified experience and diabolism in respect of the rest. Spiritism, on the other hand, is content with the hypothesis of discarnate minds.

The case of St. Catherine of Siena offers an opportunity to test the Church standpoint by the value of the teaching which she received in her psychic or interior states. As an example belonging to the doctrinal order—and I think that this will suffice—she was told that the smallest offence against Him Who is the Infinite Good—being the speaker *ex hypothesi,* or Christ the Lord of Mercy—demands an infinite satisfaction. Here is the old stereotyped theological argument for eternal punishment, but carried to its final issue, since it swallows up all distinction between venial and mortal sin. As regards the Church and its ministers, it was impressed upon her (1) that those in religion have been placed where they are " to announce My word " in doctrine and in truth ; (2) that the Religious Orders have been founded by the Holy Spirit ; (3) that " I do not wish any temporal lord to be their judge " ; (4) that they are the anointed ones appointed " to serve Me, the Eternal God."

It is too easy to see from what recesses of Catherine's nature this voice issued. It was not, in my judgment, hallucination ; it was not arch-deception ; it was of those who speak at the psychic gates, who utter great things on occasion—even high things and holy—but for some reason are always in mask. The channel of the recipient's personality may be itself the veil. It is easier in my opinion to infer that the kind of direction is external to the mind of the medium, though it reflects the training of her mind, than to adopt the alternative hypothesis which I have stated above ; but I carry an open mind on the whole subject of explanation, so only that I make clear my rooted conviction that the Christ Who taught St. Catherine was not the Great Master.

It should be mentioned as another illustration that after the supposed exchange of hearts—after and not before—the Mystic Bride entered upon that public and, so to speak, political mission in which her capacity was shewn to an extraordinary degree. Here I need glance at it only to establish a single point. The mission was twofold : (1) the removal of the Papacy from Avignon to Rome and (2) the consolidation of the temporal power by yet another Crusade. That these projects were near to the heart of Christ let those affirm who dare. She secured the one but that which she hoped for most did not follow therefrom : the second scheme came, in a word, to nothing, and there is no need to add that in the alternative event its object would not have been encompassed. In the course of her activities that Divine Heart which she carried—by the hypothesis—within her fell into a few errors of extravagance, of duplicity even, as of believing that the end justified the means ; but it follows that what dictated such policy was only the eager, too zealous human heart of Catherine, and there is no need to dwell at length on these things. About her native purity of intention, utterly impersonal detachment and singleness of purpose there is and can be no question. There can be none also that she was an important political figure for a few years and one of great astuteness. That which ensued in failure did not come about through any fault of hers, but because there was greed, insincerity and the craft which is not statesmanship on the other side.

And now in recurrence to the point in chief with which I am concerned in this notice : from my study of the life of St. Catherine it is clear that in herself she was a woman of peculiar holiness and deservedly a popular saint ; but she was not a mystic and she had little conception regarding the real nature of the Divine Union. She was a true daughter of the Church of temporal power, and she made the grave mistake of believing that the kingdoms of this world were a lawful appanage of him who claimed to hold the keys of the Kingdom of Heaven. Perhaps if she had served less zealously the power, spiritual and otherwise, of the Papacy, she might have been more truly the Bride of Christ. She was a woman on occasion of high, clear and convincing insight belonging to the spiritual-intellectual order ; she was also a woman of psychic visions and communications which were characteristic of her period. Her literary remains are of unimpeachable value as records of greatness in womanhood, but this statement has reference perhaps more especially to her correspondence.

The belief that earthly marriage is inimical to the mystic marriage is not entirely characteristic of her place and period ; it is an obscure and complex question which cannot be debated here. In the ideal, which is the Divine order of things, there is no question that the first should be a path to the second, but there is none also that few of our earthly unions are of that kind which is said to be made in Heaven, and it calls to be realised that the higher spiritual dedications are exclusive and very jealous. The inscription about them is : " With all thy heart and with all thy mind and with all thy soul." When men and women who have been joined inwardly after this manner are joined also in the outward body the world will come into its own.

To the question whether St. Catherine might have become a Spouse of Heaven—within her own understanding of these words—had she been a wedded wife on earth the answer in all the likelihood of things would be a distinct negative—under every general circumstance and especially perhaps in Italy of the fourteenth century. But it does not really arise in any serious manner, for her experience in symbolic vision bears no relation to mystic union, and she was not on the path of the union, in the mystic sense. She was on that of the joys of Paradise or of the Beatific Vision—I think, understood a little in the picture-state and in a very clear distinction of subject and object. There is for this reason a specific misconception about her title of the Mystic Bride, but it must be condoned because it is inevitable. A saintly maiden in the early ecstasies of prayer and the ascetic life does not attain easily to the true mystic espousals, nor does bachelor, wife or husband. It is a high prize at the end of a long journey. But there are certain substitutes and some also of these are in the path of holiness. Had Catherine met with a man like unto herself as woman, there might have been one of those marriages over which earth and heaven rejoice; but I have indicated that the nuptial state on earth is entered seldom now, and was entered perhaps more seldom then, in the spirit which may lead to realisation on planes within.

There is something more to be said on this subject at a later stage, but its adequate consideration would demand a volume in place of casual allusions, arising here and there in a collection of essays. These cannot touch the fringe of a theme on which the higher evolution of our human race depends, alike from the physical, moral and spiritual points of view, whether these are approached within or without the question of the mystic path and term. Meanwhile the sacrament of marriage under the auspices of the very institution which has made human wedlock the outward sign of an inward grace has missed its point entirely. There is nothing to indicate that within the consciousness of the

Church Catholic the formal sacrament is a sacred and living seal placed on the life of espousals so that it may become not only a symbol of the Divine Union but a path which can open thereto; there is no consciousness that in this sense it is even a sign. When we remember the kind of material on which the Church had to work at the time that it instituted sacraments; when we remember the mental implicit which rejected the offices of Nature for the purposes of a Divine Birth in Bethlehem; when we remember the definite ruling of St. Paul—" he that marrieth doeth well, but he that marrieth not doeth better "; when we remember in fine those early Christian centuries, with their hermit and anchorite lives, their Syrian and Theban deserts; the wonder is not that marriage was brought within the Christian law and order as if with an air of reluctance and a certain grudging note but that it was ever brought at all, and much more made a sacrament. The spur of necessity drove, but Apoc. xiv. 4, remained the secret feeling of the Church and the spirit of its perfect counsels,

VOICES FROM CARMEL

THE voice of the silence of Carmel may be the voice which speaks most eloquently at this day to the soul that knows the Mount of Vision and the great tradition of its mystery, as if a secret and sacred wisdom came down from immemorial ages, when a higher law than that which was delivered from Sinai reposed in the heart of the elect. But the voices to which I refer are those of the mystics of Carmel, and seeing that they are many in various paths of devotion or at various points of attainment, it should be said that I am concerned with two only, at once greatest and earliest in the sense of attainment—St. John of the Cross and St. Teresa. Their voices are in all men's ears who have heard the call of the Spirit and have uttered as they could their glad and loving responsions. Now, it happens in the harmony of such things that these voices are like that of the silence of Carmel, which gives tidings of those who are taken by God, as Enoch, or ascend like Elias into heaven : they are witnesses to the same rapture and the same elevation in the spirit. The Castle of St. Teresa is built upon the slopes of Carmel, if not on its summit, while the soul's ascent to God is compared by St. John of the Cross to the ascent of that holy mountain.

There are certain names the utterance of which seems to work on the soul with a power that compels at least reverence and sometimes love, according to the particular departments wherein their rule operates. The name of St. John of the Cross has a penetrating influence of this kind, and it may seem scarcely less strong in those cases when it awakens but vague echoes or stirs doubtful wells of memory. Even then it is a voice which speaks, in however strange a language, concerning great experiences and achievements of the soul. He was a monk of the Carmelite Order in Spain of the sixteenth century, and I am not concerned with his life because it is either known already to those who read or there are easy sources of reference and I should be retracing therefore only a travelled ground. The appeal of St. John is of course to and from within that school of Mysticism which is the spokesman at the highest grade of Latin Christianity. Every line that he wrote on the subject which was not only his life but the life of all life within him has been available for long years in English and in more than one translation. It is to be wished that as much could be said of certain other lights belonging to the same school and great also in repute, like the Spanish reformed Carmelite, but for want of translation not so well known by their writings as one might be disposed to assume from all that their names imply. Some of them wrote in Latin and have remained therein. Some of them were transferred into that tongue from their respective vernaculars, as if from a quiet stall in the chancel to a side altar in one of the transepts or aisles. But this was in the days when Latin was read and written as the chief means of communication between men of learning. In this respect it may be said to have died a second time, and the books which are left therein are entombed therewith. Until Maeterlinck rendered into his great French the Flemish ADORNMENT OF THE SPIRITUAL MARRIAGE, Ruysbroeck was but a rumour outside his own country, for no one read him in the limpid, unruffled and colourless Latin of Surius, while an anterior French volume of excerpts based on Surius is a modern redaction of Ruysbroeck, in which the divine contemplations of the original are but an echo of a far-off voice. We owe therefore a debt of gratitude to those who in these days put the Christian mystics into modern tongues.

The ASCENT OF MOUNT CARMEL, the DARK NIGHT OF THE SOUL, the SPIRITUAL CANTICLE and the LIVING FLAME OF LOVE are at once a chronological enumeration of the mystic's written memorials, the epochs of his inward life and the stages which mark his ascent of that mystical mountain the summit of which is the attainment of Divine Union. It signifies nothing that the first two appear to have been composed in the same year, namely, 1578, for many years of spiritual experience lie behind them. Within this narrow period the ASCENT OF MOUNT CARMEL was first in order of time and is more than twice the length of the later treatise. I do not propose to affirm that the DARK NIGHT is definitely more important in a vital sense, for the distinctions and analogies between the two works, which are both commentaries on successive lines of eight metrical stanzas, placed as a proem to each, go over for the most part an identical ground of experience. They are concerned in the first place with what is called the night of the senses and thereafter that of the spirit—the state of neophytes beginning to advance therefrom and the state of those who have reached the second degree and are called to the master-grade. They are otherwise a history of the soul in its progress from the life of meditation to the truly contemplative life and then to its deeper modes. But it should be added that the longer text contains what ostensibly at least is an extra section, dealing with " the purgation and active night of the memory and the will."

It is not difficult perhaps for even a beginner to realise that the DARK NIGHT is in reality a more advanced work, by which I mean that it deals in the later sections with states of the soul which are not subjects of consideration in the larger thesis. The disciple is brought at the end to a certain interior asylum which the powers of evil cannot enter, or those at least of a conventional kind. It follows almost obviously that the first impression which will be made on such modern readers as are capable of interpreting to themselves the messages of books like these is that the DARK NIGHT is a handbook for the guidance of souls on whom experiences which are almost untranslatable have already come down. There is little and less than little which belongs to common knowledge among those who, in or out of the world and its normal ways, have set out for the spiritual life. The result, however, recalls a bizarre point in old theosophical Kabalism, wherein the emanating light is pictured as descending from numeration to numeration, but they are disrupted speedily by the influx. In other words, the persons whose difficulties are described, whose desires and disabilities are analysed with such exceeding care and fulness, seem scarcely ripe for such experiences as are described subsequently, so common are the temptations from which they are held to suffer. *Cæteris paribus,* the earlier sections of the DARK NIGHT are comparable to a book of instructions addressed to simple rustics on right conduct in the Palace of the King, and the one unaccountable thing is that they should have been commanded to the King's Palace.

I must not be interpreted as affirming that in the great majority of natures there is not first of all what is termed the gross purgation in other schools or that it is followed otherwise than by that of the spirit. In most cases this is probably the order of the work; but the catholic mystics and indeed mystics generally have treated but seldom of another secret operation of grace and will, by which the former works immediately upon the latter outside all external conditions, and by a change in the axis of its inclination puts an end to the old order at once and, as one might say, for ever. In the face of such rare and almost unknown experiences, even great spiritual teachers like St. John of the Cross seem to be dealing with the incipiencies and accidentals; and their anxious directions for putting away pride and presumption, waywardness, concupiscence and so forth are for the threshold of the life of religion, the counsel to those who are seeking only to make the best of both worlds. The remarks which are offered here to those who read the Spanish Carmelite apply equally to readers of Ruysbroeck, though he went so far on the journey which ends in God.

If a word must be said to summarise what no skill can reduce within the compass of a paragraph, let it be said that, according to St. John of the Cross, pure faith is a dark night of the natural faculties, and this night is the purgation of union with God. It is a certain flowing in of God into the soul, an infused contemplation, an instruction in the perfection of love. In respect of its condition, as in respect also of that which is destined to follow it, we can think of it as analogous to the physical darkness in which the body is itself developed. This comparison may contain a great truth, if it is not pushed too far. The years of spiritual life on earth are as certain moons following conception, during which the form of divine desire is developed within us; and in due season we shall issue forth to see with our own eyes that which all things now foreshadow, all faiths make evident.

As regards Divine Love, St. John of the Cross presents it as a work of the Holy Spirit which breathes into the soul and quickens or awakens that which was previously as a thing dead within us or plunged in the lethargy of sleep. The SPIRITUAL CANTICLE and the LIVING FLAME are songs of the triumph of love, and amidst their aspirations and raptures they belong also to the records of experience. He who has implied that it is always latent within us, who says that it is raised into life by the work of God in the soul, has reached that state of love in which he can shew forth its full stature of activity and some of the fruits thereof.

The second voice of Carmel is that of St. Teresa, the contemporary of St. John, who worked with her as his senior at the reform of that Order to which both belonged. She is an eloquent witness on finding God within, on the dignity of the soul, which is like a Palace for the Great King, and on that complete dedication of the mystic life which surrenders it wholly to His Presence. Her chief states of Interior or Mental Prayer—Prayer of Recollection, Prayer of Quiet and Prayer of Ecstasy or Rapture—are to be interpreted simply as stages of growth in love. The first is laborious, as the beginning of a great work, and is comparable to the difficulties of meditation for those as yet unaccustomed to thinking in the heart. The second corresponds already to a first sense of the Presence within the soul. She says that the soul is led captive by the love of God : it is a state of contemplation, wherein is a certain stillness, for which reason St. Teresa says also that it is listening rather than speaking. The third state is compared to " a fresh baptism of the Spirit," a state of deep calm and a sleep of bliss. The work is done for us and in us, but it is the Divine Master Who has taken it all upon Himself. Her diagnosis of this condition is that " the soul has entered into the secret place of the Most High " and is abiding " under the shadow of the Almighty." But the Prayer of Rapture signifies an epoch of plenary grace descending, or of the soul ascending as if above itself, entranced and carried away. It is said that " the soul wings its flight into the unseen " and that this is also an epoch of fruition.

The Prayer of Union is likened also to a first meeting between the Lover and Beloved and to a Spiritual Betrothal, while the

Prayer of Rapture is the ravishment of the soul's aspiration towards union with the Spouse. In St. Teresa's CASTLE OF THE SOUL she describes the ineffable state of Divine Marriage and the new life which follows it, being that of Christ in the soul. She affirms concerning it that the place of the Presence is in the centre of the soul and in another manner of symbolism that the spirit of the soul becomes one and the same with God. It is added that the state endures always in the centre of which she speaks, and it is understood also as being a state of Prayer. As such it has no formal name assigned : it is, however, the Prayer of the Living Presence, as between the Lover and Beloved.

POST-REFORMATION MYSTICS

BEFORE the voices of Carmel were raised in the reformed Friaries of Spain, the Reformation was already in the world, and about the time that St. Teresa and St. John of the Cross were called to a deeper knowledge of God and His union the strife of sects in Germany was driving many in search of at least some intellectual asylum, if not of a deeper peace in the knowledge of Divine Things. The close of the sixteenth century and the years that followed thereon begot among other things much mistaken zealotry on the downfall of the whole external order and the Second Coming of Christ. There was also the zealotry of reform in things other than religion, and new stars in heaven were taken as portents of new eras and great revolutions everywhere. The Rosicrucian Brotherhood arose with pretended schemes backed by mythical claims : there were prophets also in the highways and byways, with all Scripture behind them. The event which loomed on the threshold was not, however, either the coming reign of Antichrist or the Second Advent but the Thirty Years' War.

The first Protestant or Lutheran mystic was Jacob Böhme, who was born at Gorlitz in 1575 and died in 1624. As a man of vision and a psychic of the highest order, he offers a notable contrast to the purely intellectual theosophist and cosmical philosopher Robert Fludd, his contemporary, who does not connect with the mystics, except in moments of rare illumination. The great Teuton stands therefore alone—as at his place, so also at his period. I shall take him in connection with a later name belonging to the Latin tradition.

The name of Jacob Böhme is in all men's ears who know anything of the mystic life, its travellings, its strange researches and the grace of its literature ; but his place in the annals notwithstanding Brother Laurence until recent days, when he came to be translated and edited, was scarcely known in England. Böhme belongs—as we have seen—to the end of the sixteenth century and to the first decades that followed it; Brother Laurence is later by forty or fifty years. The one was born and bred in Luther's Reformed Church and, for all his visions and revelations, he took at no time any overt step to leave it, though it denounced and excommunicated him. The other was a serving brother in a monastery of Discalced Carmelites, and he died as he had lived always in the communion of the Latin Church. Jacob Böhme was a shoemaker by trade, and so earned his bread to the day's end; Brother Laurence had followed arms as a common soldier, till he exchanged by way of promotion into the monastic kitchen. History does not tell us what reputation or success attended the one at his last or the other among his pans and kettles; but I judge by the spirit within them that they did in a good and workmanlike manner that which it was given them to perform in that way of the outward life to which it had pleased God to call them. Such election within as was theirs is usually a recommendation for service and a character in daily paths.

Jacob Böhme is the deep unto deep uttering voice and the height unto height shewing knowledge. Brother Laurence is the scullion in the kitchen of the King, saying that the King's kitchen is like the King's Sanctuary, because of God's Immanence and God's transcendence. And if on the High Altar there repose in the great white tabernacle those elements of bread and wine to which the Presence of God in Christ is most sacramentally allocated, not for this shall the scullion fail to find the Presence of his Master, even His hidden voice, among the furnaces and stewpans of his humble material alchemy, so only that he maintains in the kitchen the same spirit that he carries to the steps of the Altar. It is possible therefore to serve both God and man no less as cook in the kitchen than as thurifer or acolyte at Mass. Yes, even, in the last resource, there is not wanting a natural analogy between him who sings Mass for God's purpose and him who cooks common meats to place on a refectory table, or for that matter on another board anywhere in this world of ours.

So also Böhme and Brother Laurence are divided by gulfs on the surface, yet are they one in the great concern—the mighty cosmic seer and the humble maker of maxims, bright as are seeds of pearl. They differ only after the manner of true voices bearing witness to the one subject. Brother Laurence discoursing of perfect union between the soul and God in his simple and glowing language and Böhme in his grand, rough, strangely intelligible periods telling of the finding of God, in Whom are all things, assuredly answer one another, exchanging the watchwords of progress on the great ascent. At least in the WAY TO CHRIST and the PRACTICE OF THE PRESENCE they are saying the same thing and shewing forth the same end, each in his own tongue, even if one is like a master sitting in the chair of doctrine and the other like a monitor supervising in the lower classes. They are each of the Holy Assembly and its high apostolate.

The fear of God drives many and this is well, but God's love drives the elect of God and this is better. They belong to that unincorporated fraternity of grace and the spirit in which all mystics desire to be registered, though not all can be classed—by us at least—in the same school or rank of that Holy Assembly to which I have just alluded. How shall we place, for example, that Gerard of Zutphen who wrote the SPIRITUAL ASCENT ? St. Thomas à Kempis tells us that when he passed from his cell to the church and so only frequented the streets of the city, he regarded the worldly crowd which surged to and fro about him as if they were a herd of swine. Compare the patience of Böhme, the large charity of Brother Laurence, the spirit of St. Francis— him of the " little flowers " and the lover of Lady Poverty ; compare any and all of those who have aspired to seats of the beloved in the eternity of the great goodwill : was not the crowd for these the material of a salvation which is to follow ? It did not come about therefore that Gerard brought tidings of experience concerning the Grades of Love. The SPIRITUAL ASCENT exhibits by stage and by stage the whole steep stairway of the ascetic life, but it is neither the deeps nor the heights. There is much concerning the holy fear of God and of God's love it is as if Gerard had dreamed a little ; but as to the love of one's neighbour and the path which is possible therein—notwithstanding certain cold counsels towards the end of his book—it is as if he were in dark night. It is certain that the path of such asceticism is not the path of union. It is to be affirmed that the love of a little child in the sense of Christ is better than all the houses of asceticism that are apart from charity. The last of Böhme is better and so is the jack of Brother Laurence.

The question which remains is the appeal of Böhme's doctrine to mystical Christianity. Much as I love and admire the author of MYSTERIUM MAGNUM and THE WAY TO CHRIST, I can make no claim to a seat among his truly informed exponents : he is the study of a life rather than of such hours as I have been able to spare for his great volume of work. If I speak on their subject therefore it can be only with a certain reserve and while certifying to my own limitations. There is no question that the Teutonic Theosopher is of importance for certain aspects of Christian Mysticism, but he is not—so far as I can see—in the great tradition. He does not enter into the golden chain which began with pseudo-Dionysius and St. Augustine : if he could be said to have antecedents at all one might look for them behind THEOLOGIA GERMANICA, behind his contemporary enthusiasts, Valentine Weigel and Guttmann, among the rumours of things and persons which move about the period of Merswin and the Friends of God. But I think that he stands alone, his own and no other's, so that there is no ground for his comparison with any seer or saint in the Christian centuries. If Eckehart, Ruysbroeck and St. John of the Cross are typical witnesses in the forefront of Christian Mysticism, he is so much out of focus with them that it seems difficult to term him a mystic, and yet he is, but in another school and speaking another language. He is a man of revelations, with a great scheme of the universe and a spiritual history of man—both pregnant when they are approached with an understanding mind.

As a Christian, he appears in my own mind a little nearer perhaps to Catholicism than to the Lutheran sect of his particular place and day, but he is of either only in the wayward turn of a glass of dream. As a seer, he beheld in his well of vision not only that which was essential to his own concern but vestiges and reflections of things which belonged to other systems. He connects in this manner with important schools, one of which is outside Christianity, though two centuries at least were passed by a section of scholarship in attempting to prove that next to the Old Testament it was the chief independent witness to Christian truth. I speak of the Jewish theosophy known under the name of Kabalah. He reflects also from alchemy, which at its apparent beginning in Byzantium had Gnostic elements, at least in the form of expression, but at a later period—as I am disposed to hold—was taken over into the mysteries of " grace and experience " which lie behind Catholicism. It is said that when the writings of Böhme began to be known in the world the masters in alchemy felt that their Secret Vessel could not much longer remain in reserve among them. The reason why it should remain would in such case also have reached its term.

Jacob Böhme comes before us as an exponent of that " spiritual mystery of life " which is attained in Christ, and on this account I call him not only a mystic but one among mystic teachers. So far as records are concerned, he is the first who reached a considerable grade of first-hand inward experience and yet owed nothing to the ascetic rule. At the same time it seems to me that the last end of the human soul in Divine Union passed seldom within his sphere of vision, and his doctrine of the after-life can belong at best only to intermediate stages. It is hampered, moreover, with the separation-scheme of everlasting punishment. This notwithstanding, he had some conception of the soul going forth to God and entering into His love—with the unspeakable joy of that love—and also into the mercy of God. But Jacob Böhme was more especially a macrocosmic philosopher, concerned with the genesis of things and the whole order of manifestation. His scheme is strange and significant, but those who can take it into their hearts are a small minority, and I question whether it has any real message for the present age. To his serious students I have one counsel to offer, and that is to collate Böhme with Jewish macrocosmic theosophy, as contained in the ZOHAR. There is otherwise still a work to be done : it remains for one who is really familiar with the texts to take out the great mystical *dicta* apart from their systems and let them stand in an ordered collection at their own value. I believe that the result would be like a new light on the Teutonic Theosopher and a treasury of pearls of price. That he belongs meanwhile to our subject is shewn in many places, as for example in THEOSCOPIA, which speaks of the will in its turning, whereby it is born anew " in the Divine outflow of love " and enters thus into the state of Divine Sonship, in which it is " united with the Unity " and becomes " one with all things."

MOLINOS AND THE QUIETISTS

THE day of great names was over, the great testimonies had been borne, the sixteenth century had closed, and after voices of the mystic saints there seemed to be heard only, because there resounded everywhere, the clamour and the conflicts of reform. The Church whose office it was to carry the beacons and banners of the Prince of Peace had illustrated its view of His message with fire and sword through the centuries. The witness of the faith once delivered to the saints had been formulated in a plenary sense by events like the Albigensian Crusade and by the Massacre of St. Bartholomew, this last so late as the days of St. John of the Cross. It was to receive a further formulation in the life-time of Molinos, the Spanish mystic, by the Revocation of the Edict of Nantes and all that followed therefrom. It was to be exemplified also in the person of Molinos himself, of Fénelon and Madame Guyon, who represented in Spain and in France a school of Mysticism which the Church condemned and sought to extirpate under the name of Quietism.

Molinos was born in 1627 and died in a dungeon of the Holy Inquisition at Rome in 1696, after years of imprisonment. His life is well known, as also the kind of considerations and interests which led to his proscription. Of Fénelon I need scarcely speak, because the MAXIMS OF THE SAINTS are in the hands of all and nothing that is new to our purpose arises therefrom. Madame Guyon and that for which she stood will be therefore the chief concern of the present essay, which is not on account of her greatness or the living import of her message but because she exemplifies rather typically the class of testimony which was borne under the Christian ægis after the great witnesses.

There are admirable things in Molinos, but they are in the occasional and sporadic rather than in the sustained sense. Like certain other doctors of perplexed souls seeking their term in the centre, he is perhaps more especially a memorial of old evidence rather than a living guide now upon the chief subject of debate which fills the universe. Molinos, Madame Guyon and Fénelon are three names, practically concurrent, which stand for an identical motive and path in the inward spiritual life. The qualitative value of their appeal is about equal, but I do not think that the deep had shewn them its most hidden secrets or the height its final hope of attainment. THE SPIRITUAL GUIDE relates what has been learned by its writer concerning that secret place of attainment wherein God "communicates Himself with incredible intensity" to those who enter "the sure and perfect mystical silence." The way of its attainment is called Nothingness by Molinos, but the word is not used in the sense of Dionysius, John the Scot or even the author of THE CLOUD OF UNKNOWING : it is not, I mean, an intimation concerning the Divine Darkness wherein the uttermost of Divine Transcendence is withdrawn, according to these great masters, nor is it the soul's privity in the hiddenness, apart from all the images, where the great light shines in the great emptiness. It is the native nothingness of the soul itself, and that is a false counsel which seeks to glorify and approach God by disparagement of the one vessel that, within our direct knowledge of the cosmos, is capable of receiving His presence. The first realisable truth concerning the soul of man is the native nobility of that which can dream of union with God, can also attain it, according to the faithful testimony of lords and princes of the life within, and by the experience of such attainment discovers that in the soul itself and not otherwise—as if without or beyond—is God realised and known in the sacred nature of things. Meanwhile it has nothing to renounce on the inward way but that which does not belong to these its royal prerogatives. As it stands therefore, THE SPIRITUAL GUIDE must be said to confuse the issues. And yet it has great moments.

For Molinos the life of the Presence is the life of prayer, and in his particular manner of symbolism the soul becomes Prayer, which is described alternatively as a loving and "habitual recollection" of the Divine Presence. It follows therefore that in the terminology of the Spanish mystic prayer is a synonym of love. His so-called Quietism is only the doctrine of conformity expounded by the development of all that is implied therein. Beyond the normal counsels of submission to Divine Will, which are in the alphabet of spiritual practice and in their lowest reduction are a process for making the best of things as they are, there is an active side, which is that of willing co-operation with the providence of God in all things, mischances, sufferings, sorrows and the rest of the " crosses " being included as part of the providence. But beyond this Molinos explored a state of inward passivity, in which the soul received from God by the way of simple surrender and interior devotion. In the contemplation of this state and its practice, the false idea of the soul's nothingness passed from the mind of the mystic, and it becomes comparable for him to a strong castle which could withstand the beleaguering of all its enemies, a sanctuary of inward peace, a habitation and a Kingdom of God. There is nothing which differs herein from the testimony of all who have witnessed concerning the way of the soul in union, but as I have shewn elsewhere it incurred condemnation because its interior practice appeared to reduce the necessity of certain external offices which insured power to the Church. A similar fate for the same reason befell concurrent French Quietism, which was in the likeness of that of Spain.

Fénelon and Madame Guyon are both beacons on the mystic path, but I think that their light is thrown upon those directions wherein there is no final harbourage. Between them there stands the circumspect figure of Bossuet, as an undesired moderator between them, carrying all official warrants, to all of them loyal, signal as the author of Variations of the Protestant Sects, but ultimately almost negligible as a teaching authority on the great subjects—perhaps, it may be said, more especially as he appears in the once celebrated and now forgotten Instructions on the States of Prayer—whatever their evidence in respect of personal sincerity and devotion. Here was a remarkable, even a momentous conjunction and opposition of planets which do not group usually after this manner. It is not easy to characterise or to compare them. It is not quite easy to adjust them to their environment or to their brilliant, faithless, dissolute and embroiled period of Louis Quatorze. It would be *ultra vires* at any time to set Bossuet in judgment on Fénelon or Madame de Maintenon on Madame Guyon, giving the best intentions to all parties; yet Bossuet was the spokesman of the Church and Madame de Maintenon was in a certain fluidic sense one mouth-piece at least in the political party. There is a great deal to be said about the position of Bossuet, who was in the face of a grave difficulty; but he had the incompleteness of the logical under-standing when it seeks to deal with those highest subjects which exceed its canons. There is a great deal to be said about the position of Madame Guyon, against whom he was instrumental in moving the vast machinery of the Church; but she had some errors of the mystic consciousness married to a mental endowment which was equipped imperfectly at the best. This notwithstand-ing, she was also a shrewd woman after her own manner and manifested on one occasion an extraordinary aptitude for business of a complicated kind.

As regards the deep things of inward experience which are involved in the whole subject, I set down as I conceive them their broad principles in the first place and as follows: (1) Hereof is the purpose and term of the inward life—that a man should know in fine Him in Whom he has believed at first, which itself is the justification of that faith whereby it is said that in the beginning we ourselves are justified; and this was the condition which Madame Guyon claims to have attained in the repose of her own soul. (2) It is that state of which the men and women in the world do not know, and there are few who can instruct them so effectually that even a preliminary certitude can enter their hearts: it is also that state of which people under the external obedience and ministry of the official Churches for the most part dream only—even if they dream indeed—and it is at a long distance. (3) If I may speak for a moment in symbolism, the root of our consciousness can grow into a great tree, by which we shall ascend into Heaven, and so did Madame Guyon ascend in her spirit, according to her unwavering testimony. (4) The ground of our possible attainment is that we belong to the true legitimacy, are Sons and Daughters of a Royal House in God, and the fault may be ours if we do not enter into our own; but

in respect of Madame Guyon, she had come to know of her in-
heritance, that this was indefectible, and though she did not
read perfectly in the language of Divine Law, she had begun, as
she best could, the investigation of her title-deeds. (5) She did
not understand fully that it is by no means in respect of our
imputed " vileness," our supposed miserable plight and the
compassion which this state is held to kindle, but because of our
genealogy and because of our ingrained capacities that God has
given to His elect that which we know to have been given. (6) The
secret of the heights which begins in conformity is the great secret
which ends in Divine Union, and—within and without—Madame
Guyon knew certain depths and some of the heights which can be
encompassed by the uttermost subjection of the will to God. (7)
She knew also that the way of subjection, of conformity and of
advancement by one step at a time is the way of love.

Since it must not be assumed that I am writing altogether
as a mystic for those only who have accepted, intellectually or
otherwise, the dedications of inward life, it is desirable at this
point to give a short account of Madame Guyon on her external
side and its relations before proceeding to the real matter of the
present thesis. Madame Guyon, *née* Jeanne Marie Bouvières de la
Mothe, was born on April 13, 1648, and she was still in her childhood when Queen Henrietta Maria, widow of Charles I, King of
England, visited her father at Montargis in the province of
Orléanois. This is sufficient to indicate the social condition of
her family, and I have said previously that in France it was
the epoch of Louis XIV. Jeanne was a child of conventual life,
almost from the beginning, a neophyte in Ursuline, Benedictine
and Dominican schools of teaching, and—under whatever limitations—she not only learned early but realised something also
concerning the ways of God with man, in virtue of which the
chosen souls are drawn " from tents of Kedar to Jerusalem."
She was married in her sixteenth year to Jacques Guyon, who
was approaching forty, and by the intervention of his mother
she was brought too soon, and indeed immediately, into familiar
acquaintance with the sorrows of a persecuted life. It was not
otherwise a happy, though apart from her it might well have
been an endurable life. Madame Guyon became the mother of

five children, and she lost her husband when she was still under the age of thirty years. There are grounds for believing that her dispositions towards the spiritual life had helped to alienate his affections : in any case, his death brought about her liberation from the yoke which her mother had imposed. It should be added, as a note upon minor inflictions, that her considerable personal attractions were ravaged by smallpox. She lost also two of her children, to all of whom, in the midst of her religious dedications, she was attached deeply. Those dedications passed through the familiar stages which characterise the life of the soul in all the Christian records—seasons of joy, seasons of illumination, seasons of sanctifying grace, and in fine a long period of privation, drought and inhibiting darkness. But perhaps her signal misfortune was to mistake the absence of joy and consolation for a sign that Divine Grace had been withdrawn as well—by which I understand the Plenary and not what theology calls the Sufficing Grace. Such privations seem to carry with them almost invariably an implied guarantee, seeing that in the annals of sanctity there is no instance of their endurance beyond a specific period. In the case of Madame Guyon they lasted, I think, longer than usual ; but they ended, as such experience ends always, more suddenly than they began, and this was in response—as she tells us—to the concurrent prayer of herself and her spiritual director, Father Lacombe. The change came in July, 1680, after which there was no reaction to the dark experience, and she felt in possession henceforth not only of that God Who is power but also of the consoling God.

There is evidence that at this comparatively early period she had taken a certain place already as a teacher of the inward life ; but it was assumed and reserved always within the immediate circle of her private acquaintance, of those who sought her, and of the poor and distressed, to whom also her material wealth enabled her to minister materially. She was at no time in public evidence as an instructor, reformer or prophetess, while it is to be noted especially in her favour that although she was the recipient of many " sensible favours " in vision, she never presumed upon them, as if they constituted warrants of themselves, but relied upon that which had been given her otherwise in a palmary degree, the realisation of Divine Life communicated in supernatural faith.

As regards her outward condition at this stage, she was drawn so much towards retirement that she thought seriously of the conventual life. She renounced it on account of her children, as later—but for other reasons—she renounced an episcopal offer which would have given her high conventual status, nominally at least. On the other hand, she was approached in three instances with a view to her second marriage, and it seems certain that in one direction she was conscious of natural predisposition, but she had resolved already on belonging only to God. She continued therefore for the moment her own way of dedicated activity in seclusion. With an audience which grew insensibly, she spoke—as I think—not of herself but of that which had been given to her in trust, and she exercised such influence that even in the case of her director she led rather than was directed. In conjunction with him and with D'Arenthon, Bishop of Geneva, she was for a period at Gex on the Swiss borders, where she devoted herself to works of charity and religious instruction. But that which had come to be termed the new doctrine—though it was briefly and simply the old and almost familiar notion of sanctification by faith—had gone abroad as a rumour in that part of the world, from the centre-in-chief at Paris, and it was thus that her trials began. Father Lacombe preached on the experience of holiness and incurred the displeasure of Bishop D'Arenthon, largely through the intervention of the latter's advisers, and he who had welcomed at first both Madame Guyon and her director, allocating the spirit of the teaching to her whose teaching it was, resolved to terminate her work within the limits of his diocese, unless he could adapt it expressly to his particular ends. Originally he had designed that work solely as a ministry of good works, not of religious teaching, with which object he proposed now that she should become the prioress of one of his conventual houses. Recognising that in this manner a period would be put to her mission, she left Gex as an alternative and repaired to Thonon, where, however, the feeling of ecclesiastical authority towards the inward life was illustrated by the burning in public of books devoted thereto.

It was after her practical expulsion from the diocese of Geneva that some part of Madame Guyon's experience began to pass into writing. A thesis entitled SPIRITUAL TORRENTS was composed at Thonon, and at Grenoble—her next place of sojourn—she began her mystical commentary on the Old and the New Testament. She appears also to have held private assemblies for prayer and religious discussion. But the cloud which may have been no bigger than a hand at Gex extended over this the first book and began to break in tempest. Under friendly episcopal advice, she left Grenoble for Marseilles, but there opposition was stirred up against her speedily. She found refuge for a period in Italy and thence returned to Paris in the summer of 1686, being still under forty years of age. Here there was a lull of some months, and Madame Guyon gathered into her circle several who were distinguished by their rank and some by their sanctity. But scarcely had a year elapsed when the first bolt fell from the sky of Rome, working through the Court of France, by the imprisonment of Father Lacombe, who, for the remaining seven-and-twenty years of his earthly existence, was consigned from dungeon to dungeon, with the Bastille as a beginning and the Castle of Oleron as a term.

It is pitiful to record that the instigator of this transaction was a certain Father La Mothe, the half-brother of Madame Guyon, and there is no question that through her spiritual director he was attacking her. This policy continued, and after a period of slanderous accusations, involving her personal character, she herself was imprisoned in a convent. There, amidst privations and indignities, she had at least the opportunity of writing, and her own extensive memoirs were—I believe—the chief result. Through the good offices of Madame Miramion, who is known otherwise to history as a woman of spiritual life, the influence of Madame de Maintenon—though previously hostile—was brought to bear upon the throne, and Madame Guyon's release was secured after a confinement of eight months. This act on the part of the King's morganatic wife brought the two women into acquaintance, and the one who had misconstrued the other now learned to admire her.

It should be observed that it was subsequent only to Madame

Guyon's first imprisonment that the star of Fénelon rose over the horizon of her life. It was not therefore, as casual readers have supposed, an early or very long acquaintance that sprang up between them; and as no one was in a better position to be informed concerning her than the Archbishop of Cambrai, he must have acted from the beginning with his eyes open. There is little doubt that into the spiritual side of her heart he was taken at once by her; there is no doubt that she appealed to him as to a new director, at least on the doctrinal side of her literary work; and there is finally no doubt that she did bend or awaken him towards her mystic purpose in the world. Between them there was long and frequent correspondence and between them there were various meetings. He on his part became an apostle in a manner of the inward life; but though he could counsel at need and correct perhaps at need, in matters of technical doctrine, he could save her so little in extremity that he was almost lost himself. His patronage therefore availed little, except that it increased her vogue. In 1689 her book upon Prayer was burnt in public by hundreds, and about the same time those who on a previous occasion had sought, it is said, to ruin her by means of a forged document are believed to have tried poison through the offices of a bribed servant.

The next event in her history was the intervention of Bossuet, who—in a book which I have mentioned already—pronounced somewhat late in the day against her opinions, but without involving her name. He sat also in judgment upon her, with other commissioners, but there was no specific condemnation, and it seems certain that his overt actions resulted rather from the pressure of her enemies than his own direct inclination. The outcome in either case was her second imprisonment, this time in the Castle of Vincennes. Subsequently she was removed to Vaugirard and thence to the Bastille, where she remained for four years and was then at length released. She lived thereafter as an enforced exile at Blois, where she died in the year 1717, having —all her vicissitudes notwithstanding and all her persecutions— attained the age of nearly seventy years.

We have now to consider a much more important matter than one of external history and of the suffering thereto belonging:

it is the attitude of ecclesiastical power towards that which it termed Quietism, or alternatively to the attained condition of repose in the inward life by an identification of human with Divine will. The official Church, even in her most intolerant form, is not of necessity an enemy of the interior life because she is the custodian and teacher of outward doctrine, with the practices and ceremonies attaching thereto. There are many for whom this statement will have almost the idle aspect of commonplace, but there are others for whom there is no ground of correspondence between that which is without of the Church and that which is looked for within, while we have to face further the strenuous fact that in her position as keeper of the faith she did proscribe the doctrines of inward life as expressed by Madame Guyon and Fénelon. At the same time the mystery of that life, the counsels of perfection which belong to it and the sanctity which has been its witness are written over all her literature. I am assured also personally that as the vital organism of a corporate body the Latin Church is conscious—and conscious keenly—that all which belongs to her without depends from her as she is within. She may affirm—and otherwise she would be scarcely an external Church—that her teachings are to be accepted in their literal sense ; that her practices are the rule of faith ; that her ceremonial is authentic and holy ; but she has never said that the mysteries of Divine Truth do not exceed all measurements of mental conception and hence all dogmatic expression, while no Christian institution has maintained more continuously that the Kingdom of Heaven is within. But this being so, why did the Church persecute and imprison either Molinos or Madame Guyon ? Why did Rome close the mouth of Archbishop Fénelon by a quasi-condemnation of his MAXIMS OF THE SAINTS ? I believe that there is a very clear and cogent answer.

We must take in the first place the case of Molinos, who was actually the antecedent of Madame Guyon. He taught in Spain that which at its root was the same as Madame Guyon witnessed a very little later in France. He was still in the prison of the Holy Office at Rome when she was in danger of the judgment at Vincennes. Though so nearly allied in time, there is no reason to suppose that she knew of him then otherwise than

o

at a distance; but at some later period of her life THE SPIRITUAL
GUIDE may have come into her hands, though in spite of certain
forged letters—or letters so accounted—it is unlikely that her
name and repute ever entered within his horizon, seeing that his
outward life was restricted within the four walls of his dungeon.
The sum of those principles and of that practice which received
in the case of Molinos the name of Quietism—by the way, it was
a term of contempt—corresponded sufficiently to the principles
and practice of Madame Guyon for her system to be designated
by its enemies after the same manner.

Molinos taught the doctrine of present and effective sanctification by the way of faith. Madame Guyon taught the mystery
of entrance into God through Christ, also by the way of faith, the
necessity in all things of complete dedication to God, and the
ministry of inward holiness as the consecration of outward life.
The end on earth was the attainment of that state which she
terms Pure or Unselfish Love, the nearest approach to Divine
Union of which it was given her to speak. I see nothing in this
naked expression of principles to which Rome need have taken
exception; I see nothing which it did not at need approve. As
it so happens, however, the formulation given does not exhaust
the content of that which was implied in the principles, and there
is hence a certain intellectual warrant, for the sake of the truth
of things, to exercise justice towards that Church which has
arrogated to herself a licence for the extermination by all means
of whatsoever she regards as heresy. We know that this title
does not inhere in Churches or other institutions, however consecrated, and we may reserve all rights as to how we characterise
the claim. But at the moment this exceeds the issue, and the
fact remains that the Church, from her own standpoint, was
confronted by a movement which, quite unconsciously to itself,
tended—as suggested already—to make void her office. After
common Protestant heresies had divided the world from Rome
there seemed on the point of springing up within its own bosom
and claiming to be a part of itself a school of secret thought,
as the prince of some other world wherein the Church had not
anything.

Quietism was a product of its period, and at the root it does not differ from the universal principles of the mystical life. It was an inclination of the axis of the period which caused the Quietist to say that mystical love at its highest forgets solicitude even for the loving soul's salvation : that was its answer of the hidden heart of man to the doctrine of rewards and punishments —with its accretions and concomitants, the commercial transactions in forgiveness and indulgences, its trade in prayers and masses. It was also an answer to the imposed rule of ascetic life, though those who put it forward were not aware of this fact and themselves, in the person of Madame Guyon, adopted on occasion revolting forms of penance which belong to the world of mania. But in the last resource Quietism signifies the repose of the soul in God as the resting-point of all that ardour of activity which takes the soul to the centre. It is obvious therefore that the relations between this view and the doctrines of the union, as expressed by the great company of all the saintly doctors, is one of identity rather than analogy. Moreover, it has been pointed out that Margaret Mary Alacoque was beatified—under popular pressure perhaps, but beatified she was—for saying the same things after nearly the same manner as Molinos did before her— both being Spanish contemplatives—and things far exceeding Fénelon, who in addition to the mystic consciousness had the logical understanding in the reasonableness of sweet marriage therewith.

When Fénelon, by a necessity of things, was driven to try conclusions with Bossuet, and with the power which was behind Bossuet, it is said—and credibly enough—that he regarded the doctrine of the interior life as being itself upon trial, and as that life signified for him Christianity in its essence, therefore Christianity also would stand or fall with him. The bone of contention was the little work entitled MAXIMS OF THE SAINTS, and the complicated issues which were involved, owing to the position of the writer, caused the condemnation which overtook it to be worded with such caution that it fell upon constructions which were or might be put on it without accusing the mind of Fénelon of being at variance from the mind of the Church. This wonderful policy notwithstanding, the book offers fullest evidence that a sister-tree to that which had been cut down in Spain was putting forth strange branches and strange blossoms in France. The most express points which can be cited as part of the evidence exhibit the following claims : (1) that a holy soul may deduce important conclusions from the Word of God which would remain unknown otherwise ; (2) that the decisions of a soul in the state of continuous faith are the Voice of the Holy Spirit speaking within the soul; (3) that souls which have experienced the higher sanctification have not so much need for times and places of worship as others.

The fact that these statements are moderated and even minimised as the spirit of a prelate intervenes could make them little less unsavoury in the mouth of the Church, and there is no doubt that what is negative and implied in Fénelon becomes positive and explicated in Madame Guyon, who, by her doctrine of justification through faith apart from works, had passed without intending it over to the camp of Protestants. On all higher planes the issues for her are between the soul and God, whence I find no room in her system—if indeed it can be regarded as such—for the intervention of the Church and its sacraments. I do not wonder therefore that Madame Guyon and Fénelon shone forth as signal dangers to the great, jealous, exclusive institution which claims to be the sole depository of faith and the sole interpreter of its purport. But seeing further that in their particular quality of light and their grade of sanctity I do not find the mystic light of all ; that in Madame Guyon the mode of expression is too often one of sentiment passing towards hysteria, while too many of the MAXIMS OF THE SAINTS are scarcely saved from commonplace ; I recur to the point whence I started and record in fine that their theosophical realm offers no abiding harbourage.

It follows from all considerations which have been enumerated here and now that Madame Guyon had the consciousness of the mystic term and I am assured that she had some of its experiences. Perhaps in his own more reposeful, more reasoned and reserved way, Fénelon saw a few things more clearly ; but he too was in the initial stages only, so far as his records testify, and I am by no means condoning the ways and methods of that Church to which they owed their first inspirations if I add that they, and she perhaps more especially, would have done well to recognise more fully that the gate of instruction *ex cathedra* is a gate through which all must pass if they would be grounded in any learning, while that of ceremonial, strict observance and sacramental offices is not only of sacred significance but can admit souls to the path. With a little more wisdom, with more of authentic and catholic illumination, Madame Guyon would not have been chastised and might have been even beatified. Above all, she would have done her work better.

Here also is one morality at least which arises in a broad sense out of the whole subject, for to-day the mystic life is again on its trial, but in a different sense than it was at the time of Fénelon. It is not before the Court of Rome or the Court of King Louis, for in the sense of arbitration and its office such arbiters have passed. But the *vita sancta* and *theosophia magna* of that which is called Mysticism are before the face of the intellectual world as the one claim which remains to be tested after all other modes have been found wanting and those who had the highest stakes in them have confessed to their failure. It does not rest upon individual witnesses, even though their long line goes back through all the centuries ; it does not depend from any system of official doctrine, and much less from the approval and authentication of hierarchic keepers of doctrine ; it is not of philosophical persuasion ; it is a claim put forward on the part of a great experiment by those who have tried it. It is open to all who are conscious of vocation in the world to which it belongs, and if it must be admitted that there is a sense in which it is hidden from the rank and file of humanity, from the man of business who is nothing but a business man, from the mere sportsman and worldling, let it be realised also that in something of the same sense the higher mathematics are hidden—shall I say ?—from myself, while the great circles of technical arts and sciences are realms beyond the ken of those who for want of vocation have not been drawn within them.

LATER WITNESSES TO THE LIFE OF LIFE

THE byways of mystical literature and the quiet annals of obscure mystical lives are things that repay study in several ways and some of them may seem to be not unimportant within their own directions. To the critical and expert mind they offer testimony in full to the fact that there are no great books on the life of the soul in God which have failed to emerge into the light of general knowledge and that there are no records of attainment which have remained hidden from our view and yet belong on examination to the first or any high rank. There is nothing in Dutoit-Mambrini—of whom I shall have something to say at a slightly later stage—which deserves to be compared with Saint-Martin and nothing in the enthusiast Pierre Poiret which shines with the light of Fénelon. The vast memorial of Ægidius Gutmann, entitled REVELATIONS OF DIVINE MAJESTY, and the tracts of Valentine Weigel on the eve of the Rosicrucian Mystery will never cause anyone to forget their contemporary and fellow-countryman, Jacob Böhme. So also the great official DIRECTORIA of the Latin Church, like those of Scaramelli and Antonio a Spiritu Sancto are not likely to be obscured by some later writers who are still among us, or perhaps even by Schram, excellent though he be in his way. The IMITATION OF THE POOR LIFE OF CHRIST, ascribed falsely to Tauler, will never replace the original and genuine IMITATION, nor Tauler's own INSTITUTIONS. Yet those who have recourse to these—and other texts by the score in the same degree—will find things that are precious and so obtain their reward.

It is possible to quote many names which belong to the literature of Mysticism within and without the folds of the Christian Churches, and a few at least from which appeal would perhaps seem perilous. But we can almost calculate in legions the names of those who, in virtue of some limitation, either through stricture in their surroundings or deficiency of faculty and grace, appear rather as dwellers on the borders of that which for every mystic is the Life of life. They have left their memorials behind them, and these indicate that the threshold on which they remained had open doors through which they could and did behold not only the Sacred Rites celebrated in long cloisters, but something of the Grand Mysteries which are particular to the Sanctuary itself. One of their characteristics is therefore an experience which, of its kind, is obtained at first hand, and this has always its grade of value ; while, seeing that so many of us, for whom the greater experience of the mystic has become the one thing desirable, may seem, by our callings and their environments, precluded from nearly everything excepting the simple intellectual realisation and occasional sudden awakenings which abide like a blessed memory in the heart, it happens often that such memorials can offer us aids to reflection in ways that are comparatively easy, sometimes almost elementary. In this manner the " second best," though it enters into no comparison with the great good, brings to us precious gifts, as the Kings of the East brought gold, frankincense and myrrh—gifts which signify all that is beyond themselves and the givers.

I propose some brief excursion into these paths, now almost untrodden, taking as exemplars certain writings and their authors wherein I found aids to reflection—somewhat far in the past— and believe that they may prove of service to others. It should be understood that in the historical sense we have finished with the great epochs of Christian mystical testimony and are in the day of the aftermath. In St. John of the Cross the voice of Carmel and the voice of the Dark Night had closed long since the canon of the Latin Church. As intermediate between him and the witness of " reformed " Churches—with which I am about to deal—the Quietists represent already a lower groove.

One of their memorials has been known for many years to a few collectors of minor curiosities of the soul, which scarcely lean towards greatness, under the title of LE MYSTÈRE DE LA CROIX, AFFLIGEANTE ET CONSOLANTE, DE JÉSUS CHRIST ET DE SES MEMBRES, ÉCRIT AU MILIEU DE LA CROIX AU DEDANS ET AU

DEHORS. It has suffered from the neglect of centuries, and perhaps it has suffered also from the zeal of its rare admirers.

THE MYSTERY OF THE CROSS has a literary story which is at once unusual and not a little suggestive. It was finished, according to the original title-page, on August 12, 1732, and it was published in the course of the same year without apparently attracting any marked attention. This notwithstanding, it appeared in a German translation at Leipsic in 1782, and it has been stated that in this form it was long read and highly prized by theosophical circles of the period. It was re-issued also at Lausanne in 1786, or 1791, under the attributed editorship of Philippe du Toit de Mambrini, who, adopting a certain guise of Protestantism and an assumed name, published a number of volumes which are adaptations of Christian Mysticism conceived in an errantry of the spirit that is not less than bizarre. The first French issue had become very scarce in his day, and there is ground to think that it was misconceived by the alleged editor, who refers to it in his own works ; but I have no record of its destiny under his fantastic hands. Probably it perished, almost without a sign, and was unheard of until it attracted attention from the anonymous author of a book called A SUGGESTIVE ENQUIRY INTO THE HERMETIC MYSTERY, published originally in 1850 and withdrawn at once from circulation. Ten years later the French work was reprinted in London, under the auspices of Williams and Norgate as publishers, by an English editor, also anonymous, who neglected the obvious precaution of translating it, so that it is still under its first seals. A rendering in manuscript does, however, exist, though I am unable to speak of its claims or its present whereabouts. The author termed himself simply " A Disciple of the Cross of Jesus," and till 1877 it was known only in Germany that this pseudonym covered, or is said to have covered, the identity of a mystic called Douze-Tems, described as a countryman and spiritual kinsman of Madame Guyon. Dr. Otto Zoeckler, who furnishes this information, does not appear to speak with any first-hand knowledge ; it seems probable from its form that the book was, as its writer hints, the work of a man experimenting in a language not wholly familiar to himself, and it is possible at least that he was a German of

French descent. Dr. Zoeckler's work errs unfortunately in several ways on the side of imprudence, as its English translation in 1877 veers perilously towards the illiterate. There is no reason, in any case, to suppose that a name like Douze-Tems is itself anything better than a pseudonym. On the whole, we must rest content with the scanty particulars which have been transmitted, chiefly by report, concerning the writer, as follows :—

1. That his ancestors were French Protestants of the Desert— meaning perhaps that they were Albigenses in their day.

2. That he sought an asylum from persecution in the dominions of the Elector of Saxony.

3. Finally, that for some unknown reason he was imprisoned at Sonnenstein on the Elbe.

The last statement rests on the authority of the book, and is the only certainty concerning the author, though, in spite of one whimsical remark, somewhat after the manner of Leibnitz, it is difficult to suppose that he was wholly unconnected with so much of the Rosicrucian movement as was abroad in Germany at his period—otherwise, the successors of Sigmund Richter and his activities *circa* 1710. The connection is to be assumed, at least tentatively, from a number of his allusions and generally from his affiliations in Mysticism. On this subject it is scarcely possible, or indeed necessary, to enlarge in the present place, nor does it signify much what was the author's private history or what his real patronymic. Perhaps, in the last resource, it would also not signify seriously to the mystic if the Fraternity mentioned had been itself, as Douze-Tems suggests, only a beautiful invention, though projected in good faith. It is possible, however, that the remark may call for a certain interpretation, and is an instance of that precaution concerning which the author has warned the correspondent whom he addresses, and readers generally through him, namely, that several matters have not been fully treated, and that about others his prudence has counselled him to maintain a certain reserve. The various chapters are indeed sown with maxims extracted literally from published Rose-Cross documents, and it is difficult to account for such uniform fidelity in citation if Douze-Tems did not possess affiliations which he disavows informally. However this may be, he has signal connections in literature which are of the esoteric order outside anything that he may have derived from sources ascribed to the Fraternity. He recalls continually the later Kabalists, for one example, and he must have celebrated many unusual marriages in books before he wrote his own treatise. I mention these points because they will interest people who are concerned rather with historical issues, and on this account they are not less than important.

I must confess perhaps to some personal predilection derived from strange ways of reading, if I express the opinion that it is probably from the later Kabalists that Douze-Tems drew part at least of the intellectual generosity which is one of his most attractive characteristics. There is nothing to shew that he knew them at first hand, but there were many treasures of learning then available in Latin books which presented Jewish theosophy as an eirenicon between the Law of Moses and the Law of Christ, and which sought at once to lay the foundation of lasting peace in Israel and to heal the many dissensions of the several sects in Christendom. From sectarian bitterness Douze-Tems was wholly free, and though certainly not a Catholic he speaks invariably with an enlightened indulgence towards the Latin Church and its mystery which, at his period, was exceedingly rare in those who did not belong to it. As the work is so little known and in no sense readily accessible, I must not permit it to be inferred that its Rosicrucian and Kabalistic connections make THE MYSTERY OF THE CROSS beyond measure obscure and difficult. On the contrary, it is a manageable treatise which, supposing discrimination in the student, is full of wise guidance and ministries at the initial stages of the life within. It has, in an unusual degree, that seal of conviction which I have already mentioned; in spite of certain limitations that are sufficiently obvious, it is the work of a man who has been in those high places of which he discourses, and there will be the less disposition to challenge his claim to the use of one daring statement which appears in his first lines : *Absque nube pro nobis.* It is drawn from one of the memorials of the Rosy Cross. What was that mystery which for him had ceased to be clouded and of which he claims to have written both " within and without "—that is to say, with a plain external sense and yet with an inward meaning ? Who was this

pilgrim through eternity who could cite yet another maxim:
Dulcia non meruit qui non gustavit amara—which bitterness is
actually the experience of that cross the mystery of which he
unfolds? He says further, with the Rosicrucian Masters who
went before him:

> *'In cruce sub sphæra*
> *Venit sapientia vera.'*

Here there is no opportunity to discuss questions of symbolism,
but the simple planetary figure of the star Venus represents, for
those who used it after this concealed fashion, the crucifixion
of love issuing in that wisdom which is not of this world, and is
love itself in resurrection. Those who are acquainted with
symbolism may be disposed to regard the apparently obscure
allusion as one of the keys which open the closed entrance to the
particular palace of Douze-Tems; for, in its final understanding,
the work of the mystic can only present itself to the mind as a
part of the work of that love which produced the whole universe
in consequence of an infinite clemency. In this case, the bitterness
which is inseparable from the Cross of advancement is the essential
acerbity of election, whereby that which is gross is transmuted,
and this realised, the darkness of all the Carmels is indeed no
longer clouded.

The book is divided into fifteen tabulated considerations—
on the origin of the Cross; its outward and inward providences;
its use and misuse; its perpetuation after death; the supernatural experiences which it comprises, and in particular its
lessons of humiliation and of victory in the passion and death of
Christ. It is not a work which lends itself readily to quotation,
or to any process of summarising which will carry much light
with it. A synopsis of its chapters would also suggest little,
apart from knowledge of its pages. To put the matter briefly, it
is a story of the experience of a soul to which utter resignation
has brought peace and knowledge by some first-hand contact with
hidden truth.

If the afflictions and advancements of the Cross were those
simply which are less or more with us along all our daily roads,
if they were entirely identical with our common trials and were the
common recompense of our resignations, there would be little

probably between the leaves of this book which would make its
notice seem necessary, for the literature of the lighter Mysticism
is almost as the sands of the sea ; it provides the first spelling-
books and readers of the spiritual life in all the Churches and
sects ; and it is characterised by every convention and every form
of insufficiency. On the surface, nevertheless, or at least for many
people, this may well seem to be the simple limits of the message
found in THE MYSTERY OF THE CROSS. It is certainly the rigid
term for those unversed in the separation of the inward from the
outward sense—for those to whom the spiritual expression *intus
et foris scriptus* connotes something that is past finding out. But
there are others who will understand readily enough, under what
guise soever, that the Cross about which there is a mystery is no
economy of catholic redemption, as it is no mere application of
morality, and it is to these that the obscure mystic will come with
another meaning in his message than that of light trials in life
and the way to bear them. He will say that the knowledge of
God is to be obtained only at the centre, while this centre must
be sought, which is not by any means impossible in the present
life, though no teacher can affirm that the path is easy. There
can be also no question that it carries the seeker far away from
those putative particular centres which are recognised and count
for anything in the material world. It is often claimed that a
certain knowledge of the Divine, as at great distances and I know
not under what veils, is obtainable by the testimony of things which
are without ; and it is indeed to furnish these evidences that is
the chief purpose of the multiplicity which exists in Nature.
THE MYSTERY OF THE CROSS has some of the sacramental kin-
ships which come from the touch of Nature, but it makes wholly
for that final end, of which its author truly says that there is
none other conceivable as a term of the soul. It is married, as
will be expected, to a doctrinal system which, within limits, is
characteristic of the period, though for that period it is also liberal,
in the laudable sense of the word ; it is liberal, for example, in
eschatology, not in the sentimental sense which sometimes draws
a broad mark of cancellation over great principles of equity, but
with a simplicity which is chaste, severe and conscious of the
counter-claim, yet ends as reasonable eschatology can end alone,

namely, with God as All in all for all that lives and has its being in Him.

We are not so intellectually certain at the present day that the old divines and single-hearted seers of the past, clearly as they did discern and steadfastly as they were accustomed to look, are entirely indisputable guides upon specific doctrinal points. We may not be prepared to accept literally the particular interpretation offered by THE MYSTERY OF THE CROSS concerning, let us say, the descent of Christ into Hades. Certain issues have entered into the mystic consciousness which had scarcely been raised in the days of the earlier leaders; and this is why I have referred to a saving gift of discernment as desirable in the modern student. All this nothwithstanding, the book remains, when it is taken in the larger sense, as one which will be helpful at the initial stages because it makes for that kind of righteousness which must be the first possession of the mystic, namely, the unswerving devotion to something which has to be done with our might, constituting the origin of that general and catholic Cross which has to be borne in the flesh—which is indeed the common burden, as it is also the common support, of those who have resolved steadfastly to enter the true path. That, outside all ethical questions, such righteousness has its rewards, is known early, as it is assuredly known fully. That for the world it must be always folly, because the world can judge only after discriminations of its own kind; and that it is at the same time the first step in wisdom: these things will be known also, and they are indeed assumed beforehand. That it is a Cross within as well as a Cross without the disciple has to realise profoundly; and seeing that all mystics are acquainted with seasons of inhibition, he will in due course experience what our author terms " the use and abuse of the Cross." But when he has overcome in this struggle, he will have entered already into a moderate familiarity with the designs of God in the Cross, and will be prepared to realise that, in so far as he falls short of his term, this Cross will follow him to the end of his days, even after death, at once his humiliation and his triumph.

I have presented intentionally what might be termed the metaphysical process of THE MYSTERY OF THE CROSS without guise or decoration. It proceeds entirely from the principle that it is impossible for God to do otherwise than love His children, however far they pass under the law of rebellion, and, so far as I am aware, it is to this extent the first professedly mystic thesis, since the days of Origen, concerning that reintegration of man in God which became afterwards so famous in the school of Martines de Pasqually and his successors. The punishments of the Cross after death are therefore the free workings of the scheme of redemption, and humanity ends where it began also, in the Divinity which is its home. Some ways are short and keen and splendid; some are long and obscure, with the darkness of all suspension and desolation; but the term is still the same: and sweetened by patience and clemency the mystic who has sounded the depths, but at the same time can give us a scale-plan professionally tabulated of many exalted altitudes, has come forth from the experience consoled, saying with a later adept, " that God Who alone is real and alone present everywhere, fills the limitless immensity with the splendours and eternal consolations of the sovereign reason."

The lessons of the recluse of Sonnenstein, though delivered with an accent which is individual and set apart almost wholly from the conventions and commonplaces of a purely devotional treatise, have their affiliations in mystic literature which not only deserve remark but have actually an aspect of importance, because they interlink men whose writings and lives were at the same time widely different. To simplify this point, I will mention six dates which represent the publication of as many books, the first of which is THE MYSTERY OF THE CROSS, in 1732. The second date is 1615, or coincident with the Rosicrucian fervours, when the great name of Cardinal Bellarmine was attached to the title of a tract concerning THE ASCENT OF THE MIND IN GOD BY THE GRADE OF NATURAL THINGS. The third is 1677, when the works of a lesser but still illustrious prince of the Church, Cardinal John Bona, were collected at Antwerp, including his MANUDUCTIO AD CŒLUM and VIA COMPENDII AD DEUM. The fourth is the year 1738, which saw the appearance in its first volume of THE TESTIMONY OF A CHILD OF THE RESURRECTION CONCERNING SEVERAL MATTERS OF THE INTERIOR LIFE, extending in all to nine volumes, which were the work of an unknown author, assisted by an anonymous editor, and were in their way a treasury of singular discourses. The fifth is 1784, when Louis Claude de Saint-Martin issued his ECCE HOMO. The sixth and last book appeared in 1801 at Paris, as a translation from the Russian, under the title of QUELQUES TRAITS DE L'ÉGLISE INTÉRIEURE. It connects, quite undesignedly, with THE CLOUD UPON THE SANCTUARY, though it does not possess its authority, or indeed its convincing accent. The author was Lopukhin, a Russian Freemason and Rosicrucian in the days of the Empress Catherine. I must dissuade my readers from supposing that I am making simply a short bibliographical list. The dates, if not exactly nothing, are of slender importance, and the only consanguinity between the persons is that of the spiritual order, on the principle, recognised by Saint-Martin, that all who have attained truly their spiritual majority use the same language since they come from the same country. Speaking generally, they owed nothing to one another, though the two Cardinals may have made acquaintance in the letter, even as they were united in the experience. Further, it may be true, as suggested by Mambrini, that Saint-Martin had once at least met with THE MYSTERY OF THE CROSS, but there is nothing to justify our expression of a bare possibility, from which very little would have followed, in the language of even tolerable certainty. I should say that the Chevalier Lopukhin had never heard of Eckartshausen, and it signifies less than little for the range of the documents that the unknown CHILD OF THE RESURRECTION, as well as his editor, had read quite widely the current French literature of Mysticism. At the same time, as I have intimated, they are all kindred in the root-spirit, amidst great doctrinal divergence, and the order in which I have cited them, though it violates chronology, is one which should serve to simplify the successive tabulation of their points of correspondence and divergence, as also after what manner one accounts for another, while he extends also another, each testifying to each, almost supposing each, after a tacit manner. The truth is that such books, as also indicated already, are like doors which open successively, distance beyond distance, into certain great chambers of the soul. Their analogy is hereof, and hereof is also their importance. The works of Cardinal Bellarmine and Cardinal Bona, fully differentiated as they are between themselves, constitute an introduction to a spiritual life of the active and practical kind, while enforcing the true end of that life and the particular mastery of its experience. They have naturally many elements that have passed out of the region of necessity, and they are more valuable as intimations than as precise handbooks. Shall I say that they occupy, relatively speaking, much the same position as a Layman's Mass-book when compared with a literal MISSAL containing all the local variations, all the propers of the saints, and all the rubrics ? I am speaking of course suggestively, not instituting a parallel. They contain what devotional treasuries term the Key of Heaven, but they do not always open exactly the kind of doors by which we, in these days, can gain entrance most directly into the House of the Father. On the other hand, ECCE HOMO, though it is much more profound, much more advanced, as one would say, calls for restatement and, as it stands, for some enlightened reserve, while THE MYSTERY OF THE CROSS is not without a certain fantastic spirit, and the TESTIMONY OF A CHILD is a little hindered by its diffusive sentiment. Of THE CHARACTERISTICS OF THE INTERIOR CHURCH it is more difficult to speak ; it is at once so much and so little—so much in its unconscious analogies with the far more important work of Eckartshausen and so little, since, from one point of view, it is purely a devotional treatise, one among many thousands, and not especially distinctive. But the text is available in English, and I have discussed its claims at length in an introductory notice.

It is impossible within ordinary limits to make an express summary of points of correspondence, and the bare affirmation must suffice, at least for the moment. To myself it comes with a certain quality of illumination. The different actuating influences, modes of thought, and even of point of view on the part of mystics who were at heart really one and tended to the same term are assuredly of considerable importance ; those of whom we are speaking were all after their manner remarkable ; they lie also beyond the habitual course of knowledge for those who are themselves professed mystics at the present day and are exploring one or other of the same paths, unconscious perhaps in some cases how far they have been preceded. The analogies, which are much more intimate and naturally more easy to recognise, have one advantage which makes for simplicity of treatment ; on the one hand, we are dealing with men who had attained their convictions by means of first-hand experience ; but, on the other, they had not passed into those heights of the spiritual life which spell extreme difficulty for the aspirant who is seeking to follow them. The evidences of such attainment do not at least appear in the books, which are therefore serviceable manuals, well adapted for a school of novices. The indoctrination differs, in other words, from that of St. John of the Cross, Ruysbroeck and Jacob Böhme, who are rather for the professed than for neophytes. Let me say, in this connection, that it is better, in one sense at least, to read books that are imperfect, so only that the aim which they propose is the one undeniable and true end of all things, than the reputed masterpieces which do not make for eternity ; and, this being granted, it is not only desirable but necessary that we should be proficient in the nature of their imperfections. This is why theses like THE MYSTERY OF THE CROSS are so much more valuable than any technical criticism can realise, because they teach as much in their deficiencies as they teach in their fulness, though it is true that this quality of their ministration is more strictly for the doctors than the scholars. I do not mean that THE MYSTERY OF THE CROSS would tempt even a tyro to become a protestant of the desert, if such a vocation were possible in these days ; but, its inward message notwithstanding, it might dispose him to believe that some of the great things are outside rather than within him, and that the indefectible gospel has been written elsewhere than in the soul. In other words, the path which it opens is not without pitfalls. I would counsel therefore the few persons who may fall across a work which the inscrutable star-workings have contrived again to make rare, that they should avoid above all being scandalised at its occasional touch of the grotesque and its leaning towards a few issues which deflect from the path of wisdom. To my thinking, it is of greater rather than lesser consequence on these accounts.

P

Be it said, in conclusion, that most great books of the soul call in a sense for rewriting, which signifies in all simplicity that we need others as great to follow, lifting up lamps of guidance to those who are called and chosen in these " foremost files of time." But of those in the past as of those which are yet to come, one might have some ground to feel doubtful if they offered no weak point to the strictures of their brethren. There are amazing fatuities in Ruysbroeck, though he had sailed over trackless seas, and St. John of the Cross on Carmel seems occasionally like the ingenious gentleman of La Mancha rather than Galahad at the Graal Castle ; but it is chiefly for this reason that, being that which they were, they can yet extend helping hands.

Those who have been immersed for a long period in that luminous world of dreams which is called SEPHER HA ZOHAR may turn with profit to the lighter debate of ADUMBRATIO KAB-BALÆ CHRISTIANÆ by Baron von Rosenroth. The brief study which ends at this point is written as the memorial of a period when it can be said most truly that there was little open vision, when the mystic quest was followed at the circumference of its subject and not at the centre. There were rare moments when echoes came from the centre, but speaking generally the official princes of the Church were concerned with the authentic titles of salvation as they are earned by the offices of the Church and not with exotics of attainment, or with anything beyond the everlasting joy of an external heaven. On the alternative side of testimony the MYSTERY OF THE CROSS leads into all light except that of the union, while the Child of Resurrection beholds a Spiritual Zion among hills of aspiration but not the Hidden Sanctuary, from which those who enter do not come out any more. It remains that they are profitable reading after the greater texts, like the tract of Rosenroth.

IN THE SHADOW OF REVOLUTION

THE unfrequented paths of intellectual activity are as rich in curiosities as are its highways in great landmarks ; but few have time to follow them. Few only can turn aside from the lessons of the direct road for the suggestions of indirection which are met with far from the beaten track. Outside the common ground of history and philosophy there are still many paths of thought and action which are worth hearing of, even by those who have neither opportunity nor inclination to pursue them on their own account. And of such byways none are more curious, none certainly more fantastic, than those which belong to the first half of that nineteenth century out of which we cannot even now be said to have emerged completely, except in the matter of date, so strong has been the spell thereof, and so far-reaching is its atmosphere. The quickening and fermenting which all over Europe led up to the supreme event of the French Revolution, had produced among other phenomena many curious awakenings of mental activity. There were seers and prophets everywhere ; men claiming strange powers and men possessing strange missions rose up on every side ; in feeling and in perception, as in thought, the world was at fever-heat. Even the impostors were splendid, and so fervid was every heart that many of these were at least partially sincere, however flagrant their deceptions. Before Cagliostro, Althotas—his mysterious instructor, as it is said ; before Althotas, Saint-Germain ; before Saint-Germain, Lascaris —the alchemist of Mitylene—with a score of others ; a long line of wonderful pretenders, so extensively believed in for their season that in a certain sense they may have come to believe in themselves. As the public warrant of their assumptions, there arose in its day the marvel of the mysterious batôn of Mesmer ; there was the persuasive personality of Emanuel Swedenborg ;

there were the oracular utterances of the illuminated man about town, Saint-Martin, the so-called "Unknown Philosopher," in the highest circles of the world and yet not of it; there were the enigmatic romances of Cazotte; while overshadowing and including all these were the great unsearchable claims of continental Freemasonry. Never did astrologers and makers of almanacs read such presages in the starry heavens; never was the alchemist so near witnessing the precipitation of gold in his crucible; never did strange and almost nameless Rites of magic and of necromancy so closely approach in their results the similitude of a pathological fact; never did visionaries so nearly attain in their contemplation the knowledge of things everywhere regarded as inscrutable. Unknown secret associations, practising these and other mysteries, seemed to be generated spontaneously. No one had heard of them previously; no one could guess their origin; yet expectant hearts palpitated, because all felt that they were on the threshold of some great mystery. At Paris, at Lyons, at Bordeaux—for France at least—it might have assumed a shape already. But the fever reached the paroxysm of its crisis, and then the stars had no longer a voice; all the visions were stultified and ceased; Cagliostro was in the hands of that unanswerable Inquisition which never gave up its dead, and but seldom its living; the divine messenger from Sweden had less secretly passed away, with much of the amaze concerning him. Presently the overwhelming fact of the great dictator shadowed all others, and on every side the nations seemed preparing for a coming Armageddon. No one thought of Secret Orders or personal inspirations when Napoleon assumed to himself the crown of empire, and cast down his gauntlet as a challenge to the civilised world. It was the day of the Grand Army.

In the year 1801, the subsidence of activity in those byways with which we are concerned found certain personalities remaining over from the previous century, portents which the flight of time was gradually drawing down into the past. Among them, at once pathetic and fascinating, was Louis Claude de Saint-Martin. Belonging to the privileged and therefore proscribed classes, he had lost all, or nearly all, of which the general upheaval could deprive him—dear friends, the competence which was his birth-right and, worse than these, the possibility of a tolerant audience. At the threshold of the nineteenth century we observe him, notwithstanding, still hopeful, still pursuing the career of the enlightened theosophical enthusiast, and still the most public-spirited of his intellectual fraternity, discussing now the way to the blessed life, because he was a mystic in his zeal; now the lessons of the Revolution; and yet again the mission of Consul Bonaparte—all with a correspondent in Switzerland whom he had never met. Sixty years and more were destined to elapse before his letters—one of the most remarkable memorials of that perturbed period—were to see the light, and they are now to be accounted among its landmarks. There were books, however, of Saint-Martin which, in spite of the apathy of the time, continued to make their way unobtrusively and almost negatively. On the threshold of the new age he dared to tell his countrymen of regenerated man and his nature; of the ministry of that real humanity which underlies our external being; and more persistently still, of the depths and heights which, some two centuries earlier, had been scaled and sounded by a poor German shoe-maker, named Jacob Böhme. There is no need to state that at the present day these books are generally unread, or they would have no title to be included among the obscure ways of thought belonging to the first half of the nineteenth century. But they remain with all the strangeness of their accent, which must have sounded stranger still at their period, seeing that amidst the clamours of crashing kingdoms they told the inner secrets of the Christian religion as deeply, as earnestly, though in all things else unlike, as any of the saintly voices heard century after century from the antique Sanctuaries of the Latin Church.

With Saint-Martin there had been once associated—though it is only within recent years that the fact has transpired—one wholly unknown to fame, and his antithesis by vocation, that is, J. B. Willermoz, a merchant of Lyons, who in the midst of his business preoccupations found time to interest himself in strange schemes of Initiation propagated by a mysterious adept, called Martines de Pasqually. About this individual we now know more than was known when the first biographers of Saint-Martin speculated, wondered or propagated misconceptions concerning him. He is said to have been one of the last disciples of Emanuel Swedenborg, but he does not seem to have followed the system of his supposed master, and when he produced his Secret Order it was not the so-called Swedenborgian Rite which once found followers in France, and may still be heard of to-day, but one possibly of his own devising, for which he claimed not only that it was the sole genuine Masonry, but that it had been received, if not bodily, at least as regards its inspiration, from the old brotherhood of the Rosy Cross. Two things stand out clearly in the life of Pasqually as we know it—his sincerity and his fervid religious devotion. As to these we possess witnesses between whom there is no trace of concerted action. For the rest, it must be said frankly that his Rite—except on the side of its phenomena—does not seem to have possessed any marked titles by which it deserves to be distinguished from similar inventions of that fantastic period, arrogating to themselves the exclusive title of primeval Masonry ; while the one treatise that he is known to have written, though it exhibits some slender connections with philosophical systems of the past, is in reality so confused as to be very nearly unintelligible. It has, however, some strange lights for those who can find them and suggests continually in its obscure pages that had he followed his proper dedication, its author would have belonged to the mystics rather than the experts of thaumaturgic practices. Swedenborgian or Rosicrucian, true Illuminé or enthusiast, whichever he may have been, or all in turn, Pasqually appeals to us more especially as an adept in those theurgic or magical works which at the time found votaries both in France and Germany. That is to say, he had recourse to formulæ of evocation, with which he and those about him contrived either to produce something or to sustain themselves with the idea that they did. And this brings us back to Willermoz, who, while Saint-Martin was writing great books intended to demonstrate that all external ways and all search after wonderful phenomena were full of delusion, and did not advance the soul, was occupied sedulously, and, as it would seem, also successfully in those very pursuits, and in preserving from utter destruction the remnant of that mysterious Rite which, now under the auspices of Pasqually and again under those of his successors, once flourished at Lyons, Bordeaux and elsewhere. Between the epoch of the French Revolution and that of Eliphas Lévi, who died in 1875, and has been termed the modern magician by those who regard him seriously, the name of Jean Baptiste Willermoz is alone connected with occult operations in France, so far as history is concerned. They have, however, to be distinguished in his case, as in that of Pasqually, from the ordinary ends and intentions of that questionable art. The Rite of Pasqually and of his pupils did not seek to communicate with departed spirits, like modern mediums, for that which was supposed to be obtained as a result of its procedure was the visible manifestation of a being termed the Repairer, by whom, from the evidence that is available, there can be no doubt that Christ was understood. The difference may be well enough an indication only of more profound delusion, but it serves to set apart this school of Christian wonder-working from all others of its kind, even if their Rite itself offers little to distinguish it from Grimoires, the so-called Keys of Solomon and other depraved medleys of Jewish Kabalism which formed part of the chap-books and literature of colportage in French country-places at the period. The fact is additionally interesting because, so far as we can discern, the doctrinal substratum of Pasqually seems to have been drawn indirectly from the German Kabalism which flourished in the days of Rosenroth, and was designed for the conversion of all Jewry to Christianity. It had been subjected, however, to so much alteration that it is difficult to speak precisely.

In 1805 Saint-Martin transferred by death the process of his return to that unity which he had so long desired, and he was survived by Willermoz for something like ten years, or less than half the time that he had been preceded by the Comte de Saint-Germain, the sole personage of a period prolific in adepts to whom there might be some excuse for ascribing a higher Initiation than may have been dispensed by those from whom Saint-Martin drew his early teaching. Madame de Stael represents Saint-Germain as a remarkable figure in Court circles prior to the Revolution, and as dying in obscurity and poverty overwhelmed by the terrors of a future life. We are now in possession of evidence which gives us a more correct—if not more reassuring —picture, and one by which we can at least disassociate him from Cagliostro, for whose connections with older Secret Societies, in spite of many statements to the contrary, there is no evidence worthy of the name. We can at least say that Saint-Germain was scarcely an adventurer in the more invidious sense of the term, and we meet him under circumstances which make his connection with Fraternities of the past at least tolerable as an inference. That is to say, assuming the existence of such associations at the end of the eighteenth century, there is tolerable reason to suppose that he was one of their representatives, more especially in the case of the mysterious Knights of Light. At the same time he has left nothing behind him by which we can judge him at first hand, and he produced, so far as can be seen, no great or lasting influence.

Willermoz died in or about the year 1815, almost coincidently with Mesmer, and this brings us to Anton Mesmer, who, from obscure hints in old books and other seeming accidents, is thought to have stumbled on one of the secrets of the old Initiating Brotherhoods, and he most assuredly gave forth an important psychical fact to the modern world, however much he may have misinterpreted it. His great secret was a part of the greater mystery of the will, the secret of intentness. Royal Commissions and Royal Academies went to work collecting and sifting evidence to prove or disprove the existence of a vital fluid transmitted in mesmerism from operator to subject. They found, as might be expected, that there was no fluid, and the action of mind upon mind did not apparently concern them. The brilliant empiric who owed nothing to Initiation, unless in Masonic circles, retired with broken prospects. We find him at the close of his life in a little German village, practising his cures modestly without emolument, and dying so unknown that his grave was discovered, so to speak, some fifty years later by an English tourist, the Rev. C. Kegan Paul, who may well have forgotten before he died himself that he alone it was who wrote verses to the memory of the discoverer of Animal Magnetism.

There is one other name in connection with France at this

period which must engage our attention for a moment. It is that of the Chevalier Du Toit de Mambrini, occasionally but erroneously identified by some biographers with the Comte de Divonne, who was the friend of Saint-Martin and on whom Saint-Martin exercised for a time a great influence, gratefully acknowledged. We have only meagre information concerning Mambrini, and Saint-Martin, who, despite the fact that he termed himself the Unknown Philosopher, knew nearly every one and was well known by all, seems to have been unfamiliar with his personality. He is mentioned twice only in the course of Saint-Martin's correspondence with the Baron de Liebistorf, and it must be said regretfully that it is rather a hostile reference. Mambrini was a Christian Mystic so much after the manner of Saint-Martin that he has been regarded almost universally as one of his disciples, which is not true either personally or philosophically, nor does he appear to have belonged to the sect of Pasqually or to any of the Masonic Fraternities. All that we know of him is, that about the time when Saint-Martin was himself issuing his most important and mature works, there appeared, sometimes on a much more elaborate scale, these rival handbooks of a kindred theosophical Christianity. They have their merits, and perhaps at the present day, or here at least in England, they are not much more unknown than are some works of the Unknown Philosopher. They have none of the genius of Saint-Martin, and they abound in crudities which are very similar to his own. The reference in the correspondence of Saint-Martin was occasioned by a remark of Baron de Liebistorf, who might, however, have been prepared to admire Mambrini, had he received the cue from his correspondent. But he did not receive it, for the riper thinker had read Mambrini without conviction, though he confessed himself somewhat startled. It was not altogether gracious, but we may be sure that it was not ill intended, and above all not suggested by any spirit of rivalry. Saint-Martin was fastidious in his philosophy, and in his later life it is said that he took none but Böhme into his heart of hearts.

With Saint-Martin, Willermoz and Mambrini we have exhausted this school of French thought at the beginning of the nineteenth century, and when these had departed at their several seasons, the animal magnetists alone remained.

Germany did not share to any marked extent in the particular enthusiasms of her neighbour on the eve of the Revolution. She had passed through two earlier awakenings, firstly, at the beginning of the seventeenth century, when the report of the Rosicrucian Fraternity was noised abroad in the world, and, secondly, when Baron von Rosenroth published his epoch-making work on Kabalism, placing the claim of this Jewish theosophy within the reach of his countrymen and all Latin-reading Europe. From that period Germany had never wanted exponents of esoteric philosophies, but at the time of the French Revolution the country in question, more even than France, was under the propaganda of an advanced sceptical philosophy with a defined centre of diffusion, at the head of which was the bookseller Nicolai. Its most notable consequence, so far as our subject is concerned, was the foundation of a political order known as the Illuminati, at the head of which was Weishaupt; but it is important only because ignorance still ascribes to the mystery of this political scheme the complexion of an occult mystery; and because, when the organisation was broken up forcibly in Germany, the adepts of the infidel and revolutionary fraternity took refuge in France and merged themselves in the political and secret doings of that country. Germany nevertheless, as already indicated, possessed traces of Illuminati of another order, and among these also its impostors. The adventurer Schroepfer filled Leipsic with evocations, and the rumour of evocations, and was driven to suicide in order to avoid being unmasked. He has found his apologists, however, at a later day, but the imposture is nearly indubitable. Finally, the Rosy Cross was still at work in Germany and especially in Prussia on the eve of the French Revolution and afterwards till the death of Frederick William II in 1797.

The learned and saintly Lavater is an individual figure of an altogether different aspect, and his group is one of the most interesting to the student at his period in Germany. All its names belong to those side-issues with which I am concerned here, down even to Heinrich Jung Stilling, with his suggestions of missionary enthusiasm and of a Lutheran theology illuminated by a beautiful life. But that Lavater, in spite of all this, was not specially recommended to the inward-seeking mind of Saint-Martin is not perhaps surprising. The discoverer of physiognomy, as appears by his SECRET JOURNAL, had only one thing besides a devotional spirit in common with the author of the NEW MAN, and that was an experience in those physical manifestations to which reference has been made already. Where Lavater failed in perfection from the standpoint of the Frenchman, was that he had not explicitly passed out of this elementary stage and its delusions; and there is a note of jubilation in the correspondence which hás been cited so frequently when it went abroad that the daughter of Lavater had resolved on the spiritual life. What followed from this determination is not known to history, and the group which surrounded the physiognomist belongs really to the eighteenth century, for in so far as it passed that period it passed also its consequence.

But this brief reference will serve to introduce another and more important personage, who, like Lavater, figures in the correspondence of Saint-Martin, and unlike either the German physiognomist or the French theosopher, is not the subject merely of passing mention or of frigid criticism, but of respectful reference and frequent eulogy. The Baron, who waited mostly on the superior opinion of his correspondent, introduced the Councillor von Eckartshausen with a tentative panegyric, which seemed to invite a favourable reception for one who had impressed him almost as much as the French philosopher, and with whom he corresponded also, no doubt after the same manner. Whether in this case the communications have been preserved we do not know, but it is more than doubtful. Outside the pages of his letters there is nothing to shew that Saint-Martin took any pains to understand his German brother, even when he wrote on a subject so dear to his own heart as the mysterious properties of numbers. It is, however, a debatable question whether Eckartshausen is not as great a name in their common subjects as is that of the Unknown Philosopher. He had not perhaps so much real genius, if we follow the dictum of Emerson, for he had a lesser quantity of " unavailableness." There are, notwithstanding, indications in his writings, and in one especially, that he belonged to a high order of attainment. THE CLOUD ON THE SANCTUARY is indeed an epoch-making work in Mysticism of Christian quality, and it is astonishing that its real significance and importance should have been overlooked by many whose intellectual occupations and interests might have enabled them at least to judge what books are, from their standpoint, vital. The little work is itself a series of letters addressed we know not to whom, it may have been even to Baron de Liebistorf ; and it claims to come from the centre of all Christian knowledge, indicating undeclared connections on the part of the writer which one does not dare to formulate in precise terms. The statements which it makes are possible only for those who have enjoyed intercourse before which the object sought in the secret Rites of Pasqually seems to shrink in dimension. THE CLOUD ON THE SANCTUARY claims, in other words, to be the voice of the Inner Church of Christ affirming the fact of its existence, and in such terms that the ordinary guarantees of evidence seem hardly to be longer necessary. Never had a Higher Christian Theology put forth its claims more clearly, more profoundly, or with more allurement of suggestion. We must unhesitatingly accept this work as marking in its way a new era at the dawn of the nineteenth century. It may not be without a purpose, in conformity with the astrology of books, that it was translated for the first time into English on the eve of the twentieth century, in which it perhaps has found its fitting audience and its wider mission. The other writings of Eckartshausen are like the other seership of Germany at the same period—matters which must not be named in the same connection ; but they are important in their way, notwithstanding, and it is little short of deplorable that nothing has so far been done to make this remarkable writer known in proportion as he deserves to those who should be concerned with him in England.

Without exception, unless it be that of Eckartshausen, as to which there is no evidence, all the personages who have been here cited were representatives of the Masonic Fraternities ; that is to say, they belonged to one or other of those innumerable Rites which at the end of the eighteenth century sought to propagate their particular objects under the mask of Masonry.

It was a natural attempt, rather than a device of subtlety, because it was the consequence of a genuine conviction that the Rites of Masonry had once at least covered a great secret. It was the design of every such attempt to restore the lost treasures to the rifled Temple. Naturally also, as we have seen, every new Rite, representing some one or other of the occult arts, was regarded as the only genuine Masonry, because each one was actually seeking to manifest what was held to be its true purpose by the inventor of such Rite. It is customary at the present day to speak derisively of the innumerable grades and systems which thus sprang into being, full grown and vested like Minerva. Masonic writers tell us that they are not real Masonry, which, like some other assurances of the Fraternity, does not need much authority to affirm and does not much signify, having regard to the present intellectual status of the Masonic subject. But they are serviceable for the history of the movement, because they undoubtedly helped to spread it, and because, after all eliminations, if anything remains in Masonry, it is assuredly the shadows and reflections of a mystic end. At the beginning of the nineteenth century most of these Rites had already perished, and so far as regards the vestiges of such corporate associations, the interests which they represented had seemingly fallen asleep.

It could scarcely be said at the period that they had even awakened in Italy, though we have the authority of Saint-Martin's correspondent, Kirchberger, Baron de Liebistorf, that in 1796 " inward works " were translated into Italian and Spanish even at Rome. The governing centre of the great State Church was too near, the proscription was too rigorous, the penalties were too heavy. All the mysteries were confined therefore within the circle of the Church, and stood or fell by their accommodation to its official dogmas. But even within the domain in which the mystic alone received a charter and enjoyed immunity from danger, there had been seldom any special diffusion of light, and at the period in question it may be said that there was almost none. Church and State were alike distracted, and at such moments the life of contemplation is scarcely possible even in a Trappist monastery. But if there was little or no Mysticism in Italy, there was beneath the ferment on the surface of life an old deposit of superstition, as replete with corruption as the tideless lagoons of Venice. And the exhalations of that sediment were still given up in the shape of Grimoires like the BOOK OF HONORIUS, of Black Magic and Black Masses, nameless corruptions for which Petronius could have found no language and Trimalcyon no appetite. Superstitions belong to folk-lore rather than to the side-issues of thought, and such corruptions have no history, or none at least that can be written. Occultism in Italy may be summed up in the one fact that, after a poor attempt to propagate his so-called Egyptian Masonry in Rome, Cagliostro was seized by the Inquisition and died, so far as we can tell, in imprisonment at St. Angelo. The nineteenth century was still within the shadow of the future. Obscure booksellers went on producing and reproducing the Grimoires; loathsome priests provided the Sacred Elements for profanation; occult arts, like others, stagnated under the shadow of the Vatican. It is only at the present day, and now only in a minor degree, that Italy has begun to enter into the history of these byways.

Under much the same domination there was some difference in Spain at the same period, but this country has at least possessed always a mystical theology because it has had always a fervent devotional spirit. On the one hand, St. Teresa and St. John of the Cross, both canonised, and one named the Mystical Doctor; on the other hand, Molinos persecuted, imprisoned and despoiled; afterwards, as a link between them, Maria d'Agreda, scarcely different from Molinos, but with the voice of popular feeling on her side, and beatified in consequence. Between the influences of all, Spain could not want her mystics and occasionally produced an adept, but in their particular missions they belonged really to other countries, since they found no field in their own. Spain therefore does not enter specially into the subject-matter of this memoir, and, speaking generally, it was the land of bondage rather than of secret philosophy, nothwithstanding that it was in some sense the birthplace or at least the schoolhouse of Kabalism, the home of Moses of Cordova and Isaac de Loria. It will serve no purpose to catalogue the countries of Europe which did not contribute anything to these interests at the inception of the era with which we are dealing; to say of Portugal what has been said of Spain ; to exhibit how slight was the influence of Jacob Böhme on Silesia or of Swedenborg on Sweden. The places which do not understand them now did not understand them then. It is curious to observe that one country from which we should expect nothing, offers seemingly something to our purpose, though it can be told in a few words. The Rosicrucian movement passed from Germany into Russia, where it abode for a period, more or less under the veil of Martinism and side by side with Masonry.

If we turn now to England, we shall find that matters here shew some contrasts and some similarities in comparison with France at the same epoch. Among the contrasts is the fact that there had been no such activity as was found across the Channel in 1789. Cagliostro was welcomed, it is said, by the Masons in London, and given the place of honour to which his status in the Craft entitled him ; his biography also was published by a contemporary, but his claims did not move the English mind. It was indeed not a little contemptuous. On the other hand, Saint-Martin found good friends in England, and retained loving memories thereof. The inference is that, while there was not much love of the marvellous, or inclination to be deluded by a splendid adventurer with a budget of prodigies, or much field for novelties in Masonry, there was at the period a certain school of deeper Christian thought in England, and this was assuredly the case, nor is its interest slight or its claim to be passed over lightly. It was the school of William Law, of Jane Lead and of Pordage. It was also the school of Jacob Böhme, within which the English translation of his works was undertaken. It offered conspicuous differences from the French school of Christian thought, even when modified by Saint-Martin in the Böhme interest. It lacks the colour and the richness ; it savours of the nonconformist " broken meat and garlic." Divorced as he was in his heart from all official ecclesiasticism, and closed by his principles to the devotional impression of the senses, Saint-Martin has always something, nevertheless, of the odour of the sanctuary, and he suggests the Graal even when he denies the Sacrament. But the English school had directness, strength and clearness—in a word, all that which the French philosopher never succeeded in obtaining, strive as he might, and there is evidence that he did strive ; it was wanting also in Mambrini and was deficient even in Eckartshausen. It must be added unfortunately that this directness was purchased as it is almost always purchased, and that to state it is really another way of saying that the school in question remained more in the letter, and was therefore less profound. There is palpable proof in both cases. No one has read Saint-Martin and dreamed that he was other than a mystic ; thousands and tens of thousands have read and drawn something of spiritual life from Law's SERIOUS CALL without ever suspecting that the author had a tinge of Mysticism or had a hand in the production of the works of Böhme in English. In the most popular of all his writings there is nothing to suggest Law's acquaintance with the MYSTERIUM MAGNUM, or with a deeper " morning redness," than that of the Eastern horizon. Some early members of the school, and Jane Lead as an instance, were more openly and unmistakably mystical, but their books are of the visionary order and do not offer any real substance to the inward needs of mind.

Another analogy between France and England at the beginning of the nineteenth century is found in the secret associations which existed here. They existed, of course, on a very minor scale. There was no period at which they could be said to have flourished, with all deference to the estimation in which some people have held the spurious Rosicrucian revelations of John Heydon. But if they ever flourished, they were then languishing. We must remember, of course, that it was England which gave to the world the Secret Initiation of Masonry, but the significance inherent therein was confined to a few symbols and a strange dramatic mystery, while no one then had and few possess now any real notion as to how it obtained them. Outside the symbols, and apart from any forced construction of the legends, the highest object of English Masonry was the diffusion of simple ethics, having much the same motives as those of any society for mutual improvement and edification in any village of the kingdom. It was not till the art had passed over the English Channel that it assumed another aspect, and this has never been acknowledged by the Craft, except in the minds of a few.

The societies which did exist and were, as I have said, stagnant, were not native growths, and to both of them a very curious history attaches. One was the Rose-Croix in the guise of Masonry and the other the Templar chivalry. If we take the case of the former, it is very difficult to determine the date on which this Order entered England. We know that Robert Fludd created an interest concerning the original form by an apology which appeared very soon after the first accounts were made public concerning the Fraternity. We have heard also that Fludd's enthusiasm was awakened through a visit paid him in England by the alchemist Michael Maier. Some years after the death of Fludd we find John Heydon affirming that the Fraternity was then dwelling in Wales, but the whole account is obviously mythical. About the same time we have the one mystic alchemist of England who would have been selected on *à priori* grounds as the most likely to hold a high place in such an institution, going out of his way to state that he did not belong to it. It may be argued that, by the rules of the Order, this course would have been incumbent on him in any case, which is true enough if the laws published by Sigmund Richter in Germany, late in the eighteenth century, are to be taken seriously ; but even then the circumstances attending the denial of Thomas Vaughan were not sufficient to occasion its necessity in the absence of its truth. From the period of Fludd to that of Vaughan and Elias Ashmole we hear nothing of the Order. The Oxford antiquary, who has told us that in things Hermetic he knew enough to hold his tongue but not enough to speak, appears to have been acquainted with an obscure alchemist and supposed Rosicrucian, whose confidant he became, and it is reported that about the same time Sir William Moray, a personal friend of Vaughan, and others also, had become members of the Fraternity. As these persons are important in connection with early Masonry, it is supposed by some that the Craft assumed its symbolical aspect under their guidance, and was thus a kind of transformed Rosicrucianism. But these things are dreams.

The Templar encampments, which are mentioned by Godfrey Higgins, were in existence before the year 1830, and there is no question that they were a survival from the previous century. Like Rose-Croix Masonry, they are still in evidence, with greatly increased prestige, among the High Degrees of Masonry. As such, they scarcely belong to the byways of secret association at the present day. It was to some extent different at the beginning of the nineteenth century, when their history is doubtful and legendary. We may speculate whether the Order of the Temple, as we now know it, was imported from France, like the sister-Rite. Unfortunately, we can only speculate, because the materials for a decision are entirely wanting.

In the year 1801 a book was published in the French language, in London, by one who signed himself " Clerk in Holy Orders," an exiled abbé, a derelict of the French Revolution, who had found an obscure asylum in England. Unknown, rather than forgotten, this work is perhaps one of the most curious which was ever issued from the press of a London printer, and its clumsy title is in keeping with much of its matter. WHAT WE HAVE BEEN, WHAT WE ARE, WHAT WE SHALL BECOME, written by the Abbé Fournié, appeared in the first days of the nineteenth century. The reviews of the period contain no mention of the fact. Probably it fell dead from the press, which is scarcely surprising because it is quite certain that no one would have understood it who was on the staff of the literary journals of that time. This work contains the doctrine of Martines de Pasqually, as it would appear after passing through the alembic of the mind of a catholic priest. If it were nothing more than this it would be exceedingly interesting for purposes of comparison with the same doctrine as it was developed by Saint-Martin, who had few clerical sympathies and was nurtured on a Lutheran method of self-knowledge ; but it is much more than this—it contains an account of the author's familiar relations with Pasqually, including a narrative of communications held with that personage years after he had passed away in the flesh. However we may regard its story, or the doctrine which it develops, this almost unheard of treatise is the most remarkable contribution to its subject made in England during the early part of the nineteenth century. The author died, as he had lived, in obscurity, and we have no record as to the date. He belongs to the school of diluted Christian Mysticism. His transparent sincerity is one of his most conspicuous merits, and though it is easy to regard him as hallucinated, there is very little in his pages to give colour to this supposition, except to those for whom experiences such as he relates spell only delusion or imposture. It must be added that he does not present the philosophical or doctrinal side of the school of Pasqually in a manner which would dispose us to regard it as, even from its own standpoint, other than a fantastic system. He may be said, indeed, to misrepresent it, and it is certain, at least, that he tinged it ; but there are many aspects in which he seems nearer to Pasqually than Saint-Martin, who originated more than he derived. There are striking points of likeness, outside the general drift of teaching, between the work which we have been discussing and Pasqually's long unpublished treatise concerning the RE-INTEGRATION OF BEINGS. Among the lost treasures, or at least curiosities, of the nineteenth century, it would be fair to include the second part of Fournié's treatise, which was promised but never appeared. The first part itself was held over by the writer for five-and-twenty years, and this, in the absence of corroborative testimony as to the events recorded, is assuredly the best guarantee of a presumptive kind that it was not a work either of haste or violence, and must not, however it may be regarded otherwise, be ranked among mere errors of enthusiasm.

With this account of the experience of a Frenchman in London, at the beginning of the nineteenth century, we may contrast a more lamentable history, not inferior in its sincerity, yet not undeservedly characterised as a fanatical delusion ; it is that of Joanna Southcote. It is needless to say that all common estimations of this extraordinary victim of hallucination miss all the important points. The historians of her tragedy—which is that of the soul entirely, for she was not in any conspicuous manner a subject of external visitations—have not endeavoured to convict her of imposture, nor have they erred in the general estimates of her hallucination. The most important of the points which have escaped them is that in her insanity as in her shrewd-ness, and the shrewdness is well attested, she was one of the martyrs of transcendentalism. It is quite impossible for any unbiassed student to deny her possession of extraordinary gifts, among which that of prophetic utterance may be named first, since it is of the obvious order. It was because she had those **gifts** that it was possible for her to be destroyed as she was.

Another important matter, and that not so obvious, is that she seems to have passed through many of the inward experiences of older Mysticism, as interpreted by unchallenged authorities of the Latin Church. When she proclaimed herself to be the bride of the Spirit, it is almost beyond question that she did so on the ground of that experience, and that the latter was similar to much which we hear concerning many early ascetics and saints of the past. In most of these instances they had the authority of the Church to guide them, and were thus saved from aberration by a direction which, whatever its imperfections, is shrewder than the shrewdest of the mystics. There is reason to believe that her life was altogether exemplary, nor will those who have studied it sympathetically deny her the seal of sanctity. It must be confessed, for the rest, that the Christianity of her period in England—which she regarded, by an instinct rare for her period—as only partial and introductory, most assuredly stood in need of completion, and the only regrettable circumstance is, that she was not competent to supply its deficiencies. The success of her mission, the environment of her later life— when the unlettered peasant, daughter of a small farmer in Devonshire, saw herself surrounded by fourteen thousand followers —may indeed have intoxicated her, but no intoxication, and even no ordinary measure of vanity, can render less pitiful and less dreadful the catastrophe of her closing years, when the seeress, believing that she had conceived miraculously, though approaching the age of Sarah, and that she was to bring forth a new avatar, was finally awakened from her vision by the fact of physical disease. The pyre of Joan of Arc could scarcely have exceeded that awakening or approached that disillusion. With her sad history closes the first cycle of the movement with which we have been dealing, during the course of the nineteenth century. We see that all its great names, and these are few, while they are not of the greatest, were remainders brought over from the preceding epoch. When these had passed away there were no others to replace them, and all things fell gradually into abeyance. It was a melancholy period for philosophical and intellectual thought. The desolation of the time found voice in the OBERMANN of Senancour, which reads like the world's dirge over its dead aspirations. The air was resonant with the uproar of thrones falling and the thunder of conflicting empires. The hiatus is filled only by mesmeric phenomena. It has been said that mesmerism is the key of all these secrets, and while there may be a certain sense in which such a statement has an aspect of truth, it should be added that those who were in possession of the keys could not discover the lock, or, at least, that the door which had been so far opened was not the right door. At the same time the key of Mesmer was destined before many years had passed away to open one door in the outer world with such consequences, that the sleep of the " secret sciences " came to an end abruptly, while its awakening was unlike anything in previous centuries.

The close of the eighteenth century signifies a great admixture —I had almost said, contamination—in the matter which belongs to our concern, being the witness of the soul in manifestation by the way of sanctified life and the abiding of the soul in hiddenness. But it was more especially an epoch of occult pursuits, amidst which in reality one voice alone was raised concerning the secret paths that lead into Divine knowledge. I am thus excluding Mambrini with reluctance and regret, though also with a certain subconscious questioning of heart whether in a day to come it may be given me to see more deeply within his clouded wells.

I have borne my witness to Saint-Martin in many places, but remembering always that he issued from an occult school and did not emerge fully. While its art and practice became unto him anathema—perhaps too strong a word, but they were at least cut off definitely—it seems to me that he remained for the most part within the pearl-mist and light nebulæ of its mental atmosphere. They dissolved in his great moments, the lucidity of which is penetrating, but these are not of his ordered theses, of his system—if such he had in any definite sense. On the path itself of the union, above all in its further length, there are no books needful, except for joy and consolation, and I am very certain that among those written by the Unknown Philosopher there are several which will afford both.

And now I have adverted in this study to many things which

lie outside the quest, for these were characteristic of the intellectual time with which I have been dealing. It is a little like taking the closing in a long tale of redemption, ere night comes down on the records. But we shall see in the next essay that there is one little star in the dark, so that in reality the tale goes on. There are also suggestions of a twilight which comes before morning. These essays written in humility are therefore looking to the East.

A MODERN DAUGHTER OF DESIRE

WE are living in an age when " God fulfils Himself in many ways," and if some of them are the old ways, under honoured sanctions of the past, it is for us to recognise the fulfilment wherever we meet with it, in a true catholicism of the heart. Assuredly there are many witnesses to the great truths, and if there were several centuries of this Western World of ours when the testimony to the Life of life was uttered only from within monastic walls, we should feel no sense of astonishment that there are witnesses still within them. If we have found on our own part that there are many paths which may lead to the centre, those which were travelled of yore by innumerable sons and daughters of Divine Doctrine are not for that reason to be held as henceforth of no service in respect of the end proposed. I am speaking, of course, to those who realise—in whatever measure— that there is a life of the soul possible on earth by the following of which it can enter into the experience of God dwelling within the soul. It is more than probable that their understanding of the kind of life is remote from that of asceticism ; in the ordinary meaning of the word I hold no brief for its defence as the best way at the present epoch of the world, and much less as the only way ; but I have in mind the memorial of one whose name filled for a period, and that somewhat recently, the whole world of Latin Catholicism. The episcopal process of her beatification was closed in 1911, is yet in the hands of the Sacred Congregation of Rites at Rome and will be followed no doubt, or has perhaps been followed already, by the Apostolic or Roman Process, the result of which is probably regarded as certain by thousands of devoted hearts. Marie Françoise Thérèse Martin was born on January 2, 1873, and she died of consumption on Thursday, September 30, 1897, in her twenty-fifth year. She is therefore in the plenary sense of the term a contemporary instance of that which is represented by her life, the external particulars of which, for the purposes of this brief notice, can be given in a few words. She was a child of profoundly religious parents and, bearing as she did from her tenderest years all signs, characters and seals of an uncommon election, she had leave—after much difficulty, involving appeals to the Bishop of Bayeux and even Pope Leo himself—to enter the Carmelite Convent of Lisieux at the age of fifteen. This was on April 9, 1889 : in conventual language, her " clothing day " was on January 10 of the following year, and she was " professed " on September 8, 1890. It was not long before the charge of the novices passed into her youthful hands.

The life and the spirit have naturally evaporated in this bald recital, nor can I say that her published life itself conveys more than an intimation of the influence which she exercised within the " Carmel " walls of her dedication. It is rich, however, beyond words in other and more essential respects. It contains in the first place her own " story of my soul," and this memorial is of permanent and living value. It is followed by an account of her death by the Prioress of the Carmel, extracts from her correspondence and certain other writings. Most of the remaining pages are concerned with events after her death which made her name for more than a brief moment something like a household word throughout the Roman Catholic world.

Now, it is out of the simple and general matters of fact so far related that the two main points of our concern arise : one is the manner in which Sœur Thérèse appeals to mystics, while the other is her alleged connection with extraordinary phenomena which were once in evidence among us, and for all I know to the contrary may still continue. In respect of the first, her rule of life was the perfect and zealous pursuit of the severe regimen prescribed by the Carmelite Order, and she raised it in her own case far beyond the ordinary formal degrees. Whether we like it or not, the lesson which her story conveys is the quality, depth and extent of the grace which remains in the ascetic path for those who are still called to follow it—few and far between, as we tend to think, but more numerous perhaps and signal than we may care to dream. I speak as a Christian mystic and as an apostle of the alternate ways, believing that Thérèse might have reached her term otherwise, yet recognising her particular fitness for that state in which the Divine called her. I need not add that such practices are of themselves nothing : it is the motive which makes them aids. Her secret from the beginning was the all-secret of love, and this is why I have called her—in the words of Richard Crashaw—a " daughter of desire." It was in virtue of love that she could say that " days of earth become days of Heaven." She spoke also of " the delicious fruits of perfect love and of complete abandonment to the Divine Will." With her it was loving union in the mode of purified mind. She was spared for the most part the " visions " and " locutions." It must be said also that her experience was rather by the way of faith in a childlike spirit than by mystical realisation understood in the sense of the mystics, and this notwithstanding that she found high lights in the works of St. John of the Cross. Her first reception of the Eucharist was the great turning-point in her story. The event and that which it signified offer an aid to reflection that while many beautiful and sacramental signs communicate under their respective veils the same deep, mysterious and holy things, it remains certain that no mode practised in external religions is so efficacious towards realisation of the Divine inwardly as the Eucharistic Rite of the Latin Church. On the day of her First Communion " all the joys of Heaven " came down into the heart of Thérèse and Heaven itself dwelt in her soul. The beginning thus made was continued to the end with ever-growing frequency and fervour. It was doubtless thereby and therein that she was truly in touch with the infinite and had the gift of being lost therein. So also her story is one of stages in " the science of love "—an expression of B. Margaret Mary Alacoque. Thérèse reached the fulness of the state of love on June 9, 1895, and so found that her vocation was love simply. But that was a question of consciousness, for this had been her call from the beginning ; and hereto was due her valiant chivalry of aspiration, by virtue of which she dared, even as a child, to be a saint in resolve, dared to believe that she was " born for great things,"

said to herself ever and continually : " I shall be a great saint."
Yet the valiance was one of all humility—in virtue of the vesture
of Christ. So also she was catholic in the best sense, in the
encompassing sense of love. The whole of the Christian world,
that world which she could enfold with love in her consciousness,
became to her a garden of the soul and a " living garden " of
the Lord. Though she called herself only " a little flower," she
reminds one rather of that lady, " the wonder of her kind," who
tended " from morn to even " a certain paradise known to the
poet Shelley. Thérèse nourished her garden with her love,
watered it with her prayers, offered up her many sufferings
because of it, filled it with the graces of her days, while those
whom she brought to God were the flowers of her tending. And
so at last God called her by the " death of love." The Prioress
of the Carmel says : " Suddenly she raised herself, as though
called by a mysterious voice. . . . Thus she remained for
about the space of a *Credo*, when her blessed soul . . . was
borne away "— a victim of Divine Love, as the Prioress
says also.

Here is the first point at some length, but of the second I
must speak shortly. The desire of Thérèse was to " spend my
Heaven in doing good upon earth," to " come down " to her
friends, to spread the love of Christ, her Spouse, more fully and
more perfectly among men than was possible within the narrow
measures of personal life in this world. " After my death I will
let fall a shower of roses," and the book says that the graces
" attributed to her intercession " are innumerable. They are
conversions, physical healings, escape from death, accident
averted, even gifts of money. I suppose that the cures of the
sick will be most important as evidence to those in search of such
things ; they include cancer, loss of vision, elephantiasis—among
others numberless. I do not adjudicate upon the value of any ;
as to one which was given a place of first importance in the
popular mind about the time of her beatification, it recalls certain
phenomena of modern Spiritism ; an apparition is included
and the transportation of money and notes. But the beautiful
life of " the little flower of Jesus " became better known by these
means. Those which were purely spiritual in their compass are

of an order which is familiar in the annals of the saints, and they are distinct from psychical happenings.

I have called Sœur Thérèse a little star shining in a dark hour, and I have thought in the last essay of a morning which is possibly to come. But who can tell, looking at the danger-signals which flame about us and ahead ? She had at least the mind of the mystics, for the deep states are in the mind as of a little child. It looks into the heart of the mystery with direct and simple eye, till—apart from all the processes of hardly ordered thought— that which was seen in the distance is found in the heart of the soul, and the light thereof.

PART III

LAMPS ON HEIGHTS

MYSTICAL REALISATION

THE testimony to mystical experience has been borne in the modern world, in the main on the faith of the records, and under the Christian ægis—through all the Christian centuries—it has been borne at first hand by those who have attained therein some part at least of that which awaits the souls of men in the fruition of Divine Union. The annals of old sanctity and the commentaries of expert theology constitute together an exceedingly large literature, over and above which there is a yet larger testimony going back into remote ages and concerned with the same experience under the denominations of other religions in the sacred world of the East. Yet it seems to me that in what has been called the "general and popular world" of thoughtful and literate people there is still only a very slight and imperfect understanding of the whole subject. There is, I think, none on which statements are looser and fundamental misconceptions more frequent. The terms Mysticism and Mystical are still used to characterise the dealings of "occult science" and as synonyms for the scheme of things which are usually connoted by the title of "new thought." They are labels in common used indifferently by friends and enemies of both. Those who affirm that there are no occult sciences, though there are many grades of self-induced hallucination and many curious arts, are apt to term them mystical as a byword of reproach. Those in whose view the literary ventures which carry the mark of new thought are goods that are labelled falsely, regard it as the last word of condemnation to describe them as mystical. On the other hand, both literatures belong, in the opinion of many defenders, to the realm of Mysticism, which they understand to mean higher thought. The point of union between the two parties resides in the fact that they are indifferently misusing words.

It happens—as we have found—that Mysticism is the world-old science of the soul's return to God and therefore those who apply it to (1) any form of conventional metaphysics, (2) any branch of mental philosophy, (3) any reveries high or low, are no less mistaken than those who use it as a term of scorn. I care nothing in this connection for the etymological significance of the word, as denoting what is secret and withdrawn. It has come in the course of the years to have one meaning only in the accurate use thereof, and we must abide by this and no other—for the sake of ordered thought—unless and until the keepers of mystical science shall agree between themselves on another and more definite term as an expression of the whole subject.

I have been speaking of the outer circles, from whom it seems idle at present to expect accuracy; but there is a more extraordinary want of understanding on the part of some whom we should expect to be capable at least of thinking rightly within the elementary measures of Mysticism. Here it is no longer a question concerning the mere word, or the use of denominations in the sense of the mystical path when they belong more properly to the end, after all the travellings are over. I refer especially at the moment to misapprehensions respecting the place of the science in the life of modern man and woman, and this involves a consideration of the now recurring question whether that science can be acquired by practice in the daily life of the world. There can be no expectation of presenting in a brief space any views that will differ materially from those which I have expressed already in much longer studies; but it may be possible to offer something simply, for understanding on the part of those who cannot examine the subject in ordered and lengthy books. The question is therefore whether those excellent people are right who seem to think that the principles of mystical science may be so put forward that they can be taken into the heart, not indeed of the men in the street —though no one wishes to exclude them—but of men and women everywhere who have turned already to God, or are disposed in that direction. Alternatively, is it—shall I say?—a science which is reserved to experts only? We know that it is not possible to become acquainted readily and easily with the higher mathematics, with chemistry or biology. There are certain natural qualifications in virtue of which the poet is born, as well as made subsequently ; there is also the scientific mind, which presupposes gift and faculty, as well as opportunity and application. In the science of the mystics, in their peculiar art of life, are there certain essential qualifications to be postulated in every case, and is there a long apprenticeship ? Before attempting to answer, let us see what is being said and how far it exhibits any adequate acquaintance with the problems belonging to the debate.

It has been suggested recently that religion is at work revising institutions and theology, that reconstruction is in the air everywhere and that Mysticism needs reconstruction as much as anything else. In the face of this statement a certain caution is necessary lest we begin to talk foolishly. It appears, however, that the remark applies rather to notions, theories and systems, to " the spell of mediæval Mysticism " and to the reconstruction of these. Yet the tendency is to regard Mysticism as a mode of thought, an attitude—if you like—towards the universal, so that we can have done with archaic forms and devise others which are modern. It is, however, as I have said, a science, the end of which is attained in the following of certain methods. One does not change sciences—as, for example, mathematics—but we can reconstruct and, it may be, improve our way of acquiring them. Mediæval Mysticism is the same as modern Mysticism—if any— but there may be other ways of reaching it, in respect of the externals, than were known and practised in convents. Fundamentally speaking, however, the ways are one—whether in the East or West, for those who follow *Vedanta* and those to whom the IMITATION is a source in chief of leading. The only change that we can make is by taking out of the way that which is unnecessary thereto. As I tried to shew—it is now some seven years since—in THE WAY OF DIVINE UNION, there is no question that the end of Mysticism was reached by the method of ascetic life during many past centuries of Christendom, but it belonged to the accidents of the quest ; for other ways are possible, as I tried also to indicate.

The alleged reconstruction of religion is taking place only in a subsidiary sense, within narrow measures, or here and there in

R

the corners. The great Latin Church is revising nothing, while the Greek—I suppose—is stewing in the waters of its own incapacity. But if they were both at the work of remaking and at one in their activity with the sects and the Anglican Church, the case of the mystics would still differ, because pure Mysticism has no institutions to revise and no conventional or official theology to expand, reduce or vary. It is a path of advancement towards a certain end, and the path is one : the variations are found only in the modes of travelling. Having in this manner cleared the issues, there must be something said of the end and the way by which it can be reached.

There is a great experiment possible in this life and there is a great crown of the experiment, but in the nature of things it is not to be bought cheaply, for it demands the whole man. It has been said that the life of the mystic is one of awareness of God, and as to this we must remember that we are dealing with a question of life and a life-problem. But what is awareness of God ? It is a certain inward realisation, a consciousness of the Divine—not only without us but within. The word awareness is therefore good and true, but it is one of those intimations which—as I have suggested already—are of the path and not of the end. It is of the learner and not of the scientist. The proof can be put in a nutshell by an appeal to the perfect analogy of that experience which is human love. Can we say to the human lover that an awareness of the beloved must content him here and now ? But that which he seeks is possession, after the manner of all in all—possession which is reciprocal and mutual. In Divine Things the word is realisation, and mystical realisation is the state of being possessed and possessing. Otherwise, it is God in us and we in God : O state of the ineffable, beyond all words and thoughts, deeper than tears of the heart and higher than all its raptures. The science of the mystic is that of the peculiar life-cultus, life-practice, or quest of life which leads to this state. In respect both of path and state the word is love. The kind of loving is summarised in the grand old counsel : " With all thy heart and with all thy soul." The rewards of love are not those which can be earned by divided allegiance. There is also another saying—about the desire of a certain house having eaten one up. There is no eye on two worlds in this and no Sabbath dedication except in the long Sabbath of undivided life. Here too is no art of making the best of both worlds and especially of this one, as if with one eye on the dollars and another on God. In this kind of dedication the world goes by and the pageants of all its temples : there are no half-measures respecting it. The motto of the path is *sub specie æternitatis,* and it connotes the awakening and subsequent activity of a particular inward faculty. We know well enough by experience the power of a ruling passion, and it may happen to be one that is lawful. The man who is ruled thereby is living *sub specie illa ;* it colours all his ways and days ; it is the very motive of his life. Now, if we postulate in certain persons a ruling passion for God, it is then *sub illa specie æternitatis* that they live and move and have their being.

As regards this state and as regards its gifts and fruits, even at the early stages, I testify that the Divine in the universe answers to the Divine in man. There does take place that which maintains and feeds the passion. A life which is turned to the keynote of the eternal mode knows of the things that are eternal. It knows very soon that it is not on a false quest : that God is and that He recompenses those who seek Him out is verified by valid experience. It grows from more to more, an ever-expanding equipment in highest sanity of mind. Two things are certain : (1) apart from this high passion there can be no practical mystic ; but (2) no one can teach another how to acquire it. Once it has been kindled in the heart, the secret of the path is its maintenance, and many devices have been tried—among others those of the ascetics. The only excellent way is that of love in its activity towards all in God and God in all. This is the sense of St. Augustine's : " Love and do what you will." Hatred is a canker in the heart and eats up this passion. Universal love maintains the passion for God till that time when God enters and takes over the work : it is then the beginning of the end, and that end is the still activity of union in the Eternal Centre. It is inevitable that vocation must be postulated, but this signifies an inward possibility of response to an ever-recurring call. It is thus that the divine passion is kindled which—as I have said—

no one can communicate to another. There is something in the individual fount by which some are poets and some are called to the priesthood. For the same inscrutable reason there are some who receive and answer the call to mystic life. It may be a consequence of antecedent lives or of hidden leading from spiritual spheres : I do not know. It follows that the mystic life is reserved to those who can lead it, but unlike all other sciences the only technique connected with it is the technique of love ; the apprenticeship is that of love ; the science is love ; and the end is love's guerdon. All this being so, I am sure that there are more true mystics than we can dream, and yet they are few enough. They will grow from more to more, for love always conquers. But as to when this science of love can appeal to all classes I make no pretence of knowing : it is for those who are able to acquire it ; and so are the questions answered.

FAITH AND VISION

THE authority which is above all authority has announced to us that any search after goodness outside God is a vain quest, because He alone is good. If such is the construction placed by our Divine Master upon the claim of those natural amenities which it is customary to class with goodness, we shall be justified in looking at the whole subject more closely than is possible in any summary allusion or indeed discursive paper, for we are in the presence of an intimation concerning our end of being.

If we may set aside for a moment the conventional urbanities of polite education, and may venture to affirm what is not in reality disputed by those who have a title to think independently of the conventions in question, namely, that, taken even at their own valuation, the characteristic of ethics is insufficiency, we shall have done something already to liberate human thought by opening up wider issues than the considerations of morality can afford. The bare statement is liable, however, to certain misconceptions on the part of hasty minds, which will be apt to conclude that the insufficient is also the ineffectual. If they are told, for example, that there is very little trace in the universe of what used to be understood in the old arguments by the conception of moral order, they will suppose that it must be governed alternatively by blind fatality alone. If they learn further that the theological doctrine of requital—the system of conventional recompense and punishment—lapses with the notion of moral order, they will assume, on their own part, that human conduct is a matter of indifference, carrying no personal consequence, and that the decalogue has passed into abeyance. One crudity is thus replaced by another in minds of this type, for which leading-strings are necessary, because the moment they cease to be controlled by the stipulations of right conduct, they are impelled by the freneticism of passion. The truth is that the fundamental laws of morality are more vital in their importance the more fully we recognise the final inadequacy of any simple doctrine of conduct or any general rule imposed upon civilised conscience. Such inadequacy does not arise from the fact that, being catholic to the whole world, they are of necessity common-place in character, and by their familiarity have become platitudes in expression, though it is part of our burden that the obvious and the familiar are sources of great weariness and inward dejec-tion. It follows rather from the fact that, look as we may upon the brighter side of being, hope as we can for the future, believe as we do, not alone in the actual and latent worthiness of human life, but that we came at the beginning from afar and that in the end we return afar, it remains that, as a race, we have fallen short of the most restricted ideal, and that therefore human conduct stands in need of a more powerful motive than any which is provided by the simple moral law. This law endeavours to insure, firstly, harmonious correspondence with an accepted standard which abides in the general conscience; secondly, the intellectual development which accompanies the progress of knowledge; and, thirdly, that amelioration of the conditions of existence which is understood by sociological science. Thus, by a natural method, " devoid of haste and violence," and at work on the physical plane, it would give man at his best to the world. Because insufficiency is written upon the face of these things, they are not less necessary as titles and warrants in every postulant for admission to the Kingdom of God.

In one form or another a motive more powerful than morality has been present always in the world, and this, under the name of religion, has insisted on an excellence which is other than moral goodness, standing thereto, perhaps, in the same relation that genius bears to talent. Fixing its intentions at once upon man's higher nature, it endeavours to accomplish its objects by producing a harmonious correspondence between God and the human soul; by insuring the soul's progress in the immediate knowledge of God; by a transfiguration of the conditions of existence through the suspension of exclusive correspondence with inferior things; and by the establishment of higher correspondence—which is the aim of spiritual life. It is, in a word, the assonance of conscious being upon the inward side. In the ideological world the conceptions within and without suppose one another: so also the elevation of the physical and intellectual man cannot proceed if the culture of the soul be ignored, and the soul's growth is impossible with an undeveloped or deteriorating physical instrument. It is only at the great heights that this instrument ceases to hold an office, and so falls gradually away.

At the same time the religious motive, more powerful as it is claimed than ethics, has, like ethics, failed to accomplish its purpose so far as the race is concerned. It cannot be said that this failure must be ascribed to the fact that the two have not worked in conjunction, for it is only of late years that there has been an attempt of a methodical kind to divide them and accomplish the secularisation of morals, or, in other words, the reduction of insufficiency to suspension. On the contrary, the religious motive has insisted without variation upon the moral basis, but this insistence and that conjunction, which should have been the source of strength, have been perhaps the secret of failure. The reason is, that the nature of the correlation has been misconstrued; morality is not the groundwork of religion, but true religion is the foundation and philosophical motive of morality. The misconstruction can be realised most easily by one of its simplest summaries, as, for example, that "the pure in heart shall see God." In the merely natural order the statement seems notoriously untrue; the reference, however, is not to any natural condition of negative innocence, but to the attainment of that spiritual state which on the inward side yields the Divine Vision, and on the outward insures purity of heart as a consequence. In other words, we cannot work up from Nature to that which is supernatural, but the supernatural is so extended as to include all that is good and gracious in Nature, while it maintains and ameliorates it continually, bringing it by degrees to perfection after its own kind.

The object of religion is the development and perfection of humanity by a series of spiritual processes, and its union with what is highest in the universe, while morality proposes the amelioration of the race with the assistance only of natural law.

Religion has so far failed because it has realised imperfectly its own pre-eminence, and morality for want of an adequate recognition of spiritual law. We must know God in order to be good, but no moral goodness can bring us to divine knowledge. It follows that the Churches, as the official teachers of religion, so far from reaching their term, have not as yet entered into their true patrimony; that their higher function is before them, in whatsoever form they may be destined to assume hereafter; and that the world at large needs them at this moment more strenuously than in the past.

Whether to the messages of history or to the living facts of the age in which we move and are—wheresoever we turn, we see everywhere about us the energies of a power which makes for advancement. We see everywhere an outward and inward, a collective and individual struggle towards a higher state. But we have also to confess the presence of retrogressive forces and further of those negative forces which retard or arrest development. If we take for a moment the conventional view of evolution as it is construed by official science, that law would appear to have proceeded along its path of progress till, in the process of development itself, certain factors were introduced with which it had ultimately to reckon, namely, human consciousness, reason and free will. When these appeared, something was introduced into the sequence which could set itself against the law and arrest progress, if it chose, in that department of Nature. The cross and retrogressive currents thus put in motion are not to be identified with the simple inertia which man, in common with other forms of existence, would oppose naturally to the progressive agencies at work within and without him. He has operated against his development instead of co-operating therewith; and this constitutes what the old transmigrationist Glanvil has termed the grand mystery of sin and evil. To cope with this tendency the moral law has arisen, among other forces, and up to a certain point it assists us to fulfil the higher law of our being. But, after all that has been advanced to the contrary by the casuistry of some emancipated minds, the sanction of moral law is in the Divine Law, for which reason it does not rest on any foundation of its own, nor can it, on the other hand, offer a substantial ground to religion. We need therefore to reverse all the processes of the past. Philosophical religion is no matter of faith, interpreted as intellectual assent to the clauses of a formal creed, or as a subscription to the Thirty-nine or any other Articles of Association adopted by a particular Church : it is of experiment and experience. It has been said, as we have seen, that no man is good, but God alone, and it is only in so far as the religious experience advances us to Divine Knowledge that we begin to grow into that supernatural goodness which includes in its larger dimension the restricted, dependent and temporal sphere of ethics.

These considerations would be only in the nature of special pleading if religion could not be regarded as a practical science which obtains its results as surely as any physical science by the application of its proper formulæ. It is this scientific, philosophical and, at the same time, mystical religion which should be set at the basis of morals for their support and sanction, and it is summed up in the single doctrine that there is a way to the knowledge of God. Its first concern is to satisfy the hunger and thirst after righteousness which is the whole root and principle, the term righteousness being taken in its true sense as the direction of the whole man towards the absolute goodness, thus differing widely from those common acceptations which connect it with standards of morality less or more conventional, the prescripts of social decency, or conformity with the ceremonial requirements of the several systems of external religious belief. These things are also sacramental, but until their service has been accepted discriminately they can signify very little to the life of the soul.

It is essential to realise that at the beginning this " scientific religion " is and can be followed only by the way of faith. In one of the Conferences of the ZOHAR, Rabbi Simeon ben Jochai, the great traditional master, is said to have reminded his hearers that, at the foot of Mount Horeb in the wilderness of Sinai, the Children of Israel covenanted to obey the Law before they had heard it, the promulgation not having taken place as yet. Now, the significance of this mythos is that in the great dedications obedience goes before understanding, not indeed that obedience is blind but because it is the condition of the opening of hearts, so that the influences and graces from above may enter and abide within us. This is stating after a more subtle manner the oft-repeated maxim that those who live the life shall know of the doctrine. If we can get to see the high reason of this dogmatic affirmation we shall have reached that firm ground of faith, about which we have heard so many definitions that do not satisfy the mind and leave unmoved those higher inward faculties which communicate with the logical understanding, though their sphere exceeds it.

The beginning of faith may be no firmer than the indeterminate feeling of a poet who thought that Plato reasoned well and that therefore " it must be so." He expressed after his own manner the clouded twilight-sentiment which comes in part from intuition and in part from yearning and was voiced again by one of his successors, who faintly held " the larger hope." This has been and it remains the quality or ground of faith for a large number of people who would elect to be classified as at least religiously disposed. It recognises and cleaves to a certain balance of probability, most often because if it were otherwise those who cleave thereto would regard themselves as " of all men most miserable." It may work up to a living thing if such a feeling abides with them sufficiently to influence their conduct of life, as it does indeed and often, though perhaps also faintly, because of that leaven of doubt which so ferments the whole mass that —as a cold consolation—they have to take incertitude to their hearts and seek to warm it somehow by affirming that

> " There is more faith in honest doubt,
> Believe me, than in half the creeds."

But in the last resource this class of consolation is so cold that no extremity of need can kindle it, and if men can get no further they die of such comfort, as if stones were offered them for bread. It can help no one through the gate of death and bring none to the gate of reality. Yet it may serve for a beginning, as I have said, and we may reach therefore past it to a better ground of belief, corresponding to that covenant of Rabbi Simeon and to the interpretation which I have placed upon it.

There is something which we must do with our might if we would go further, and to begin this active work we must take that which we expect for granted. It obtains in the lesser things and as much or more in the greater. The illustration may be in bald prose of platitude, but we shall never reach Rome if we doubt all roads that lead thereto and hence do not make a start. So also he who is paralysed from the beginning by an assumed incapacity for the work will never be a maker of books. Within or without our own course, we must begin by assuming that we are to the manner born of its business—that at least we are called thereto and may in fine be chosen—if we are going to fulfil the thing which we have set before us, whether it be the creation of a new epoch in literature or the more simple undertaking to pass from Europe to Cathay, and yet again if, being on this earth, we look beyond our present level to the place of the kingdom.

Taking therefore the will to believe as granted in the first place, the course before us is that of keeping the Law before we have come to understand it, before it has spoken otherwise than dimly and unintelligibly to our hearts, and it is that of living the life in order that past the outer shell of the doctrine we may enter into the secret region of its inward being and soul. It is this essence and *summum bonum* behind the doctrine which is called in the ZOHAR the sacred day of the Sabbath, while the Sabbath is a symbol of that Land of the Living which is called the world to come and the world of the spirit. The counsel may seem out of reason for the cynicism of strong minds, but the ruling is not in their hands; it has been transferred long ago to those who are called children according to the Secret Doctrine and according to that sense in which it has been said that " a little child shall lead them."

It is affirmed also by the same traditional source that one light creates another, which signifies thus in the uplifted sense of its symbolism : from the light of the will directed to the clearer light in conduct; from the lamp of conduct to the first and hallowed lights which shine in the world of conformity; from its turning of the self towards God to the integration of all intent which can follow thereupon, and from one to another it moves, kindling the greater lights. Hereof is the path of faith which becomes the path of quest and so leads on to the vision, that last great sacrament in all the world of images, beyond which is the union.

That which is termed in symbolism the Divine Vision is in its valid understanding the state of knowledge attained. But we must beware of being deceived by the representations which we make unto ourselves in the pictorial imagery of mind. Though the Latin Church at its highest must recognise assuredly the vital truth of that inspired covenant which assures us that " it hath not entered into the heart of man to conceive what God hath prepared for those who love Him," it has formulated the eternal future of the elect in the terms of Beatific Vision, which notwithstanding it must be realised that the knowledge of God connoted by those talismanic words is not a condition in which A contemplates B as an objective desire of the eyes and heart. Knowledge is an inward state of our own essential being, and the object of research is beheld within the subject, as in a state of still rest and exceedingly great simplicity, in which there is nothing corresponding to a picture abiding in the mind or an idea formulated and fixed therein. It is a continual and ever deepening awareness of an Indwelling Presence, penetrating the whole being. It becomes almost idle to affirm that there is no passage from subject to object. There is indeed, as it seems to me, no distinction between the Presence and the state attained. It is not precisely that the subject absorbs the object or that we become in fine that which we sought at first, though by these alternatives we may attempt to formulate the living experience to our active minds or to those of others. If the state is indeed ineffable, there is obviously nothing concerning it which can pass into expression, though the mind may vibrate continually between those two opposites in its inevitable search after terms to provide a true formulary, seeing that the office of mind is ever to manifest the word in the sacramental flesh of expression. It is to be doubted further whether we diagnose the mode of being by such a formula as Thou art That. It is true of the state itself, but this is not permanent during the life of manifestation, though its aftermath remains with us like a luminous reflection. I have known the intellectual understanding quiver on the verge of plenary comprehension of the whole mode in certain anæsthetic states, but the anæsthesia has worn itself out before the threshold is crossed. In the living mode itself there is no thinking thereon, as if we would subject it to analysis. I have said that we are in still being, wherein the Presence abides, apart from notion and distinction, in the rest of the knowledge which is That, the beatitude which is That and the fontal life.

The kind of faith which leads to this vision of inward knowledge in realisation is at the beginning an intellectual assent to the possibility of such a field of experience, and that which should follow is endeavour to explore the field. There are aids to preparation for the experiment everywhere in daily life, but the first condition is obviously a sense of dedication, corresponding to the old idea of being called and chosen, though scarcely in the old sense, as if there were an external will operating to select and set aside. All who can consecrate themselves to the work are *ipso facto* those who have a warrant to begin and discover for themselves how they may fare in the path which passes through the field. It is peculiarly possible to reach the state of consecration amidst the activities of daily life, and they are better for the most part than a life of ease. There are at the present time many admirable persons of both sexes who earn their own means of subsistence and that of others in all kinds of business, and the fact does not prevent them from devoting some part of their days, and even of each day, to purely mental pursuits. There is always a way found wheresoever the will directs, with desire behind the will, and it is certain, God willing, that never the will to God shall fail of a way which leads or of time to walk therein. Of that which must be put aside I do not need to speak, because it is known beforehand, and I have said enough —as it seems to me—concerning the moral law. The work of consecration has only two aspects : we must renounce the will to evil and we must beget the love of God. When this love is begotten the will to evil dies, though it follows by no means that all temptation is over or that all our weakness has been turned suddenly to strength. Our safeguard herein is to see that the love is nourished and that the love grows. It is nourished by nursing, and this is thinking in the heart or dwelling on the love-object. There emerges at this point our next matter of research, which is called the contemplative life. We know that it was followed in the past by all mystics and is still pursued. That which it is and that which it claims is therefore to be studied from the standpoint of present possibilities and present needs. The research with which we are occupied has no concern in the past save only by reason of its appeal—if any—to humanity here and now.

THE PATH OF CONTEMPLATION

THE true Path of Contemplation is a manner of life in love, and this is the mystic Path, which has been termed in these studies the Path of the Union. There is nothing in the whole world which is so utterly apart from processes. Those who have entered into the state of love are in need of no teacher as to that which shall be done therein. It follows that the formal methods can serve only to attain the state, and in so far as they are valid in practice, or practical aids on the Path, the reason is that the Divine Object is within us and not before us: it is seen only with the eyes of the soul and realised in its heart alone.

I am about to delineate some of the processes and to summarise briefly certain results of reflection thereupon in a far past of the years. They embody records of experience, but I hold otherwise no brief about them, because it happens that I am not one who can be helped materially by methods sharply defined, while it is indubitable otherwise that each one of us must discover his own way. The Path of Contemplation is an experiment undertaken in the individual mind and must differ as minds differ. There can be no life in mappings out and in scale-plans. But the things which have helped others in days of old may still offer shadows of aid and perhaps more : they are at least indications of things that are signified and involved by the attempt to follow the inward life, while at most they are doors which open on the early stages. They do not unfold the living secret of the inward way. That is found for himself by each, and as shewn in the next study there is no one on earth who can teach it, because it is love's secret.

It must be understood, for the rest, that all mystical knowledge is either of the intellectual order and realised as such in the logical understanding or it is reality as experienced by love, and in the

Divine Order the synonym of this is sanctity. The Path of Holiness in love is the Path of the Union, and there is no other : in accordance with that which a man would reach he must first live. It follows that this essential condition is presupposed by all the methods which have been practised by masters of experience and formalised into high conventions by scholiasts thereupon. It is possible by the mystic life to attain consciousness in unity, and this is God realised within. No one has dared to say that the path is easy, but seeing that its term is the end of all our being there is no insuperable hindrance and there is no barrier which cannot be taken out of the way, including those substitutes which come in the guise of attainment but are its remote reflections only. Their characteristics are peace, light and extension in light. The final term exceeds all pre-realisation, though the heart depicts it to itself. It must be added on the basis of all the records that it is not permanent in our manifested life on earth, but there is a perpetual aftermath, more precious than the kingdoms of this world, their altars and their thrones.

But the first and last counsel of the Path of Contemplation should assure us that a single handful of coins from the mint of love is worth all the treasures of formal method in the garners of its sacred houses.

PART I

THE PREPARATION FOR THE PATH

1. PRELIMINARY CONSIDERATIONS

THERE are certain distinctions which it is necessary to make in the first place, so that there shall be no misapprehension as to what is involved by a subject which is concerned with deep states of the inward nature. In the common use of words, the terms Contemplation and Meditation usually merge into one another, and there is a disposition to regard them as synonymous —which is countenanced by popular dictionaries—but they are not so identified in mystic literature. More especially in the holy Christian schools, Contemplation is regarded as a simple intuition of truth, and the act thereof is a pure, quiescent work of mind, the external operations of which pass away utterly in those later stages of which something will be said hereafter. Meditation, on the other hand, is that course of the reasoning mind wherein it proceeds from one point to another of a given subject and attempts an exact research into its several aspects and circumstances. Meditation is therefore an activity of the rational faculty, which works from without to arrive at the inward nature of any given object. Contemplation is the repose of that faculty when it is so fixed on the subject that the realisation of its inward nature replaces the outward apprehension. It has been said still more shortly that Meditation is seeking and Contemplation seeing. There are several recognised degrees of both; but it is enough at the present moment to create a clear distinction in respect of the elements.

So far as the definitions have proceeded, they have said nothing in respect of purpose, and it is of course understood that concentration and the normal processes of applied thought have more often than not some worldly, material or personal object in view. We are dealing, however, and intending to deal only with the quest of the spirit of man after its end in God. In all times, among all peoples, and by every form of religion, the inward way, the way of thinking in the heart, has been found to be that path which alone leads to the end as here specified.

This is not a polemical treatise, embodying a philosophical criticism, and I do not propose to consider whether there is an alternative or whether several roads are conceivable, nor—in the case that a Path of Contemplation is the only way to reach the end in view—shall I seek to establish the intellectual grounds on which the fact must be held to rest. It is not, *ex hypothesi* at least, a matter of speculative assumption but one of experience, which can be tested by each man and woman who is called thereto in the person of each. There are some for whom, in a comparative sense, it is held to be easy, as if they were born to the work; but it is not pretended that it is otherwise, or for such reason, an easy path to all. There are some for whom it is indefinitely difficult; but it must not be thought that it is impossible for anyone. As an almost universal rule, it does not come within the aspiration—or even the horizon—of those who are not in an elementary way fitted for the experiment. Finally, a few make it resolutely and continually without getting to any term, though they may proceed far enough to know that the term is real and that it will recompense those who can pursue it further. If this is a second best, it is at least much better than the reasonable persuasions on which we are content to base most of our opinions : it is a certitude justified by experience, so far as this has proceeded, and the faith in which it began has been transformed practically into knowledge.

2. CONCERNING THE PARTS OF PERSONALITY

Before entering the Path of Contemplation, to attain any degree of experience therein, we must seek to understand ourselves, so that we may know what it is that contemplates and after what manner the quest of the soul of man can, by this path, come to its end in God.

There are several methods of dividing and subdividing the human individuality, but they make for the same understanding in the last resource.

There is that of Christian Mysticism ; it recognises the triad of body, soul and spirit, which is perfectly satisfactory in itself, as the triad always is ; but it suffers so much from vagueness in the mode of presentation that, for all practical purposes, the triad seems to pass into the duad, as body and soul only. Eastern Theosophy recognises the physical part manifest in Nature ; the psychic part—which is mind in its broadest sense—as the seat of personality ; and the Divine spirit. Subject to the reservation which I have made, this division may be taken as substantially identical with that of Christian doctrine, but the reservation in the latter case may imply a tacit and even unconscious intention to lend the aspect of permanence to a more transient side of our personality.

Having mentioned one Theosophical School outside Christendom there is something to be said of Kabalism, which offers a remarkable division and subdivision as follows : (A) *Nephesh*, which is the animal soul, in immediate connection with the body and the latter is sometimes held to be included under the distinctive name. *Nephesh* is referred to *Malkuth* and the Fourth World, or *Assiah*. (B) *Ruach*, which is the mind, the logical understanding, the rational nature. It is allocated to *Tiphereth*, the Second World, or *Briah*. (C) *Neshamah*, the seat of individuality, sometimes termed the spirit, or more loosely and less correctly, the Higher Aspirations of the soul, the soul in its exalted mode and the supernal part of the mind. It is ascribed to *Binah*—because this *Sephira* is the fount of souls—and to the First World or *Atziluth*. Such attributions are, however, essentially arbitrary and are moreover subject to variation, for there is more than one distribution of *Sephiroth* in the Four Worlds. *Neshamah* is subdivided into (1) *Neshamah* proper ; (2) *Chiah*, which is the living principle therein ; and (3) *Yechidah*, of which the Latin equivalent is *singularitas*, the individual principle.

Alternatively there are said to be five divisions of personality distinguished by these five names : *Nephesh, Ruach, Neshamah, Chiah, Yechidah*. But the last three—or *Neshamah* in its widest sense—are the shadow and the reflection of a celestial and perfect prototype which never leaves *Atziluth*—the First World. This prototype is called *Tsure* and signifies the archetypal form, otherwise, the imperishable spirit in the world of Deity, or the eternal idea—pre-existing in the Divine Mind—of every individual being destined in the evolution of worlds to come forth into manifest existence. This is man in the noumenal mode, or that which we are in God. It is said that by inspired devotion the will of man directs *Neshamah* to the *Tsure ;* the *Neshamah* endeavours to leave the body and attain reunion with *Tsure*—otherwise to go back whence it came. The latter responds ; and the two are united by the drawing up of an invisible thread which always connects them. This thread seems to correspond with a mystic path of ecstasy in Kabalism.

It will be seen that what is here intimated is a marriage of the Divine and human in the union of *Tsure* and *Neshamah*, so that individuality is immortalised by the hypothesis of Kabalism. But beyond *Atziluth* there is the withdrawn world of *Ain Soph Aour*, which is the inmost abyss of the Godhead. We have no authority for saying that there is an union possible at this centre, but if so all that we understand by individuality, which reacts upon itself in order to the realisation of self, must dissolve therein : it is the peace of consciousness in eternal love. This is the state in which God is All in all.

Alternatively, *Nephesh* could be allocated to *Malkuth ; Ruach* to the *Yetziratic Sephiroth* of *Netzach Hod* and *Yesod ; Neshamah* to *Tiphereth ; Chiah* to *Geburah ; Yechidah* to *Chesed ;* while *Tsure,* as the supernal part which does not leave the Supernals would be referable to *Kether,* and the aspiration after union therewith is the desire of retroversion towards the Fount of Souls. As realisable here and now, it can be referred only to *Daath,* which is Supernal Knowledge and the state of Divine Sonship.

It follows in any case that the three modes of division which prevail in Christendom, Indian Philosophy and Kabalism join in the recognition of an imperishable part of man and in its capacity for Divine Union. But orthodox Christian theology does not acknowledge that it is a Divine part, and this is the great crux of the West in Mysticism, as it is indeed of the whole subject, because the state of oneness cannot be predicated except of things that are alike in their essence. If there were a marriage of heaven and hell, each of them would become the other. Even in the figurative or substituted union of earthly marriage the two physical personalities are held to be made one flesh.

Some further considerations on the life of union belong to the close of this study, but the mystical doctrine on the subject which emerges from a cloud of intimations may be formulated for the time being as follows : In the deep states of Divine Love there is a point of awakening to the Presence of God in the soul, and beyond this are all the states of the union which are on record in the annals of experience. It is called sometimes the state of the self-knowing spirit in union. Dionysius certifies unawares concerning the essential difficulty of its formulation when he says in his paradox that " if any one sees God and understands what he sees, he has not seen God at all . . ., who exists above all being and is understood above all understanding."

The practice of the Path of Contemplation follows from the Doctrine of the Union, and its end is to attain the state, to such extent as may be possible in this life, according to our several measures. It tends to be missed sometimes because contemplation as understood by true mystics is not to be identified solely with concentred thought.

3. THE LIFE OF DEDICATION AND DETACHMENT

Contemplation in the proper understanding is a governing preoccupation of life in love, and it belongs to the entire life ; it is a permanent disposition and direction of the whole concern of being. The distinctions created between our parts of personality are largely apocryphal, but we must give the whole heart, the whole mind and the individual soul if we would attain the great ends. The life of letters, the life of art, the life of research demand the entire man. If we take up these things sporadically, we cannot attain their perfection. A capricious *nostalgie de Dieu* is little more than a mood, and if it is far better to experience such unstable emotions than to have no sensibility towards Divine things it remains that they are not to be counted as sources of true light or real leading.

On the other hand, the permanent disposition or direction does not mean that day in and day out we must be engrossed consciously and without intermission on the one subject. It is a wholesome counsel of prudence that we should not be looking exclusively at any single point, lest we should cease to see at all. But in a sense our accepted purposes must be always with us, and this is assumed from the beginning in respect of the spiritual life, when that has become a vocation. It is desirable to establish this point clearly and to indicate—even at some risk of repetition —that he who thinks in his heart now and then only—whatever the end in view—is not going to reach the result of those who think well and frequently, whose life also becomes part of the thinking. So also he in whom love of God is a kind of mental notion is not in the Path of Love. At the same time, to enter the Path of Contemplation does not mean a continuity of any single inward state. We may be leading a most active life.

There is an activity without, which is a symbol of activity within, and this activity is greatest at the centre of all. Dedication of the kind which I am bringing under our notice here implies an ordered detachment, without which there is no inward progress. Detachment does not, however, consist in cutting off correspondence between one's manifest part and external things, but in a right attitude toward things that are external. The outer interests do not suffer from such detachment because it has a sanctifying motive, wholly distinct from the satiety and nausea which so often comes over the worldling, disqualifying him for daily interests and communications without drawing him towards the Kingdom of Heaven. On the contrary, we can do more good outwardly in proportion as we are more set apart inwardly and taken over to the Divine Side. Detachment in other words is the correspondence of our inward nature with temporal things in the sense of those that are eternal. It is the antithesis of engrossment therein for their own sake. It connotes also a revision of material, mental and even moral values in the light of those values which are spiritual.

Still less does detachment signify absolute isolation, which is a state of loss on both sides : the one object is attachment to God. When we have attained the holy and salutary loosening from self-interest in the bonds without and the devotion which is Divine dedication—or liberation in universal love—it is claimed that the Path of Contemplation may be entered with a full assurance that it will not be travelled in vain. The sense of attainment therein may come in a shorter or longer space of earthly time, and it is not suggested that there should be no deeper reflection while we are striving to reach this point : but ordinary meditation and the concentration thereto belonging are preferable in the early stages. The distinction is idle, however, because true contemplation produces true detachment.

The practice of detachment is that which regards all things *sub specie æternitatis*. In the first stages there is a cultivation of general intention, so that it shall become a state or habit of the mind, remembering always that this is insufficient of itself, for the will must be ready indeed, but the will must act, ever converting the time-values into those of the eternal mode. As the opportunities arise in life, the intention must be applied to particular cases, by taking one of them, whatever it is, formulating the intention to transmute and concentrating on this idea to the exclusion of everything. A moment will come when there is a sudden turn of the will and the wish together in a leap of activity, as if a wheel were set suddenly in motion, or a cannonball were shot to a mark, and we know at once that the thing is done. The axis of inclination has been altered not only in respect of the particular case, but in a catholic sense concerning all temporal things.

We may also, with the same object, make use of the great mystic formula : " For Thine is the Kingdom, the Power and the Glory, world without end," beginning with the verbal utterance and then doing it in "a more and more interior way," till the words are lost and the conception only remains. The mind becomes that conception, which is, so to speak, " the only ripple moving on the waters of the mind." The turning of the will is aided in this manner, and the will turns the personality towards any mode of the external and creates the higher attachment. It must be remembered always that this manner of conversion is a sacrificial, holy, religious act, not only for consecrating and transmuting things without in environment but for those which are of our own personality. It is good on occasion to look on it from this point of view, by making our gift upon the mystic altar of the heart, which is dedicated in this manner to God. It is indispensable that the offering should be complete by intention, and it is so made first by an act of will, but afterwards by a zeal of desire. If it is made sincerely, the act passes into life and when it so passes, the transmutation of life has begun. When we experience the first sense of its tincture, the power of ordinary temptation will diminish and the experience of this kind of conversion will move from more to more. It is part of the Mystery of Conformity.

Lastly we should bear in mind that, as a mystic once said, many fail because they turn towards God without turning from themselves.

4. THE INNER DOCTRINE OF THE PATH

(1) It is understood now that the ineffable union which is the end of mystic life is the integration of the self-knowing spirit of man in the eternally Self-Knowing God, knowing and being known therein.

(2) This is the attainment of God, and it is the great work of our manifest life, for those who are called thereto, but it is not completed here.

(3) We can attain here and now (a) union of will, (b) union of motive; and these can become permanent. They are the state of sanctity. There are various degrees in the sense of conscious union, which can be attained also here by the following of the inward life; but the records tell us that in the fulness of its highest experience it is possible for brief periods only. So far as it is possible to discern, the absolute union of our higher consciousness with God would involve ceasing from manifestation.

(4) The Divine Union in its plenary sense is all-inclusive; it is union with whatsoever abides in union.

(5) We possess all things in God which have their part in God.

(6) Raymond Lully said long ago: *Dominus non pars est sed totum;* and that which is left out is nothing; it is the nothingness of sense and illusion, of the lesser and fluidic personality.

(7) When the consciousness is directed to the universal and essential instead of to particulars and externals, it is in that state which may be called the threshold of union.

(8) The Path of Contemplation—as set forth—has its term in this state, and it is therefore a Path of Freedom. It is wholly a work in consciousness.

(9) Let us remember at this point that our true self is a mirror which contains all things: that the mirror of the universe is for this reason within; and that if this mirror of consciousness does not reflect God, it reflects that which tends toward illusion.

(10) The reflection of God therein is in virtue of some high-uplifted summit of our nature, a Mountain of the Lord on which the Lord abides: were it otherwise, we could not conceive of the union. It follows that the Path of Contemplation may be

described as the Path of Ascent into our higher being, and this is an ascent in love, for it is only in the tongue of symbolism that we can speak as if spatial distance intervened between the states.

(11) The normal personality does not cognise this supernal part of being, but we must not be deceived by the idea that their separation is on account of a distance intervening in space: it is because of the restriction on self-knowledge in the normal state.

(12) The essential mystical nearness will be understood if we pay attention to the word consciousness—of which we have no ground for supposing that there is more than one kind in the universe, though the modes are not one mode.

(13) The Path of Contemplation is for the opening of a gate in consciousness, and it must be realised that it is a holy gate.

(14) It is therefore a Path of the experience of sanctity, beginning in purification and working for the expulsion of the evil power from the world that is within us.

(15) It can never be an easy Path, as I have indicated otherwise—for not in an hour or a day does a man attain union with God, or love encompass its object. At the same time some of its stages are easy to some aspirants.

(16) Let us realise that it is useless to think of God as without: God is within. There is no part of our experience in God, man or the universe which arises outside of consciousness.

(17) If we say that there is something which is, as it were, ineffable in the world above, we need not think it unattainable in respect of ourselves: it may be an untrodden field of our consciousness. The universe itself is that which bears witness to us and does to us manifest. If in the sense that has been explained already we are a mirror which reflects Nature, there is another sense in which Nature is itself a mirror, wherein we behold ourselves.

(18) Let us seek on the threshold of the Path to open the first Gate by long contemplation of eternal things. Let us unfold in particular the deep sense of God realised in the heart.

(19) It is good at this stage to repeat inwardly: May Thy Kingdom Come; then adding: The Kingdom of Heaven is

within; and then, with a deep assurance: Thy Kingdom has come within.

(20) If we can formulate this, realising that there is nothing so much that is to be desired in the whole world, the moment will arrive when we shall know that the Kingdom indeed comes and the grace thereof.

(21) If we be faithful to the aspiration, the realisation will be true to us.

(22) It may come like a thief in the night, at a point where we least expect it; the Gate of Glory opens and we see that God has His Throne in the highest part of our nature.

PART II

THE PRACTICE OF THE PATH

1. MEDITATION AND CONCENTRATION

THE three stages of spiritual practice on the side of methodised processes are (1) for the attainment of detachment, understood in the sense that has been indicated because of the many pitfalls which encompass ascetic life; (2) meditation on Divine Love for the realisation of that which at first is an image of the mind as life itself of the soul; (3) contemplation which leads to Union.

There is no question that ordinary meditation for the attainment of Divine Love should precede all other methods. It has been regarded always as initial, and in the terms of the Christian writers on spiritual life and recollection it is called discursive in its mode. It reflects and compares—as for example, the things that perish with those which remain for ever. It is therefore an intellectual process; and it should be remembered in this connection that the living knowledge of God is not attained by reason. Its pictured representations are but a figure or shadow of the greater work; it is water in comparison with wine.

It is the faculty of thinking deeply and with order on the one subject and of driving out from the mind by will whatever distracts therefrom. As a preliminary to the Path of Contemplation, it should be unnecessary to say that the subject of such concentrated thinking should be the Divine Union, which is the sole concern of the Path. It must be actuated by the love of God, for there is no other way than this in the spiritual life, and that love must be fostered daily by the will.

Here is a counsel for progress of this kind : let us enter into our daily meditation in the love of God ; let us come out from it in the love of God ; let us live in the love of God and let all external charity be practised with God as its motive. Let us seek in love for the centre of Divine Love ; let us strive to cast our whole being therein ; let that love be behind all our intentions, our acts within and without.

Again, this does not mean that the ordinary offices of daily thought and life are (*a*) to be abandoned in favour of the one thought and the one office, or (*b*) that before thinking and acting we are of necessity to set the Divine Love before us in the first place. It may be desirable to do this when it occurs to the mind spontaneously, but each day must be begun with the conscious dedication to God's love of all that belongs to that day. We can then go about in the perfect freedom which is the life of that love. A consecration of this kind is the greatest safeguard in the world from what is called sin in common parlance. It is also of great help as preparatory to so much of daily meditation as our circumstances in life allow. There is no rule as to this, and all that makes for bondage must be avoided ; but subject to this provision, it is better for the most part to have stated times for retirement into the temple of the heart, where and whensoever place and period will best serve the purpose.

Be it realised, in conclusion as to this part, that the meditation here recommended may be called love in devotion, after which there is love in contemplation : several stages have been recognised therein, from that which is termed by Eastern mystics the Lower *Samadhi*—or meditation on a subject held in the mind and the control and extension of the ideas which well up in the mind on the subject—to that last state when Divine Love and desire have so entered into the heart of man that it has begun insensibly to pass into the first beginnings of realisation. Then has been the deep path opened towards the centre and the great path to the height. In other words, mind has passed from the excursive method to that unity intent which is understood here as contemplation.

But the attainment of this state in Meditation will seem in most cases at a far distance from the Novice. The sense even of sincere attraction and aspiration towards mystic love may be quite rudimentary at the beginning. The tide of worldly interests flows in continually upon the soul and mixes its waters of Marah with the waters of pure emotion and seas of holy longing. There is no need for depression or distress at such times; it is the natural working of the law and the way to the crown for him that overcometh in the end. The will must strive through all, cultivating dedication to the higher and real things, to all that makes for attainment. In a last resource of all, the will becomes the act, and this is merged in its object.

We are dwelling already in that love which is wedded to its source in God and our inward higher nature has become a channel for its expression in all the outward ways. The sense of goodwill towards man, to whom peace on earth has been promised, will be exalted with the love for all which the personal human heart can as a rule conceive only for one or for a few. This is the spirit of love apart from the body of desire and it can open great gates.

2. THE COUNSELS OF CONTEMPLATION

The state of contemplation is attained in the suspension of active thought. It should be realised that the work is not one of thinking deeply about a subject, as if I should set myself to excogitate the plan of a mystical thesis, taking out the heads of the argument and contrasting the for and against. That is meditation concentred on a given end and surveying all its aspects. Let it be assumed that the subject is that which it can only be, realisation of the Divine Union. Such a state is either possible to our consciousness or it is not; but the fact that so many persons have at least conceived it as such shews me personally that it is; and the first preliminary for its attainment is to set aside all the difficulties, all arguments on either side, and even all the examples of those holy people who have attained therein. These are not of our purpose at the moment. It is assumed that we have traversed the Path of Meditation and opened the gate thereof which leads to a way beyond. A beginning of our course therein may be made after this manner, it being understood that it is still a mental process, though it is hovering on the border-line : meditation is merging into contemplation if the attempt comes to its term. Let us formulate the idea of an union between God and the spirit of man ; let us set aside everything else, and let even this one thought at last die within us. When this has been done, it may come about that we are in the Presence and the Presence is in us. There are rare cases in which there is nothing amazing, or sudden, or even strange in the transit. In other and most instances there is at first, on the contrary, a great sense of strangeness. In any case, there are three stages : (a) separation of all images, except a single image ; (b) contemplation of the loving union, apart from all divergence ; (c) when there is nothing else within the horizon and when the last high thought has dissolved, the sense of the union is there and the grace thereof. It is sometimes so clear and so keen that it includes a certain foretaste of the great realisation which belongs to a later stage.

The peace of this experience will be carried back into daily life, and we should seek to live in its motive, returning thereon as we are able, and the more that we return the more will this first sense of the union abide with us and actuate all our being.

There is also that process which I will call Ascending the Mountain of the Lord, but it is to be understood that this Mountain is that of our own nature. The instruction hereof is as follows :

(a) Put aside the part of our body and the sense thereof. This is casting out the images of matter. It is an application of the counsel : Love not the world nor the things that are in the world ; if any man love the world, the love of the Father is not in him. Rise towards the love of the Father, Who is within.

(b) Put aside the part of material thought. This is casting out the lower images of mind. A man cannot, by such thinking, add to his valid equipment for the ascent towards God. Do not cleave overmuch to mental concepts of any kind : it is easier for a camel to pass through the eye of a needle than for a man who has an abundance stored up in the treasures of normal thought, and keeps his vigil about them, to go upward and enter the Divine Kingdom. Let the mind conceive the hunger of God in its own emptiness. He hath fed such hungry ones with good things, while the rich he hath sent empty away.

(c) Pass into the higher part of mind; it is the angelic part, the higher part of soul. Take it up through the bond of union, with the Divine Presence dwelling on our mountain top. Attain that sacred summit. If we can do this and dwell in it, we are in God's own White Light, but it is our light also, for the light of God is in us.

(d) It remains to say that there are states beyond this state. We have not cast out the images of mind utterly, for the light itself is an image.

(e) Beyond Divine Light there is Divine Darkness. It is a vain attempt to penetrate this Darkness till the body of this world has become the robe of Christ.

3. THE ATTAINMENT OF THE INWARD STATE

We have seen that the attempt to go inward depends on the casting out of (a) the images of matter and (b) the images of mind. These include the sensations of the moment, mental pictures, thoughts and visions. If we cease to think of anything, the world will go by, with the pictured pageants thereof. God will fill the soul which empties itself of all but the desire of Him; and the soul attains some measure of Divine Realisation when it has put aside all things else. Seek therefore to go deeply inward and to go more inward till the first absorption of the union begins to dawn in the soul. It comes in stillness; it comes as peace; the sense of it passes into ecstasy; and the repose in the heart of ecstasy is the inward mode in which the realisation comes. This state of rest is really one of transcendent activity, for it is integration in the heart and centre of cosmic movement.

"It is love which makes the world go round," says an old, familiar adage, which is used in the lightest sense and is cheapened in this manner, but the truth of all is behind it.

Let us be thankful that in this manner there are no great distances to travel, no quarters of the external world to visit or examine. It is all close at hand: the will is the way; our consciousness is the one field. The door is always there; we have only to knock.

I have not concealed that to attain this state there is generally a long apprenticeship, but it is also credible that some may have served previously. There are cases in which those who are called, simply arise and do that which it is given them to do. They do not seem especially to strive or think or watch or pray; they have made already their daily life a part of these offices. They do not in an especial, toilsome and over conscious manner put aside the lower self; they open their hearts to the union, and the union is declared in the heart. This is the process without haste or violence, by the continual maintenance of an ordered state.

It is in this state that the waters of God flow over us, as the still heaving of a tideless sea vibrates from point to point. In this state we may come to bear uninterruptedly the first sense at least of the perfect union within us; the seal of the Eternal, as it seems to me, is set thereon. While we are aspiring to reach it, let us think therefore continually of the oneness to which all our nature testifies; in the earlier stages of contemplation, let us make the idea of unity the one vibration of the mind. We are not the body; we are not the mind; the external personality is not our true selves; it is but the vehicle of a higher mode of being.

Let us remember that the great research is concerned with the questions which arise out of that one versicle: World without end. Is there a victory in the grave? Is there a sting in death? The negative answer is the affirmation of eternal life. The manifest world testifies to the perpetuity of life amidst perpetual transformation. Is this law of transformation inseparable from all life? Can the fire of our personal Mercury—in the eloquent symbols of alchemy—become constant and free from mutation? The word personal intervenes as a key to the alternative. Change, transformation and evanescence are resident therein and they are not apart therefrom. Now, this phase of us may sigh for the glory of " going on and still to be," but the yearning itself is transitory and subject to all the influence of its invariable companions—sickness, satiety and the summary of those distracted emotions which find their *terminus ad quem* in suicide. But there is the sense also of a holy desire for permanence ; it comes to us as if from beyond ; it is of consciousness in the higher part of us ; and it is in this direction that we must seek an answer to our eternal questions.

It is another lesson that all things are within. " Behold, I shew you a mystery." It is in ourselves that we die mystically, in ourselves that we rise gloriously and are translated by a great ascension into our own heaven. And when the Comforter is known by each one of us, it is the eternal spirit of God declared within us : it is not a descent from without—as if from a star in the zenith to this earth on which we dwell.

PART III

THE PATH IN CHRISTIAN MYSTICISM

I PASS now to a consideration of the Mystery of Union in that phase which has found expression at our very doors in the records of Christian Mystics. Perhaps we shall find that we have been seeking to realise the same thing for long and long in our hearts; some of us—perhaps also—have been trying to express it with our lips.

The Path is always described as perfection in the Divine Love, whereby we who have begun in the flesh as it is said—but *absit omen*—may at last end in the spirit. This love is followed in a state of recollectedness or introversion, and in it the man of desire aspires to the purest summit of his own inward being, the abode of the Holy Spirit—that he may possess and contemplate God. This summit is otherwise explained—as we have seen—to be the top of a man's secret nature, above all sensible phantoms, where God is most perfectly seen.

The Christian Mystics tell of the internal solitude, in which—creatures being banished—the only conversation is between

God and the soul herself, in the depth of the spirit. There are several phases of this state, and there is one which is called being drowned in a deep contemplation of God. It is identical with that of St. Anthony, wherein no image at all, even of the Divinity, is mingled, which does not admit the least memory, character or representation of anything spoken or done.

This state of introversion is the end of religion, the immediate union of spirit with God by love, and the passing of the perishable part of self is its indispensable condition. This is the mystical death in grace, that the soul may rise again into infinite and holy life, the contra-distinction in the heights of the death which is of sin in the deeps. The counsels in the road are many. There is the continual realisation of the presence of God, which is one of the things that sound almost elementary and are sometimes neglected utterly because they go without saying. There is the doing of all things which in our state it is given us to do, by an outpouring of love upon them, or as if with the whole heart and undivided mind. There is the attainment of constant peacefulness and tranquillity of mind, because that must be worked for at first which will be enjoyed after. There is especially what is called the repose of soul in the stillness of the Divine Spirit. Bonilla on the QUIET OF THE SOUL says much of this interior concord.

Another counsel is the service and love of all men, not in themselves, but in God, and it arises from the fact—realised rather than expressed—that all our evil is the deordination of our love.

The degrees of our interior life, the experiences of going inward, are usually classed in three : Purgative, Illuminative and Unitive. Broadly speaking, the first is the way of cleansing ; the second is the beginning and continuation of the life of grace ; and the third I have already described : it is the union with God in spirit by perfect love. Barbanson—among many others—calls it simply the progress of prayer, and classes its grades as follows : (1) The exercise of the understanding in meditation. (2) The exercise of the will without meditation. (3) The experimental perception of the Divine presence. (4) The great desolation. (5) The sublime manifestation of God in the summit of the spirit.

T

(6) The most secret way of perfection, not otherwise described because of the transcension of this state. Therein the activity of the understanding abates continually; the activity of love continually increases till its operations become imperceptible: it is the motion in the rest at the centre.

Finally, as regards the state which is called union, two kinds are distinguished: (*a*) that which is active by the elevation of the spirit, and this is freed from the distraction of material images in the world within; (*b*) that which is said to be not a state but grace in the extraordinary degree, in which God communicates Himself. In its last form, He is realised apart from all perceptible images. The understanding is said to be in darkness, but really this union passes above the understanding and the will, in that supreme region of the spirit which is visible to God alone, which He alone can inhabit. It has no name, though some mystics have sought to name it. The continuance of it—in terms of time—is very short in this life: according to St. Bernard it seldom lasts more than a quarter of an hour; but its fruits are enduring.

There is, however, another state or grace, which is descried or attained, and it is cryptically called the perfect union of nothing with nothing. All that can be understood as quantitative in our nature has dissolved; the soul is nowhere; it is in the qualitative spirit above all the faculties. The soul, while it lasts, is in that true being which is in God. This attainment was described of old by Dionysius when he recommended Timothy to relinquish the senses and sensible exercises, the intellectual operations, and to raise himself, in the renunciation of all knowledge, to an union with God above all knowledge and substance. This is the true casting out of the images of mind.

Such are the indicated results of Christian exploration in the almost untrodden grounds of our consciousness. We also have heard of these ecstasies, of these rare travellings through the most hidden places of the world within. Some of us have memories of such entrances and of the exits which come after. We know therefore of that great desolation of which Barbanson speaks, as also that it is utterly apart from the ordinary spiritual lassitude, disappointments, inhibitions, failures of light and privations which characterise the beginnings of the inward life and move, turn and turn about, with its consolations and its raptures. It characterises the approach towards the height rather than the early stages of ascending the mystical mountain. We must be careful that we are not deceived herein and that we do not interpret our lesser interior crosses as great crucifixions, our ordinary gardens of bitterness as the true Gethsemane, our hills of contrariety as Calvary, or we may only draw our own vanity after us when we are uplifted thereon. The great passion is that in which there perishes finally whatsoever within us does not belong to the Eternal.

For the rest, in the actual, intimate, high experience at first hand, it seems to me that the Christian mystics attained that for which we are seeking. They confess also to the same limitations of our own manifest life. The ascent was hard for them; there is not one of us who can say that it is easy. Their experience at best was brief, and we have not in our yearning and inreachings towards the Divine Spirit been able to remain at the height for more than a very short space, when we—a few of us, if indeed any —confess that it seems to have been attained. How can we lengthen the state of the Divine experience? How can its illumination be more fully reflected into our normal consciousness and carried down into our daily life, that we, having suffered transmutation, may become tingeing stones? It is another secret of the will in love. We must take into the heights that which we bring from the heights after another manner—namely, Divine Love, which is the root of all catholic experience, while the union is the fruit of this tree. It is insufficient, like Abou Ben Adhem, to say to the recording angel: "Write me as one who loves his fellow-men," unless, like Abou Ben Adhem, we have been made bold by that "exceeding peace" which is attained in the Divine Love. But the lesson is the true lesson of bringing down into daily life that which we have found above. He who goes up the mystical mountain carrying the Divine Love, like the cross of his passion, shall come down from that mountain as one who has risen indeed, and in God he can ask to be written down "as one who loves his fellow-men" in the sense of their salvation. So are there true marriages made in this world, and having so descended, the mystic saint becomes a tingeing stone.

The last counsel of the Path of Contemplation addressed therefore to the proficient and not the beginner, is to empty ourselves of all things. When the personal self has passed ; when thought is dead ; when the sacred darkness has supervened upon our whole nature, in the stillness of all normal faculties ; when expectation itself is over ; and at the back of the suspended mind there rests only the undifferentiated and unexplicated love of the omnipresent God ; when He fills that love within us ; we are then on the threshold of realisation. And that which follows—when indeed it does follow—has never been put into language. We know only that the so-called union of nothing with nothing is the unity of the One Who is all. The reflection which remains in the mind after this state has passed can scarcely be called its remembrance ; but it is a reflection which in this life abides for ever. We know whence we have come and whither we are going.

THE WORLD TO COME AND THE WORLD OF
THE HOLY ONE

AMONG many definitions on the subject of mystical theology which have been bequeathed to us by St. Thomas Aquinas there is one which will abide in the memory of those who are open to its message because of its pregnant nature. The definition in question is contained in three words, and it tells us that " Contemplation is Love." In the East and the West of to-day and the ages behind us there is a very large literature that unfolds and methodises the modes by which the mind of man can practise the arts of concentration, meditation and contemplation, and I have given an illustration at large in the last study ; but here, as if at the centre of the great complex, like a pearl of great price, there has lain scarcely noticed this brief sentence of a mighty master of the schools. It is the key of the inward life, when the inward life is directed to the Divine end of union. However elaborate and on what authority soever they may rest, the processes apart from love have no relation to the mystic end. It is the spirit and the grace of all. My thesis is therefore that this definition is the great Lamp of Christian Mysticism. From this Lamp have been lighted through the later centuries those other lamps which are my concern in the present paper : they are further delineations and developments of the central doctrine.

I am addressing men and women in the world who know that the way of the saints was a way of particular vocation, considered very hard to travel and travelled only in virtue of a high election in what is termed the world of grace. The way of the mystic saints is accounted the hardest of all, and comparatively speaking those who travelled it were few. We never know in these days who are listening and reading, but I am not addressing exclusively those who have been called in the higher paths of sanctity ; when, however, certain typical developments of the Thomist doctrine have been indicated, it may prove that there is a speaking message for all and sundry which will or may find its application in our own paths of life ; and this is the sum of my intention.

It will be seen that for my purpose the Lamps of Christian Mysticism are not so much personalities in the annals of sanctity as specific developments of a single basic principle. The names will serve, however, to present the notions. Now, love in its mystical understanding is the desire of Divine Union, and hence St. Thomas in another definition affirms that love is unitive. It is, I think, Ruysbroeck who is the greatest of all the lamps of the Thomist doctrine that contemplation is love. There is no fire like his, when we see it burning at the brightest ; but it is still fire. His long book DE VERA CONTEMPLATIONE is a methodised treatise on love and the art thereof. Ruysbroeck distinguishes four modes of love : being (1) the lowest, which is fear of God mingled with love, operating in external virtues and good works ; (2) a second mode, which draws life from God in spirit and in truth ; (3) an elevated and transcendent mode, illuminated with Divine splendour—the state of being rapt away by the Spirit of God ; but (4) the last is a mode of union with God in naked love and Divine light, above all activities, beyond all " amourous " experience, consumed and (as if) anni-hilated. This is his lamp of contemplation and such the love thereof. His whole mystic doctrine of the union is a doctrine of love and its metaphysics.

It is the state in which the soul puts off limitation and is so hidden in the infinite that it may be said to become the infinite. At a later day Molinos bore witness continually to this absorption of the soul in God : it is the state of love in love, as the work is love for love. Ruysbroeck is to be understood in this sense when he affirms that we are the eternal plenitude and that God is our *superessentia*. But Walter Hilton says that the gift of love is God ; and this is the bond of union—that God is love and love is also the soul. St. John of the Cross speaks of that contemplation in which the love and knowledge of God possess the soul together.

I have forestalled already the next stage of my subject, which is the kind of end in love. Ruysbroeck testifies that in the attainment of this end we are engulfed in eternal beatitude. Surin speaks of a perfect transformation into God. Tauler says that the spirit is submerged and absorbed in the depths of the Divine ocean. Schram tells us that the soul is saturated with God. Many voices make use of this overwhelming image. St. Thomas Aquinas uses the pregnant formula—one with one. Ruysbroeck bears the same witness in another manner of language when he affirms that there is no distinction found between loving and being loved. It means that in reaching this state of experience we have been removed from our self-centre, which is the whole barrier between us and Divine attainment. The passage from subject to object has passed in love. It is not—in the deep understanding of this mystery—that the soul strips off self by the old laborious and ever painful modes of the ascetic life : the self dissolves in God. It is part of the loving mystery. We do not cease from self-knowledge by an overt act : it has been said that we flow back into ourselves, as by an interchange of the union. Molinos speaks of the state as that of being lost in God. It is of course only caught at now in our deepest states.

The methodising doctors who knew such states mainly by reports concerning them—shall I say Chancellor Gerson ?—were quick to bring virulent charges of heresy against those who knew them directly, like Ruysbroeck. A host of others, like Scaramelli, Schram and Poulain, have reduced the past experiences within an almost iron rule, to which the field of spiritual experience cannot be bound—because it is living experience and varies with each life. It is only with difficulty that an original genius, such as Ruysbroeck, can be brought within formal measures, for which reason he is cited comparatively seldom, and then upon the lesser issues. Eckehart is never cited, and it seems to me because he falls only within his own measures, though his condemned propositions may offer a more obvious reason. Eckehart dared to say that in the mystical experience God is All in all, and this was more than official theologians were born to tolerate.

I have gleaned very briefly only from a wide field of intimations on the state of union, but there are records at length elsewhere in my other writings. The next point belongs more especially to the path and not the attainment. As to this, the key given by the mystics is one aspect of a very old and very familiar theosophy, for they say that the Divine Lover is within. I have followed all the records of the quest and have not found another. St. Augustine recounts how he wearied himself overmuch in looking for God without, when His habitation is within. St. Alphonsus Rodriguez calls the feeling of the presence of God in the soul a spiritual and experimental certitude, adding that it is received from on high, as if from that extreme summit of our own spirit of which St. Jane de Chantal speaks, calling it " a very simple unity " and the place of that union which she describes in terms identical with the condemned and imprisoned Molinos, when she says that there do souls " unite themselves to God and lose themselves wholly in Him."

Out of this thesis that God is within—and His kingdom—arises the practice of contemplation, meaning the practice of love. It is called the practice of the Presence. Brother Lawrence has held up a lamp on this part of the work, and it shines brightly. At the beginning of the inward life St. Ignatius speaks of " loving attention to God," as present with and within us. St. Bonaventure speaks of an experimental knowledge, which is the act of knowing the presence of the object. There is also the " Prayer of the Presence," which is an inward reflection of intent love, and when it passes into the deep states it realises that which it seeks, for the Presence unveils. The other side of this golden sphere is called habitation in God, intimating the soul's relation to the Divine immanence in the universe : it is said to be primarily a work of the will, but this rules assuredly in all modes of the practice and is a great key of the beginning. It is the beginning of the life of mystical experience, as it is that of the life of faith. A door can open thence on an infinite sea, and it is possible *in hoc vastissimum Divinitatis pelagus navigare*. The encouragements and consolations of this beginning are the begetting house of love. I have said that in the terms of another symbolism it is a house of experience : it is not a house of doctrine. It brings to birth, however, a doctrine of experience, but this is of another order than the doctrines of instituted theology. It is a great House of Quest—

> " A wilderness of building, sinking far
> And self-withdrawn into a wondrous depth,
> Far sinking into splendour."

It is most surely that House not made with hands which is eternal in the heavens. Those who enter the House and those who dwell therein know that it is not of their building.

If the Kingdom of God is in the soul it is also without in the universe : within and without is God ; and perhaps one line of criticism as regards mystical theology is that it has dwelt too much in the inward man and passed thence too seldom into that which lies about the soul in creation. The Divine in man is not in separation from the Divine in the cosmos. Again it is one with one. The side by which we realise God in the universe —following no doubt the line of least resistance—is the side of its grandeur and beauty. The way of this realisation is a way of loving correspondence : the new gates open then and the Heaven comes down. We have thus the inward place of the Presence, the outward place of the Presence, the bond between them, as if between the Father and the Son, and this is a bond of love, which is a Holy Spirit. Here is a kind of Trinity about which it becomes profitable to reflect. Coleridge says that " in our life alone does Nature live," and I question whether a greater truth of its kind has ever been put into words in any poetry. It does not of course mean that there is no such thing as Nature outside ourselves, but that the infinite universe lives and dwells within us in proportion as we can receive it. It is the correspondential reception of the Divine witness from without by the Divine witness from within, and the proportion is governed by the extent to which—through our own efforts and the Divine guidance—we have awakened the Divine sleeper. It is in this sense also that God lives in our life to the extent that we can receive Him. But another truth testifies that we are an immeasurable faculty of reception in the knowledge which comes from love. " O shew me an end of knowing," said one maker of verses : there is no end, thank God.

Have you realised what it is to be engulfed, perhaps suddenly, in some great manifestation of beauty ? The word engulfed is not exaggeration, and it seems to me that such an experience is not altogether infrequent. So long as it lasts there is no thought of self. The saying is that we come back to ourselves subsequently, which is an exact statement. This is like the Divine Union and may be even a flashing part of it at a moment. In the Divine Union, as understood by the annals of sanctity, we have seen the same term employed by Ruysbroeck and its synonyms in symbolism by other masters of experience. Here also we come back to ourselves in the end, by which I mean in this life. But we are looking for that state which doth not yet appear, when we shall return no more upon ourselves, when we shall become that which we desire. This is the Molinos state of being lost in God, though I think that we are found rather, as in an universal mode of being, and it is the Tauler state of being submerged in the Divine ocean.

But if the mystic transports are short and also the ecstatic realisations, according to the faithful witnesses, there are certain lines of venture into the great unknown, where experience is not in the rapture, but in a certain loving stillness of withdrawn mind, which has cast out all the images—nearly or almost all. I have called it elsewhere a state of continuous preoccupation. It is like another way of the mystics and is scarcely found in the literature, unless in shadows and reflections belonging to the first steps : it is rather an inference from all the rolls and records. There is more perhaps in Saint-Martin than in most of the other seers. It is like a quiet night leading to a perfect end, or a still light shining in a secret place. But perhaps the best symbol is the Lamp of the Sanctuary, ever trimmed and burning before the Presence.

The world goes on meanwhile, and we also in the world ; but a time comes when use and wont enable us to open at will the door of this Sanctuary and know the light in the stillness. The door is open always at the back of the natural mind. Perhaps I should say that the door stands ajar and that the light comes through which enlightens us in our highest moments. The word-making part of the mind receives the great intimations ; hence come the imperishable part of mystic literature and the plenary inspiration of the poet. We have all waited on this light, when the rational mind has done its most and best and now for the time being can fare no further. It is then as if a spirit which is above the logical understanding came through the symbolical door, to work with us and through us. We do not achieve the very great things of thought and literature on our own part utterly.

This is the kind of work which seems of God in the mind and of mind in God, which brings the good things from a certain Land of the Living, and to which the painful faculty of research contributes nothing. As one who has served long apprenticeships in that unresting realm, it comes to me sometimes, with a sudden dread of heart, that one has stuffed the mind with so many records of research that there is hardly room left for the realities of God. It is true, of course, that they give us warrants and titles, things which stand at their value. It is my justification in speaking and writing on the subject-matter of the mystics. It reassures those who hear and those who read, that I and the others who testify know at least the witness of the past and the great precursors. It was these who told us in the past, in our first days of zeal, that there is a Mount of Carmel in the Lord and some part of that which had come to them in the course of its ascent. And without the great Vedic saints we should know nothing of what has been reached in the East or how the same thing is everywhere in the records of first-hand experience, and that the mind and soul of man enter into reality from many points of a vast circle of being.

I shall be judged as one who has been guilty of a clear digression and yet there is a subtlety within it. If there is a sense in which research and its book-learning can contribute nothing to the great inward realisations, I have shewn in what manner they may tell us that the realisations are possible, if they are an erudition in research which belongs to the subject; and this helps me towards the next point of our consideration. Is there not perhaps some way in the lives and vocations of each of us by which the loving doctrine of mystical contemplation and the testimony of those who have followed its path, even to the end thereof, can come to us with a message, for the hallowing of these our lives, though we may never look for inclusion in the annals of sanctity ?

I have been charged with dwelling on the difficulties of the mystic life, as if they were difficulties of so-called occult sciences : but the kind of love which is implied in the Thomist definition is not brought to birth easily, and it is implied from the beginning of the life. May I put it in the most familiar of all language by saying that it is proposed from the beginning that we should fall in love with God ? The expression is very common and I suppose that it would be called vulgar, but like many such formulæ there is a real truth within it, and I am haunted with a feeling that it was used once by St. Thomas. Most of us have known its experience in the human order. The fall is from the sufficiency of self in its own centre. The love of any object in humanity decentralises the true lover. It transfers preoccupation from the self within us to the self without of another. It is an absorption in contemplation of the visible beauty. But mystic love implies the secret of contemplative absorption in an absent beauty, and it is the realisation of this beauty in the heart of mind. Realisation depends on love, and the difficulty is to begin by loving that which is unrealised, or God before we have found Him. The absent Beauty is not indeed really absent if God is always within, but we have not found that centre wherein is His sanctuary. How are we to reach the " pure and deep centre " wherein—according to Molinos—abides the Image ? It is said that the deepest love is called forth by a known, experimental possession of God ; but how is that love called forth which leads to this state when we are far indeed from its attainment ? The very language of such love is an unknown tongue to those who have never fallen from their self-centre.

Poulain expresses a great truth when he intimates, a little obscurely, that the will to love is the first secret of love. Now this lies within the capacity of us all, and this is the first step. It is the putting forth of such will in exercise, the continued maintenance of its activity, and unreserved abandonment to its direction. In the steadfast simplicity of the whole subject it may be termed otherwise the will to union. It is also the state of loving God always as the chief implicit of the mind. The great gifts of the spirit and the unspeakable gifts of understanding come to us in this way, by a continual occupation of the mind with the Divine object, in a practice followed by the whole mind. In the proper understanding this is a state of mystic prayer, and such prayer is a state of life. I have said elsewhere that the human lover needs no counsels of preoccupation with the beloved object and no processes to insure it. It belongs to the kind of devotion which cannot help itself. Devotion is love, says Ruysbroeck, or at least the flame of love. The work of the will can produce this state within us in respect of the Divine object. There is no question that at the beginning of the business the work of the will has to be done with our might, and if I must use the terms of convention there may be solitudes to seek and hours to set apart for the construction of loving purpose. The daily work indeed is auto-suggestion of the mind towards God, and that which it brings to pass later or sooner is a telepathic communication between the mind and God. I can tell you that the time comes, and rather soon in many cases, when the work does itself within us, and while it suffers little interference from the ways of life without, it does not hinder these.

When once the ground has been thoroughly broken up—to use rather a crass image—it is not essentially more difficult for a man of affairs who is a man of spiritual honour to be a true and living lover of God than it is to be a human lover in any houses of exchange. The condition is of course trueness, which seems to me another term for unconditional devotion. The secret is the leading of the spirit : and the "kindly light" leads. It is even from step to step, from the wordless prayer of purpose, shaping will, to that ever deeper prayer which marks the stages of experience in union with Divine love. As the Curé D'Ars said, the best prayer of all is that of delight in the Presence, when the Lamp of the Sanctuary shines at the hour of Exposition on the Altar of the soul. But this is the Prayer of Attainment.

I do not think that—except in the most ordinary sense of the virtues—we have to labour at leaving anything. Our part is rather a reservation of free space through which all may pass off that cannot help in the quest. It is the Christ-spirit within Who will drive the money-changers out of His and our own

Temple. If we are busy about the one subject and—in the common saying—can get a real move thereon, the things that do not belong to it will pack out of the way. Our personal office herein is not one of macerations and scourgings. There are indeed the crosses of Divine love, but they are not conventional, instituted or arbitrary : they are the occultations of the Spouse of souls. The hart is then panting for the waterbrooks, but for the time being it knows not where to find them. All this is of the yoke of our humanity, and the law which imposes the burden also removes it. The vistas open again through pure and universal love : again it is a world of wells. There are other personal offices which prevailed in the counsels of the past but are not of the golden way. Bossuet's penal practice of detachment from self and from created things is beginning at the wrong end, not to speak of its clumsy process, laborious and painful. Attachment to God accomplishes more in a day of all that it stands for than this other can do of itself in a year. The reason is that God is enough—enough in attainment reached at the end of quest, enough in defence as a buckler.

I have been concerned throughout with the work of the mind in God, as it has been given me to understand the mystery of union, and I have spoken of the heart of mind, in which desire is spiritualised. It seems to me as the poles asunder from that internal recollection of Molinos which is said to be without affection and without emotion : mystic love is the very essence of these, but when they have attained stillness at a centre. Perhaps Ruysbroeck was referring to this state when he—who knew all its ardours and all its changeless simplicity of naked, constant fire—declared once that love is neither cold nor hot, neither light nor darkness, and that nothing can be compared therewith. He was stripping off the terms of sense, even as St. John of the Cross when he said : " It is in the night of the senses that the sun shines in the spirit."

On such considerations, and at least for my present purpose, I am setting aside therefore those modes of experience which are described so familiarly by many mystic saints and which seem psychical, abounding in physical reflections. I do not deny their reality, but it is impossible not to see where they may lead, pur-

sued especially in the life of the world. I have been dealing with
a different subject, with the repose of the mind in God by a loving
realisation in the mind. This state is apart from physical reactions
and apart especially from those which are on the threshold of
sex-experience. It does not deal, moreover, in those pathological
anguishes of love, descriptions of which are furnished by its great
experts, St. Teresa, St. John of the Cross and Rodrigo Alvarez.
The terms of delight and suffering are terms of sense and depend
from Thomist psychology. It is for this reason that certain
doctors of experience on the intellectual side, in dealing as experts
with the so-called " wound of love," speak openly of the " physiognomy " of this state. They are scientifically exact in doing so.
St. Teresa knew that beyond the emotions and the ecstasies,
beyond the sense-reactions and beyond the ardours to which
St. Stanislaus de Kostka administered by means of wet cloths
placed over the region of the heart, there is one in which the
soul is asleep, according to her description—that is to say, in
suspension so far as sensible things are concerned. The state
in which there is no passage from subject to object is not one
of the emotions. They have never known the experience and
will know it never : our earthly unions have no dream, much
less any experience, concerning it. But so restricted are our
measures of language that after all renunciations and all protests
we continue to use the sense-images as symbols, not because
we are satisfied with their capacity for adequate communication
but because we have no others. They are our cloud upon the
sanctuary, when inward experience passes into outward expression
for the work of testimony. It is no more possible to avoid them
than to avoid the terms of pantheism. Yet most Christian
mystics had, rationally speaking, a militant hostility towards
the latter, for it ran counter to their whole intellectual and
theological curriculum, while they certainly never intended to
explain spiritual beatitudes by the analogies of carnal delights.
There is another cloud upon the sanctuary, as to which the
Dominican Bartholomew of the Martyrs warns us, that the presence
of mortal images introduces into the deep states something
between God and us and makes therefore for separation. Blosius
calls the desired condition a going forth into God " without any

images in the mind." Yet it is always the mind which goes forth— I mean the mind of soul—and undertakes the journey into what he terms otherwise " the vast solitude of the Godhead." And the driving power of the mind is love, as heart of the mind, heart of the soul, and heart of our very being, stayed on God. Within and without the images of God are everywhere, and it is true indeed that on the quest of reality instead of its symbols we have had enough of images. As we go forward I am sure that our progress is marked by their successive dissolutions, until that remains only about which I have quoted Molinos, the image of the pure and deep centre. But it is a Presence rather than an image. When the soul reaches this Real Presence within her and the veils fall off there follows that which has never been put into intelligible terms by any book of the mystics. It is not possible any longer to speak of the Presence or of the conscious soul ; there is no longer either subject or object but an ineffable *tertium quid*. The path has been travelled then and the union reached. Ruysbroeck has navigated the great sea of Divinity, Tennyson has done more than behold his Captain face to face, and Plotinus has borne the Divine within him to the Divine in the universe.

I have delineated in frail and failing characters some part of what it means to be in love with God, some part of that which may follow it. I have tried in halting language to shew how a beginning may be made, but not indeed how to reach the blessed end. What heart can teach another the secret ways of love ?

Love is the bond of union, and union is realisation centred on God. It is love which honours the bills and meets the cheques and backs the drafts on Zion. It follows that love is enough. There is only one word more. We are delivered from all evil by attachment to the Presence. The practice of this attachment is a better and more healthful exercise for souls than all the mental systems, heaped up and overflowing. The mind grows in God ; the thought brought back from God is clear and keen and righteous. The one great medicine of the mind is God.

And this is the world to come, brought within measures of our manifest being in the here and now. We have been told on high authority that " it doth not yet appear what we shall be," but a key has been placed in our hands, or a golden clue leading through labyrinthine complexities of worlds without to the simplicity of the centre, which is that of eternal being. And this is the world of the Holy One.

GROUNDS OF UNITY IN GRACE AND NATURE

This life of ours is like a journey undertaken by the soul for the study of Divine Aspects, and of these is the pageant of the cosmos. Or if the soul has entered into manifestation and the way of generated life through some event corresponding in the spiritual order of things to the myth of the Fall of man, then the universe into which he has been brought is the consequence and term of his coming forth, as it is the way also of his return. In either case he would bear, as one might think, within him at least unformulated vestiges of his antecedent state, of the immemorial past in God which was once his mode of being, and our mystic consciousness of a Divine Presence within us, attained in certain manners or degrees and by the following of certain paths in life, is at once a witness thereto and an earnest of a restoration to come, because it proclaims our surviving kinship with our source. But if these things are dreams or remote and figurative adumbrations of a past beyond our ken, there is still the sense of the Presence, there is still its place within us, and before it is the external consciousness which is drawn like a radiant veil over our Holy of Holies. Now, this is our real being, and hence—as I have said otherwise—we are all of us under a veil. And Nature about us itself is another veil which hides the Holy Presence ; but it is not like that of Isis, because of its shining and because the light comes through.

There are moments in our lives which are like the kindling of a sudden awareness, and we seem to be trembling on the verge of another mode of knowledge, as if everywhere about us there arose a new witness, or otherwise as if we heard after a new manner that which has been always speaking. So near are the high things that all else passes to the verge. We stand in expectations on the very threshold of a state in which the old yokes are lifted, and there is freedom on every side. It is like an all within us responding to the all without, or a word on our threshold of utterance which must pass into speech through us or it will be spoken at the corners of the streets and by any leaf or bird along the country-side. In other moments—which after a manner are the same moments—the Divine Immanence within and without ourselves is so close behind its veils that the child amidst flowers in the garden seems on the point of manifesting it, without let or hindrance. That speaking with tongues about which we have heard of old as a language of inspired lips appears on the point of becoming a speech of entire being; and when the expectant ecstasy has passed, as it does pass, we are left wondering at our own silence, when thought in the aftermath is not only " too deep for tears " but even too high for joy, in the normal modes thereof.

It is insufficient to say that experiences like these abide with us as a certitude that God is on every side. In our inevitable terms of symbolism it is rather as if the Divine Reality were knocking incessantly at the gates within and the gates without ourselves, as if God after every manner were suing for the restitution of conjugal rights, and as if the time of our exile were a long process at law for the consideration and enforcement of the claim. From another point of view and in another manner of images, the experience is like a voice affirming that though the kingdom of this world has been placed in opposition to the Kingdom of Heaven, the one is interpenetrated by the other, so that in reality there is but one sphere and one order, which was from everlasting and remains for ever, testifying that " I am with you all days," even unto the end—that is to say, until the sense of separation has dissolved into the perfect sense of union.

If it happens on the country-side that the inward sense comes over us, which is the sense of unity between the grace within and without, if it comes in our faring through warm sunshine, perhaps on a Spring day which has almost passed to Summer, we can recall sometimes the stages, like leaves turned over and over of a Book of Truth in the Art. We have been in the midst of the thuribles, all good green things and pleasant, exhaling their odours. We have been through the aisles of the

woodland, because there are fanes everywhere, and the vista
beyond the forestry is a tabernacle of the Real Presence, while
the Sun is like a Host uplifted, consecrated and upraised to consecrate. The *epiclesis* clause has been pronounced about us
everywhere. There are many choirs invisible in the sacred spaces
of air. Of such are our aids to reflection, when reflection comes
unawares, and these are dwellers on the threshold of the inward
place. It is entered like turning a corner from one path to
another, where the beech-grove also turns. Do you know of such
ways in the stillness, where the Grace of Nature suspends and
the nature of Grace unfolds ? But in truth it is not suspension.
The scents are further away and the lark sings in heaven no longer
close at hand, but far off in that kind of distance which has the
mode of the infinite between. And the church clock strikes in
the distance, a remote message of time echoing through the
eternal. There is a stillness known as God : we have passed
within it.

"There is a sublime sorrow of the ages as of the lone ocean,"
said once in the midst of his dreaming a certain Victorian dreamer,
as he heard the roll of the centuries amidst his wavering crowd
of images. It is like the soul's desolation, sorrowing for unrealised
aspirations and the truth which it has failed to attain. But
there is also a joy of the ages, like that of the primeval morning,
"bridal of the earth and sky," in which it is said that "the
stars sang together" and that "all the Sons of God uttered a
joyful shout." It is like the soul's joy, made blessed by aspiration
that is fulfilled and sacred truth attained. There is no aspiration
and no ambition to compare with the search after truth. The
necessity of truth in some natures is as imperative as that of
love, but indeed the distinction is idle because truth is love.
It does not need therefore to say that the search is always noble
because truth is always good. There are times and seasons which
are more appropriate than others for the communication of certain truths, as love has also its moments of testimony and those
of being hidden in the heart, but truth is of all time and the love
thereof. There is no lawful activity which can be classed with
the search after truth that is not a holy thing. There is a sanctity
of learning which is the splendour of the beauty of truth, while

even the methods of science, whereby we find and learn, are hallowed like vessels of the sanctuary and the lamp that burns therein.

The pursuit of knowledge is of course undertaken with every variety of intention and for ends innumerable, but never so illustriously as when it is followed for its own sake. And yet within the limits of the phenomenal, which are those of normal knowledge, there is something unsatisfying in the pursuit. The intellect may be saturated with learning and yet have no rest from its craving, because all the research in the external does not lead to the essential that is within, the font of truth behind the outward veils, the noumena behind phenomena. And so it comes about that the seeker after truth, to the highest manner born of his great vocation, turns from the transitory world towards that wherein there is " no change or shadow of vicissitude," and that which is called in the symbolism a desire for the House of the Lord begins to eat up his heart. He is led inwardly by the grace that works within for lives of complete dedication ; the direction in which he is led is that which has been called in this volume the mystic quest ; and this is the way to God, a research in the efficacious sacrament of our own being through the deeps and heights of love. The counsel is seek in love, for there is nothing in the hiddenness as there is nothing in manifest things that is not unveiled thereby. From the quest of intellectual thought God does not hide Himself to confuse and bewray exploration, but God remains hidden, because this is not the key which opens the sanctuary or the hand which removes the veils. From the exploration of love He cannot hide Himself because love is He. Here then is the organ of Divine communication, and it has been given to every man who comes into this world. Here is the sacrament which has been placed in each heart for the finding of the grace behind it : we advance therein ; we seek and find thereby.

But he who has been called in this manner is also led outwardly, and in proportion as the mystery of God is discovered within, so is it discerned without. The work of the sacraments proceeds in both orders and fulfils its end, and herein is the ground of unity in Grace and Nature. God is a great symbolist

Who teaches from behind the outward veil by signs which He writes upon the veil. The stars are secret ciphers with an interior and Divine meaning. Everything that exists is the outward sign of an inward intent of God, and he who is led within reads best the outward signs. Behind the veil which is woven everywhere around us in the shining pageant of the universe he beholds the vision which is He. Beyond the splendours of the visible world, beyond all secondary causes, he sends the challenge of the soul, and the Ineffable Presence responds.

It is said by the mystics that the veil is dark but that it is very thin. For normal minds, encompassed on all sides by the many folds of the mysteries, the veil is indeed dark, but for the eye of the inward mind it is also thin. " In the beginning, ere men grew, the veil was woven bright and blue. . . . Over His features, wondrous, terrible, the beautiful Master drew the veil. . . . And since the beginning no mortal vision, pure or sinning, hath seen the Face." The meaning is that flesh cannot see God. But there is something within us which transcends mentality and invites us to all that is permanent in being. The Presence within testifies to the Presence without, and the heart of the mystic knows that they who are as two for the processes of thought are yet one grace, one nature and one abiding life. So the veil is dark no longer ; it radiates at every point ; it is light indeed ; and it is not a corner only which is lifted there and here. If that which is mortal in man cannot pass into the sanctuary that is beyond, there is another and a higher man who enters it from another path and out of the flesh not only beholds God but abides with Him in union. There is no sense, as it seems to me, of a passage from state to state : it is rather like a sudden understanding of that which has always been, as if we were heirs of a kingship from the far beginning of things but had now only come to the knowledge, or rather as if we had known in a long past behind and began to remember suddenly.

The supreme fact of the universe is for us that consciousness by which we are aware of the universe and of ourselves as abiding therein. It will be observed that in this affirmation there are three terms—" we," " aware " and " ourselves "—which are all synonyms of the term " consciousness." The connotation of this is that no one can open their lips without affirming it. There was a time when Professor Huxley and others for whom he stood maintained on the basis of their researches that so far from being a supreme fact consciousness was a by-product, but I believe that this kind of biology has passed away with the Victorian era. It is to be affirmed in proceeding further that consciousness has the self at its basis; that whatever exists without it by any hypothesis, whatsoever bears witness thereto and is realised thereby, is and must be always secondary in comparison with the supreme fact. Assuming that there is anything outside ourselves, it exists for us only in so far as we conceive it. In respect of such realisation or apprehension, all things are within, as the greatest of all testimonies affirms of the Kingdom of Heaven. That Kingdom is not apart from the King, and God is so utterly within that His presence is not secondary but primary, or before all things.

It has been said truly that materialism can and does deal successfully with a great part of what we know but cannot account for our knowing it. In reality nothing can account for it in all that we term science : we know because of consciousness, for which also nothing can account. The likeness subsisting between God and man is the likeness in consciousness. When the consciousness is set towards things external, it is normally apart from the sense of God ; when it turns to things within, it may enter a path which leads to the knowledge of God. The union with God is in consciousness for that which is ours herein is wedded to that which is He. This is how Plotinus bore the Divine within him to the Divine in the universe. But the first and greater journey is that which takes us on the quest of the inward God, which discovers to us that the Divine within us is that which is Divine in the universe. Be it said further, as regards our relation with the world, that the condition of all goodness is in the realisation that there is no satisfaction for our self-knowing part except in the path of the union and the term thereof : we understand the kind of goodness which belongs hereto.

Presumably no one can say after what manner the men and women in the great majority can be brought to this way of election—perhaps by a process of exhaustion in the last resource. To me it seems strong appeal enough that the position should be defined merely, and this is that we take the supreme fact of our very selves to the supreme fact of the all. On such an altar there are no lesser offerings. But it is not to be confused with self-sacrifice in the conventional and almost material sense, which belongs to matters of human inter-relationship, where the motives are mixed. The one condition is the realisation of self in the right or true sense, and herein what is called grace works in even the super-efficacious degree, because we are parts of a whole, and the whole must draw us as soon as we open our doors : this is grace working upon and within us.

There is no reason to suppose that there is more than one kind of consciousness in the universe ; but as I do not hold the keys of the spheres, I make no pretence of distinguishing how many worlds of experience and—if one cared to use such language —of incarnations and reincarnations through stars and systems, may intervene before we are joined in fine with the whole. But I must believe and long for the state in which all things are made one. It is not a state of being non-personal : it is of consciousness in the All-conscious. And now as to the work in hand : it has been said that God is a Being Who realises Himself in spending Himself for others. So also we attain ourselves in spending ourselves for Him. But we must not be entrapped by the antithesis. It is He in all and only, and we are in Him ; it is not only He and we ; it is one of either. I speak, however, of the end, as those who have seen it, however far away, cannot fail to do. The sense of the end swallows up that of the path, so that we take no thought thereon, save only to see most surely that ever it leads and leads.

We have heard of the dark night, of Carmel's laborious ascent, and I have assuredly no office to challenge these modes of symbolism. The hearts of the old masters knew their own bitterness, as they knew also how they emerged in fine. And it is not exactly in my licence to speak of another way. But we have heard also of the old order changing and giving place to that which is new, and it is not for nothing perhaps that we are in these " foremost files of time." It seems to me that the qualities of dedication differ and the modes of let and hindrance. It is not also for nothing that all our highest dedications have been delivered from the ascetic path. It were a hard task now, as it seems to me, that we should find any darkness in a path which leads to God, except indeed that dark which is like the heart and centre of an all-excessive light. Whatsoever is outside this belongs to imperfect dedication : we have not been married to the quest but betrothed only, while the lower things intervene and sue for restitution of their morganatic conjugal rights. It may be more indeed than this and that we are not in separation at all, but only failing to realise that in this present order of things he must be divorced first who would enter into real wedlock.

But for him who is dedicated, him who has burnt his ships and dismantled his own houses, who has let the roof-trees fall, I can see no path but light and no mode of the path but joy. It is said that joy cometh in the morning, but it is morning always in God. *Et cor meum lætabitur in Te.*

THE POET'S GLASS OF VISION

As all the world is aware—meaning perhaps that world which opens to gifts of the spirit—Matthew Arnold proffered a word of warning to poets of his own days and of others, that they were licensed, namely, to divulge certain secrets, being those of the lesser order and that they would be praised for so doing by a world which loves new ways, but that they must beware of revealing the greater and deeper secrets, for the world will not listen and has indeed no ears to hear except what all can understand. It may be said that the old order has passed utterly away since that dictum was uttered, and this is true after its own manner, yet it would seem that the counsel remains, even if a platitude may be wrapped up from time to time in a mystery and pass for " something rich and strange " in the veils of such decoration. It was the same, I think, in respect of the great secrets even in the old days when Plato found an audience. The poet and the philosopher could discourse of the lesser mysteries but not of the greater; but I am not speaking exactly of those which were celebrated for centuries at Thebes and Eleusis. All changing orders notwithstanding and all imputed work of that melting-pot in which all things are said to be tried, it seems to me that the warning applies at the present time, and this also without as within the sphere of poetic art—in the other departments of literature and generally in those of thought. Whosoever appeals beyond established canons to principles which he regards as ultimate must do so less or more at his peril, as regards an audience.

In things of religion, for example, although there may be numerical majorities, chiefly of a technical kind, it cannot be said that there is any preponderating religious sentiment except that which dissolves in clouds. There is a tacit agreement to abide informally by certain conventions, on condition that there is nothing exceeded outside the terms of the conventions and nothing vital even within those terms. In this manner, by one of those signal ingenuities which are of purely modern growth, the time-honoured systems continue to hold up their heads, invite and receive recognition, without any serious challenge on the part of those who count; but it is on condition that there is no authoritative or at least living construction of their importance. Hence the *chaos magnum informatum* of the modern sects, still nourishing—it is true—a certain spirit of competition which, however, is reduced and diluted by growing inter-recognition and by the indulgent indifference of public opinion. The latter is a great leveller which leaves everyone under the obedience of individual predilection, on the understanding that they will not be so objectionable as to press that predilection outside their own natural sphere of influence, because a man with a great conviction has become very nearly a nuisance. If those pregnant words of a great psalmist-king, " the desire of Thy house hath eaten me up," are to be understood here and now as the duty of going to church on Sunday when other things are equal and encouraging one's wife to look after the harvest festival, they are within the rational order, or otherwise well and good. On the contrary, if anyone dares to say that they have nothing to do with these and collateral pious practices but with an utter dedication of life and with a flame-wise longing for the beauty of a house not made with hands, for a place where that glory dwelleth which is not of the earth or even an astronomical heaven, then these things are outside the law and the order, outside the canons of convention with its grace abounding, and they are left as such to the zealot.

As the poet who speaks with inspiration of the mysteries which encompass us has usually an empty auditorium; as the religious thinker who, rightly or wrongly, believes that he has found the truth and must proclaim it like St. Paul, whether in or out of season, has all doors of exit opened by his hearers; so it is also even in the criticism of literature, which more than most things perhaps is governed by the grave considerations of certain canons that taste forbids us to ignore and that constitute the first principles determining the consideration of any given subject. If there is an unpardonable sin in criticism it is to regard any question of literature from a standpoint outside the schools, because it is obviously to set aside those canons which are of the schools scholastic.

At the end of over nineteen Christian centuries, and after the conflicts of a hundred sects, there is scarcely one person of a thousand now alive in England who can give an accurate definition of religion ; and after all achievements of the great poets, after all the subtleties, refinements, insights and dogmatic findings of criticism there is also not one in a thousand who can state with the whole truth what is the highest field of poetry, its real province and subject. Now, the sects which leave man in doubt as to the true nature of religion, the criticism which has not rooted in the minds of the people the real purpose of poetry and has assisted singers themselves to misconceive their vocation may be set aside, in spite of consecrations attaching to time and authority, looking for other prophets with other modes of judgment. The religious experiment has been cited only by way of analogy, and as regards the criticism of literature, having established a point of view, there is no need to say that I am not offering new canons, nor am I actually making an appeal to poets, that they should recognise their real vocation and should redeem literature of insufficiency in the highest of all its departments.

My concern at the moment is with principles rather than persons or canons, with that which belongs at its highest to the gift of song at its highest rather than him who is singer. In the first place therefore, all poetry which is to come—true, great and like all greatness unforeseen—will have to create its hearers, for I have no concern with the gathering of flowers which are often artificial on a Parnassus which must be accounted spurious. With such creation in view it becomes possible at once to set aside the warning of Matthew Arnold and to take out a larger licence. After all it is a counsel of prudence, and there is nothing so well lost as the mere praise of the world. The poet's day comes, moreover—" in a century or in an age "—and he more than any, with the consolation of his gifts to support him, can afford to wait for an audience. If he cannot, " through the weakness of his feeble will," it is certain that his art can. In the last resource, moreover, it would seem that the growth of the world is towards him, when he brings an authentic message, and that it does get to understand.

Once upon a time, in reality a yesterday of literature, the laureate of that moment, who was Alfred Austin, expressed before a learned society his sorrow for the decay in appreciation of the higher kinds of poetry. The casual reply of current criticism was precisely what might have been expected, an *argumentum ad hominem* in one or other of its varieties. That laureate, however, was largely in the right and his critics were obviously out of court, because it is not necessary to be a great poet in order to appreciate at its value the taste of an age in poetry. I do not know whether it has come about since Austin that the decay in question has been arrested or that there has been a new birth of taste. I am concerned only with raising in the second place a single fundamental question and finding a valid answer, which will also lead us further. What is that which lies at the root of all true poetry and has enabled even conventional criticism to rule out those claimants to the gift who in reality possess only the art of verse ? The answer is, being not indeed mine but that of the spirit of art : The poet's gift is a gift of transmutation, and his horizon is the infinite. To be that which he is, he possesses the awareness of mystery, the consciousness of the unknown, the alkahest which dissolves and purges off the accretions of common life. Most cultured people know well enough in their hearts and confess sometimes with their lips that the poet is a prophet, while as regards the scope of prophecy it is understood that this is interpretation. To interpret is, however, to transmute, for things are changed when their being of inward meaning is unfolded as a flower from the calyx of the outward sense. But on what is this converting gift of interpretation to be exercised ? In a sense and certainly, on anything, on the " flower in the crannied wall," on' that which lies the nearest, because that which is furthest is most remote from our concern and demands apprehension least and last of all.

The things which lie the nearest are the great and paramount needs of the human heart. The office of interpretation is an office of ministry to these, and it can be performed only *sub specie œternitatis*. Like Heredom of the Rosy Cross, Parnassus is not of this world or of the spirit which belongs to the world, and Helicon is not climbed with feet belonging to any sphere of sense, any more than by bodily feet. The paramount needs of the human heart are not of its temporal and evanescent but of its essential and eternal concern. That only which is universal to all men is in the last resource important to all. In other words, that only which makes for the eternal calls truly for consideration in time. It follows that in so far and so only that the poet is in touch with the infinite is he invested at their highest with the powers and graces of his mission.

If we take, on the other hand, the manifold diversities of human character, which certainly demand an especial gift for their valid interpretation to others, it is obvious that this gift belongs pre-eminently to the order of insight and as such is of the poet's dower, yet it is not being exercised in its highest field, because— speaking fundamentally—diversities of character are not of the first import to humanity at large. Man is a mystery in the midst of a mystery, and the work of interpreters is to place such a construction on the dual problem that the two aspects may be enlightened each by each. The diversities between A and B, however brilliantly distinguished, offer no help herein ; a comparative analysis of the motives which actuate A and B are beside the greater questions ; but the relations of A and B to that X which is the unknown encompassing and the unknown within them are of permanent, vital and overpowering interest ; they are the one thing which really matters in a life of trifles and artificial anxieties. It remains, however, that poets who rank as great are prized chiefly for their acute presentations of character. If they are not the less great poets because they have worked in this field, there is still the abiding fact that they have left untouched the highest theme of all, and in poetry it is our unfailing duty " to love the highest."

We may take any other of the multitudinous concerns of verse-craft, and there is one among them which from all time has been practically set apart to the poet—his country, namely, and his nation. We all know that those who make laws for the people have been ranked second in their influence to those who make their ballads; and we remember well that stirring adjuration of Scott in which he execrates the person who has never exclaimed : " This is my own, my native land." It may be difficult in the face of this and yet in the present connection it becomes necessary to affirm in spite thereof that a man's country is to him and his hearers only of incidental consequence. His eternal destiny is the one thing which signifies ultimately to others and to himself. It is not to be suggested that individual characteristics carry no consequence or that their study offers nothing to our knowledge ; still less is it tolerable to think that the welfare of the Ship of State is no part of our own welfare.

> " Humanity with all its fears,
> With all its hopes for future years,
> Is hanging breathless "

on the fate of all its vessels of statecraft. Nor is it to be said that great poetry has not concerned itself with both these subjects and will not continue to do so, all higher criticism notwithstanding. But in the last resource the fact emerges that however much the gift of the poet may illustrate character and glorify patriotism, he is or should be the expounder of mysteries and that his great concern is only with the greater mysteries.

And this leads on to two other of the universal subjects of poetry, which are love as subsisting between the sexes and the love of Nature, our endeavours to interpret the latter being, however, comparatively speaking, a growth of the modern mind. On the other hand, human love has been from all time surrendered to the poet and claimed by him as his province. It is that also which awakens in man at large the beginnings of a poetic sense. Now this is truth, and it is of all truth, and yet it must be remembered that it is only in so far as individual love enters by the fact of its awakening into universal love that it makes contact and is justified with the eternal ; that the merely sexual aspect which has been the preponderating subject of poetry can be admitted among things that are permanent only in virtue of a much more comprehensive realisation of its sacramental nature than has been granted so far to most people even in their dreams, or indeed to all churches. That which is immortal in love is that which ascends above the domain of the senses, understood physically at least, and it is only when the poet himself comes to realise how the great things of valid desire are apart from things of passion, and apart from what is realised normally as the distinctions and analogies which obtain between male and female, that his function as the interpreter of love unto itself begins to be exercised in its widest and highest mode.

As much may be affirmed of the love of Nature, which in the kind of worship offered to her in these days of the misapplication of ecstasy does not sometimes fall short of idolatry. She, more than human love, far more perhaps even than human character, calls for high insight in her interpretation, since she less than either can be said to exist from herself. It is only sacramentally, that is to say, in so far as under veils and disguises she communicates the unknown, that her mystery can be vital to the the human soul.

And now having laid down these principles, let us see what is the consequence of any attempt to apply them. It has been said that the great poets have exercised their gifts of insight without rather than within the highest sphere of its concern. It is explicable enough, considering how far our best and greatest fall short of those ideals which we are individually competent to conceive. We know also how partial at best and transitory are our highest awakenings. But there is something very curious which arises from the second point. It is more particularly when occupied with those themes which ought manifestly to exhibit him in the exercise of his highest function that the poet in the majority of cases seems most unhelped by his art. Having regard to the great claim of English song through the centuries, it must be said that what is described conventionally as religious poetry is part of our humiliation rather than a ground for pride. In many cases the poets who rank as chief among us are least in touch with the spiritual. If we take the most signal example, where is the communication of Divine Grace in Shakespeare? If it is not to be said that he is of the earth earthy, he is assuredly of the earth glorious, and so utterly in touch with nothing which is beyond or outside that his fullest moment of consciousness thereupon is perhaps the time-worn quotation concerning those undefined "more things in heaven and earth," by which no one has been moved one span across the bars of sense.

Milton is of course the most warrantable instance of what is understood by religious poetry, but he appeals to a very narrow side of doctrine rather than to vital issues, and it is precisely the kind of doctrine which at this day has ceased to communicate anything. When we do meet with anyone among makers of memorable verse who have something of the true matter within them—Crashaw, Fletcher, Robert Southwell, Vaughan, Blake, Emerson—it so happens inscrutably that they are exceedingly imperfect as artists. Fortunately, it is not alone to the professionally religious poet that we have to look for that consciousness of the infinite, that gift of interpretation which constitutes the expounder of mysteries. The vestments of an authentic and installed hierophant are assumed from time to time by nearly all our great poets, and never more greatly than when it is to some extent unconsciously. It is in this respect that Tennyson, who offers the quality of communication often and strenuously, fails sometimes of his full effect, because he seems too sensible of his ordination and its validity. In such power of inevitable communication lies the test of true poets. They must be channels—occasionally at least—of gifts and graces which do not belong to this world; they must enlighten life and its problems; they must perform the office of transmutation. It is well to be of the human humanly, but the poet must be of God Godward. If we accept this standard we shall know at once why Southey, his metrical ability and his good sound English notwithstanding, was never a real poet. It was not because he wrote THE VISION OF JUDGMENT and certain official verses as a laureate in his day, but because he never changed or converted anything, never interpreted or communicated anything. At a later day there was an instance in Swinburne of the brilliant metrical artist, almost capable of deceiving the elect, but if judged from this standpoint his claims dissolve, not because he wrote DOLORES, FRAGOLETTA and so forth, but because THE GARDEN OF PROSERPINE, with all its glow of images, its panoply of diction, is simply THE GARDEN OF PROSERPINE.

x

From the period of Elegant Extracts down to these times we have had enough and to spare of anthologies, but one remains to be done from the present standpoint—the witnesses of sacramental communication in great poets and their disciples. To illustrate how the office of the hierophant is exercised unconsciously and yet with plenary powers we may take a commemoration of the idea of infinity in Wordsworth:

> " A wilderness of building, sinking far
> And self-withdrawn into a wondrous depth,
> Far sinking into splendour."

We may compare Keats, communicating the same infinite under a simple sense of enchantment:

> " The same that oft times hath
> Charm'd magic casements opening on the foam
> Of perilous seas, in faërie lands forlorn."

Then as an example of the poet's transmuting office, let us observe the alchemy of moonlight in these lines of Wordsworth:

> " As the ample moon,
> In the deep stillness of a summer even
> Rising behind a thick and lofty grove,
> Burns like an unconsuming fire of light
> In the green trees ; and kindling on all sides
> Their leafy umbrage, turns the dusky veil
> Into a substance glorious as her own,
> Yea, with her own incorporate by power
> Capacious and serene : like power abides
> In man's capacious spirit. . . ."

The quotations which might follow are endless, and sources which are unlikely at first sight offer sometimes the richest results, for in such communications and conversions the greater poets are at their greatest, while the inspiration of the lesser assumes for the time being the strength and resonance of the highest.

It has been said that the end of poetry is beauty, a definition which if it really excludes the spirit and the truth, as well as the witness of the great mysteries to the one place of the mysteries, must far more certainly exclude also such themes as the delineation of character, with all that is understood by the dramatic element as well as the national side of song. But those who would affirm that it excludes truth and the testimony of the eternal to the soul have for a moment forgotten that " the beautiful is the splendour of the true " and that there is one Being Whose beauty like His truth is " ever ancient and ever new." We have a great deal to be thankful for in the gift of the poets to a world whose word is English ; and I at least have no desire to restrict their influence, to minimise their work or reduce their glory. I have but indicated their highest office and that secret wherein their greatness lies. It is possible—with things as they are—that such office can be assumed only at intervals, that the secret is given and cannot be sought out ; but it is a wise counsel that they should remember the vocation of their priesthood.

I put up this Lamp of the Heights as a beacon for others hereafter, because of a greater possibility in days to come. There was seldom, if ever, a time when the world had more need of poets, and it is the kind of need which may well create opportunity. It does happen quite often that the hour brings forth the man. The poet has tried many paths ; he has yet to try that of the mystics. The mystic has followed the way of the union from many starting-points : he has yet to be born also to the path of song. The man of sanctity has been often a man of affairs, but he has been hardly ever a man of letters in our plenary sense of the term : the books of the mystics do not really belong to literature, as we understand the word. I look for him who is to come, as Paracelsus for his Elias the Artist. We need a greater Dante, in liberation from all doctrine but that of experience. We need one who has been where Eckehart and Ruysbroeck went, and who, having the gift of the poet, shall return and tell us not only of " the treasure-house " and " the Master too " but where is the Master and where the House and what it means to find them. In very truth there is another glass of vision through which the poet may see. He may open another door, beyond which he shall not only contemplate the eternal but speak therefrom.

A STUDY IN CHRISTIAN PANTHEISM

In the First Epistle to the Corinthians (xv. 28) there occur the following familiar but strangely pregnant words : " That God may be All in all." They are intimations of a state which is beyond the state of which it has been said previously : " Then cometh the end," that is to say, when Christ delivers up the Kingdom to God, " even the Father." On the surface at least, and whether or not within the measures of St. Paul's conscious intention, they suggest an indrawn state of the cosmos and all that abides therein, though it is not understood in this manner— as there should be no need to say—by the official or orthodox commentators, by Cornelius a Lapide among moderns, by Gregory the Great or St. Basil in the earlier Christian centuries. In any case, as we dwell upon them, it seems to me that for us and for our dedications they can have but one meaning,—that in no sense of allegory and in no figure of speech there is a state to come in which God shall be All in all. And this is pan-theism. It connotes also by implication what Martines de Pasqually terms the doctrine of resipiscence, otherwise of that universal redemption to which Saint-Martin also alludes ; for when God is All in all there can be nothing cast out. We may remember the hope of Tennyson :

> " That not one life shall be destroy'd
> Or cast as rubbish in the void
> When God has made the pile complete."

But I am not concerned with eschatology, nor are the words of St. Paul—whatever their final significance—other than a text for my thesis. And this is that the All-in-all state of God-ness **en**counters us again in the deep searchings and realisations of the Christian and indeed among other mystics, as something belonging to their experience at the end of the long path of their inward travelling. It is this primarily that I mean in speaking of Christian pantheism; but it should be understood that such pantheism is in respect of the individual soul, and is not a philosophical hypothesis concerning the universe. Were it otherwise, it would have been no part of my concern to have discussed it in the present paper; and it would have been impossible, moreover, as historically and doctrinally there is no Christian pantheism of the cosmic kind. In the sense of devotion and pre-occupation it can be said, and is said truly, that God is All in all by the hypothesis of those who have learned after any manner that He is the one end, as He is also the one beginning. It is the postulate of the life of sanctity, but belongs as such to the realm of propositions, and I am concerned with records of experience. We shall see in due course that the experience not only verifies the postulate, but gives life of life thereto.

On the threshold of what is understood as attainment the soul of the mystic does find that God is All in all—otherwise *non pars est sed totum*, according to the memorable maxim of Raymond Lully. The manner of plenary finding is a great mystery of life in Divine Being; but it must be understood that I speak of it as the sense of this ineffable state awakens in the hiddenness of the mind, when the mind listens and the soul speaks within; for in the present instance one is not concerned only with a question of research. There are the records in the first place, and there is the manner of understanding these. The records tell us that there is an experience of unity possible to the soul of man. The testimonies concerning it are everywhere; and, when every allowance has been made for the distinctions of national mentality, for modes of metaphysical thought and the diverse helps or hindrances of official religious belief, the testimony is always the same. Herein lies the witness of its validity. But this, so far, is on the historical side, a question of texts and of authority behind the texts. There is another kind of validity,—when life answers to life, when the witness of the past awakens corresponding witness in the heart of the living present, in my reader's heart and in mine. We are linked up then into the golden chain which, so far as Christianity is concerned, begins with pseudo-Dionysius,

and we know not where it shall end. But the intimations of it
are everywhere also under the rule of the other great religions,
in all human spiritual history, outside the chaos of the savage
state. Above all, the intimations of it are everywhere in our own
spiritual history, when the obtruding personal identity has
merged for the time being in any one or other of the high and holy
pre-occupations which absorb the mind. The pre-occupation of
love is the great living illustration ; because it is the only one of
them all which is made in the likeness of the mystic state itself.
But this is love in its separation from the sense-body of desire.
The explanation is that the created love is instilled by the
uncreated. But with this aspect of the subject I have dealt on a
former occasion.

As regards the state itself—on the path and even to the
threshold there is that which Saint-Martin terms so eloquently
the thirst for unity, but when the soul has "crossed the bar," it
does more than see its Captain face to face ; for that which follows
is the mode of unity attained. The true end, the high end which
emerges after all the emotions and all the raptures, is not of seeing
but of being. St. John of the Cross says that the soul is itself the
union. But there are many degrees, and they are described
under the veils of many images and similitudes. The doctrine of
the Blessed Vision has given us the immortal PARADISO ; and we
know in THE DIVINE COMEDY how the Vision was understood by
one of the great poets of the whole world of literature. On the
surface it may seem as the poles asunder from the unity of
Eckehart and Ruysbroeck, St. John of the Cross and St. Teresa.
But I am not sure that as formulated by St. Thomas Aquinas it
is so far away ; for it may be advanced that the soul in the state
of Vision is really in the state which is called otherwise Absorption, Deification and the Spiritual Marriage, and that we are being
beguiled by the fantasy of a comparison drawn from a faculty of
material sense. It must be understood in any case that the
so-called seeings of the deep states, as unfolded by many mystics,
must at their least signify an awareness of spiritual perception ;
and this is one reason why people like Poulain and most of his
precursors, with all their zeal and sincerity, only confuse the real
issues further as their pages grow in number. I set aside, of

course, the cases which can be explained psychically, like those of Maria d'Agreda, the Venerable Mary of the Incarnation, and I must perhaps even add St. Catherine of Siena. But Blessed Angela of Foligno, speaking of this state of seeing, and psychic indeed as she was, adds in a very pertinent paradox : " I see all things, and see nothing," denying also the presence " of anything which has form."

We are on other ground with Ruysbroeck, affirming that those who are illuminated by Divine Grace do find within them, " above reason and in their proper essence," the Kingdom of God and God in his Kingdom ; with Cardinal Bona : " the end of perfect life is intimate union with God " ; with Tauler, speaking of those who are " established solidly and as if naturalised in God " ; and with St. Teresa, testifying that " the spirit of the soul is made one with God." But centuries before these witnesses there is Dionysius on an ineffable mode of being in which the soul is " lost in God." This is the state which is beyond the state which according to St. Thomas Aquinas is " one with One." I have mentioned the latter in a previous essay, and have said also that it corresponds to the Blessed Vision. As if standing on a threshold, I have also characterised the state of being plunged in God as that of one in One. But this is a veridic approximation which the soul brings back on its return into the personal life. In the experience it is not one abiding within the One : it is the state of perfect unity. By possibility the Zoharic theosophist knew something, or had dreamed concerning it, when he said that " God and His name are one." It is the uttermost mode of sanctification : in the realisation it is all holiness and all saint-ship. I do not know by the operation of what law the soul comes back therefrom : it may be for the work of manifestation, for the complete fulfilment thereof, and for the business of the faithful witness in the world. In itself it is realisation of the Divine Immanence emerging into a plenary state of possession. There is no watchman to compare with this Watchman, keeping the City of God. St. Paul had entered into its great mystery of being, since he was able to say : " I live, but not I ; for Christ liveth within me." These also are words spoken in the aftermath of the experience. The state is otherwise like that of a King upon his throne when no minister is present with him in the throne-room, though they may be otherwhere and about the King's business. But in the last resource, and as there is little need to say, even this imagery fails ; for in the mystical state the King is also the throne, and the house is He. So is it put into words as best we can, and lamely : they may be sufficient for those who can hear. The meaning is that, if God is All in all, the soul is not in separation ; and hence—as the state lasts—there is no I, except in the sense that He Who is all is I. There is neither fatherhood nor sonship ; and how much more is the state of God and His worshipper in suspension for the time being ! It is the state in which those who come back repent of their antecedent testimonies, like the Angelic Doctor, who after his Mass-time ecstasy is said to have repented the SUM OF THEOLOGY, and so was put into silence, leaving it still unfinished. If we could imagine the official Church, with its Sovereign Pontiff, being integrated suddenly in this very life of very Godhead, would it not perchance repent of all its dogmas and all the high definitions ? I know not which at least should remain over, unless the Church affirmed somewhere that God is known of the heart. It might overcome the last enemy, saying that the Church is Christ, and that which would follow should be as the morning of Easter, the Lord Christ coming into manifestation out of the rock-hewn sepulchre in which we have laid Him for nigh on two thousand years. Or it should be as a light shining in the East and extending even to the West when Shiloh comes.

In the records which are continuous throughout Christian mystical literature, the deep experience passes into expression only in terms of pantheism. It is put into language of this kind for the reason that there is no other. I have shewn elsewhere that the unity-state implies the sense of identity so long as the state endures ; and more recently Dr. Nicholson, speaking of Islamic Mysticism, agrees that " the unitive state " cannot be described " otherwise than pantheistically." The Christian terminology is express and as such significant after its own manner. In illustration of this I will collect some typical examples, remembering the extraneous witness of Philo, that human reason is replaced mystically by the Divine Spirit.

(1) According to Ruysbroeck, outside the measures of the normal mind, in a superessential beatitude, we are one with the Spirit of God, above our created essence, in an abyss unfathomable, and this is the essence of God. We are dissolved in Him, meeting God by God, apart from all mediation, in rejoicing rest. The soul is said otherwise to be dissolved in Him Whom the soul loves, or it is absorbed with Him in unity. In Christ terminology, it becomes a living Christ. (2) Tauler speaks of the human mind being clothed with the form and image of God, of the soul receiving God in an altogether divine manner, of God radiating within it, and so is it transformed in Him, effectuating a supreme union between the human and Divine Will, as if the one were annihilated in the other. So far THE INSTITUTIONS, but the changes are rung, so to speak, like silver bells in the Sermons. We hear of moments when the soul is lost to itself and sinks into the great deeps of God, when it plunges with the whole being and all the faculties of reception and absorption into that which is one, simple, divine, illimitable, and from which the soul is no longer distinguishable. (3) In Eckehart the soul is not only the Kingdom of God, but in that Kingdom she and the Divine Being are one bliss. (4) St. John of the Cross affirms that the soul is transformed completely in God, that it becomes like unto God, is God rather than itself, by a process of participation. (5) For St. Teresa the marriage of the soul with God is like a stream which has been discharged into the sea, and is so merged therein that the waters of the one can be distinguished no longer from those of the other. The synonym of this is obviously that " the dewdrop slips into the shining sea." (6) But we may compare THE CLOUD OF UNKNOWING, which offers a variant analogy when it speaks of " the high wisdom of the Godhead descending into man's soul " and " knitting it " to God Himself. The substantial unity is otherwise affirmed when the Deity is defined as " the blissful being " both of Himself and the soul, which is said to be joined in the spirit with Him, apart from separation. We hear also of union with God " above all substance and knowledge." Among lesser memorials that of (7) the Venerable Maria de Escobar bears three testimonies : (a) of being submerged and lost in the Divine Essence, (b) of being united suddenly therewith

in a deep ecstasy and (c) of being plunged, as it were, into a vast ocean, which is God. (8) The Venerable Augustine Baker describes the soul as drawn gradually to God till the sense of its own being passes away and it is so lost to itself, that life and being for it are in God only. (9) The transfiguration of the soul into God is an expression of the Venerable Anne Madeleine de Remusat and it is said to be divinised by the experience.

I have given but a few examples from among the cloud of Christian witnesses. To have produced others would have sounded like mere repetition, but their records call to be studied from this point of view, taking care to set aside—but I mean of course provisionally—their own qualifications on the subject, under the regulating and chastening hand of the regnant orthodoxy. In this connection let it be assumed that for the time being, meaning in the present enumeration, I am concerned with a question of fact, not with the verity and validity of mystical experience. About this I am otherwise certain, with the certitude of the whole mind and in the spirit of humility of the whole heart; but at the moment I am dealing only with a question of evidence, the concurrence and identity of certain depositions, not with what lies behind them and not with the status of the witnesses, whether they are in a mesh of delusion or are examples of God's grace abounding in God's elect. They are all witnesses of experience at the value thereof, and I have tried in the first place to let them speak clearly for themselves on the fact of experience. We now see what it is and that the soul comes back therefrom saying that the soul is God, not as to source and origin, not as a point of doctrine, not on philosophical considerations, but on the faith of a state attained. To speak of this state, even when free from the complications of other possible issues, was a perilous thing under the ægis of a dogmatic orthodoxy holding everlasting session, armed to the teeth. It is obvious that, whether they wished it or not, the mystics had to qualify; but those, if any, who affirm that they qualified and accommodated their convictions merely to keep at peace with the teaching Church, are unacquainted with the psychology of the centuries and of the personalities which are being passed in review. Let it not be supposed for a moment that the succession of mystics represented any sect or school within the official establishment, and much less one that was in secret opposition thereto, cherishing its own designs and its own private views over matters belonging to faith. There was no school, save only an unincorporated school of saints. There were heresies enough and heresies so-called through all the times and places, but speaking generally—or at least for those that counted—they were not mystic, as I understand the term, and it seems very certain, for example, that they did not preach pantheism. There is, as suggested already, no doctrinal pantheism among the Christian mystics, but there is the pantheism of experience. It is this, I conceive, which has made the succession of mystical witnesses an element of doubt and danger in the eyes of the Latin Church. I do not mean to suggest that they would have dispensed with them gladly, had this been possible ; they were much too important and vital, and there is no trace of the wish anywhere. But of anxiety there seem traces, and it is intelligible in view of the issues, for the whole body of doctrine might prove less or more at stake, and there were witnesses, as *e.g.* the case of Eckehart, when what I have called the pantheism of experience seemed merging into pantheistic doctrine. But generally speaking, the records of experience stood at their own value, apart from dogmatic suggestions. The universe was not identified with God, and the unity of God and the soul was a diagnosis of experience, a matter of attainment, and stood forth in contrast to the formal professions of faith and the whole stream of teaching by which the texts embodying the records are always characterised. I hold sincerely that this contrast was no result of submission, performed *nolens volens*, but a natural consequence of spiritual life led within the Church, whose body general of doctrine was so ingrained that it was like second nature to the mystics, as to the lowly and unlettered monk.

The *Synteresis* of Tauler and the soul-apex of Eckehart are not conscious pantheistic propositions, any more than this can be said of the Zoharic *Tsure*, that supernal part which does not leave the Supernals, any more than it is involved by the doctrine of Divine Immanence or of the Kingdom of Heaven within. If I am right, it follows that the mystics qualified or explained their own first-hand experience in harmony with that faith which Mother-Church had delivered to them. I do not need here to quote many examples. In his long treatise on contemplation Ruysbroeck insists continually on the distinction between the soul and God, as between Creator and creature. He goes indeed further than the logic of his case can tolerate, for he affirms in one place that whatsoever has " a mode of being or a form " and whatsoever has no form are distinct " and can never become one." But this appears to challenge the fundamental message of his own inward experience. Eckehart claims· for the eye of the soul and God that they are one eye, " one mode of knowing and one feeling "; but though he wavers thus and frequently on the brink of unreserved pantheism, even as regards God and Nature, he decides that the unified soul is and remains a creature. Again THE CLOUD OF UNKNOWING, which is like the waters of unity offered in a great chalice, makes it clear from the beginning that every soul had its beginning in the substantial creation, " the which was sometime nothing." For St. John of the Cross, even in the great deeps of the union, the soul preserves the distinction from God of its own natural substance, as it did prior to attainment, and this notwithstanding that the soul is transformed in God. But an unhappy illustration follows,—that the soul is comparable to a window, the substance of which remains distinct from that of the solar rays which shine through and enlighten it. It would serve little to cite further St. Teresa, who submitted everything to her directors ; but Tauler, having affirmed absorption into something that is " one, simple, divine and illimitable," adds immediately : " I speak not of the reality but of the appearance, of the impression that is felt." He dwells also on the brevity of the experience, as if it were a further safeguard set about the difficult subject.

It is not therefore only the orthodox commentators and theologians, whose business it was to produce mystical experience in the form of a body of doctrine, to arrange and harmonise its degrees and phenomena, it is not these only who brought and limited the great range of its subject within orthodox lines. The work was done for them beforehand by those who created in this manner the title-deeds, as it were, of their real concern.

It is true that a voice of protest was raised occasionally. When Pope John XXII condemned certain propositions of Eckehart, he put antecedently the seal of anathema on several others formulated by later mystics, and though they contrived to pass unchallenged from the seat of authority they led some people to think. Notwithstanding his own dedications, the pantheism of mystical experience set Chancellor Gerson in flaming hostility against Ruysbroeck. Meanwhile the commentators and scholiasts, makers of manuals and directories, are notable after their own manner, from Corderius on pseudo-Dionysius to Scaramelli, Schram and Devine. For better, for worse they have had to accept and echo the terminology under which the deep states have entered into expression, and to use language therefore which can have one meaning only in the stern logic of things. They do not shrink from speaking with the mystics of the soul's participation in the Divine Nature, of immersion in God, of transformation and deification. And so it comes about that the witness goes on through the ages, that the roll of the Christian mystics is not only a roll of sanctity but of beatified and canonised saints. They do not walk by faith only but sometimes by sight, even through the halls of the Vatican. But it happens that their eyes can dare to turn only in one direction, lest perchance they discover to their confusion that under other names than those of Christ and in the light of other dogmas than those of the Trinity has the soul of man in many times and places attained the knowledge of unity and satisfied the thirst thereof, has returned from that centre to testify, and in its own manner of language has said the same thing. So far therefore concerning the pantheism of experience in Christian annals of the past. But there remains something to be said briefly from another standpoint.

It is questionable whether the teachings of the mystics on the basis of their experience can be counted as evidence for doctrinal or philosophical pantheism, because it belongs to the end and has nothing as such to say about the beginning or that which is intermediate between the first and the last. We may feel certain intellectually that the end is like the beginning and that thither where we pass in fine is that from which we come forth ; but the question belongs to another ground of thought. In any case, between the one and the other there intervenes a state of normal separation, wherein we become acquainted by experience with the world of external phenomena, in which we act our external part, with the self as it is so manifested, with the evil side of our selfhood, with the passions of our heart in hatred, with the will to malice ; and I do not know at what stage, if indeed at any, it can be said that they are rooted out utterly, even in the mystical life. It is very certain that Ruysbroeck, St. John of the Cross, St. Teresa and other of the paramount witnesses did not make this claim. If the serpent is not awake, it is credible that it is asleep within us, and the tiger is no doubt in his lair when he is not seeking prey in our jungles. The Kaiserism of the Great War has no part in the union, and there is a Kaiser also within us. He may be in exile and yet for all that not idle. He has found refuge, let us say, in some approximate or remote Holland within us, and he remains either an actual or possible danger. But this is for our best and worthiest, for those, as the saying is, who have entered the path, for some perchance who may stand, as it were, on the threshold of union. I do not know : it is a great day of the world and holy things may be doing in the hiddenness, as well as all the natural good which is at work amidst all the evil in the outer ways. We have heard about many being called and few chosen, but it seems to me that we are amidst great titles of election, so that many people look ready, or as if they had only to lift the latch of a certain door in the heart and they might be not so much in the Presence as the Presence might be declared in them, which is the day of understanding in Israel and of *Regnum Dei intus*. It is not so far thereafter to the valid attainment, when God is All in all without as well as within, when the soul goes forth in peace and errs no more in questing, nor is any longer in that state of dereliction in which the servant usurps the place of the Holy One.

A general testimony through the Christian centuries concurs with Tauler that the most deep experiences are brief, and seeing that at least as regards distinguished cases of election there are many worlds to conquer in lives of dedication and mission, there is no evidence before us, and there can be none in the nature of things, that as chosen souls pass on their way, performing the sacred pilgrimage of the soul, they do more, hereafter as here, than enter the unity-state for measured periods, until the great day comes when God calls back the worlds or alternatively, having fulfilled its tasks and earned its titles, the soul is called to the everlasting rest of the centre, by the operation of some unknown law in God. There is otherwise and of course a sense in which those who have known the union are for ever in its aftermath, in its transfiguration of life and personality, which in an alternative symbolism is the Christ-state of Ruysbroeck. St. Paul is the witness hereof, and it is this, I suppose, which begets the saving missions of the soul through the worlds and the ages.

This for our wisest, as Matthew Arnold says, but I speak of that wisdom which is integrated in the providence of God. For us others, let us ask to be counted among those who have received in the mind and accepted also in the heart the sacred witness to the heights, not alone to the state of the union but that which in the veridic hypothesis of attainment is described as beyond the union, which is designated in our imperfect figures of speech by such terms as absorption and the equivalents of complete identity. O sacred quest of the soul in the realisation of its own world and transformation by the ineffable Presence within the world of the soul! The heart beats on the threshold and the uplifted part of mind begins to perceive in the stillness. Between the All-in-all of God, " before the beginning of years " and the end of all, conceived beyond the years of time, can we find room anywhere in our thoughts, except for God abiding, with and within all? I have said that the end is like the beginning, and that which lies between shall be for us apart from neither. If it is not all God now, such at least it ought to become and perhaps will. For us and for ours henceforward, let us so work and so perchance attain that it shall be only and all for God.

THE GRADES OF LOVE

BEYOND the excursive and material mind, its procession of lesser graces, its treasures as of an Earthly Paradise and all its psychic states, deeply and far withdrawn, there is that part of us which knows the Presence of the King because it is the place of the Presence. It must not be affirmed concerning those inferior states that none is of the spiritual order within its particular measures, but they are not of the mystical order, which has its term in one state, and of this only is it said : World without end. As it is not entered by the path of images it appears like a remote centre, while we are relegated to the circumference in our present sphere of being. It comes about therefore that those who speak from the centre, in the plenary or highest sense, bear witness in a strange language, and their appeal comes often faintly. There are others who testify on the warrants of an intellectual realisation only, and that which they tell us remains too often within the region of debate. It is perhaps for these reasons that many who are conscious of a certain inward leading by which they might be drawn from the circumference are still disposed to tarry, " sitting late " and encompassed by " the old, familiar faces," in the old ways. The few remain, however, who, each within his or her individual measure, have begun to follow the lead and to realise in this manner that there is a mode of communication to the soul by which is awakened a consciousness of Divine Life. Like that centre of which I have spoken, the intimations reach us at first as if from very far away. But the response which follows this awakening is not to be compared with " the desire of the moth for the star": it is rather the longing of a storm-tossed mariner for the harbour which he strives to reach. It is, moreover, from the very beginning, as an act that begets its consequence on the side of Divine Life, which is waiting to communicate itself through all our earthly days, and the ground of that communication is one of consanguinity therewith in our own nature. When this truth is received and dwells in the heart the illusion of remoteness is taken out of the way ; there is no longer circumference or centre. God is not only at the door, standing at the very threshold, but He is the discovered Presence within, and the life of the soul becomes a loving contemplation of the abiding God.

But seeing that He encompasses also there is a communication opened also through external channels in the sacramental ministry of the cosmos, the symbolism of the natural world, the symbolism of the heart of human love and—as I read them—the expounded symbolism of Churches and creeds, not omitting the sacred institutes of certain Secret Orders, dwelling beyond the ken. By each and all of these channels does grace enter the soul and there exercise its own office of awakening that which is implied within us, so that we attain the secret life of the sacramental forms. After this manner does the universe without us bear its Divine part to the Divine in our own being.

This is the beginning of attainment ; but what is the path thereto ? The answer is that " love is enough," but the preparation may be summarised in the words of another formula : We must dedicate the will, consecrate the urge of motive and sanctify the outward life in all its grades and degrees, so that it can be experienced by the heart in its sincerity that we have ceased to do evil and have learned to do good. It may be questioned whether these things are possible in the round of daily existence ; but the reply is always and only that the highest grade of advancement is taken when we realise that the visible world is a great sanctuary which has been built for our consecration and when the sphere of our particular calling—with its cares, temptations and sorrows, its interests and its necessary preoccupations —has become for us truly a Church, wherein we go up to the Altar of God. Outside all splendours of the starry heavens—but often because of those splendours, if such is the line of our leading —we shall learn by fidelity to our law that there is a star within which led the Kings of the East to the birthplace of Christ in Bethlehem and that journey is possible to us also in the secret

Y

life of our sanctuary. It begins in the symbolism as if from very far away, but it ends at home. It is like Ruysbroeck's Journey in the Divine Distance, pursued within measures of experience and not of space. Its stages are those of aspiration after the eternal mode. Who are we that we should be content with a part if it be given us to attain the whole ?

I have cited the old adage which affirms that " love is enough," and the idea of its essential office in the mystic way has been with us ever or continually in all these studies. But seeing that the word love represents a state of life, as a verbal type or glyph of an image in the mind reflected from that state, it is the shadow rather than the essence of this last which is communicated by the agreed counter of expression. There is no conveyance of life by means of words : it is at once veiled and adumbrated. The tendency is therefore to go back continually by appeal from the verbal form to the mental image and from this to the living principle, in search of more valid means of expression. It seems to us sometimes that we get ever so little nearer, though the essence still escapes. But life itself in the manifest order is a quest after expression, and the urge impels us forward. And seeing that no one can speak of love as to that which it is in its own and very nature, let us try for a moment to look at the grades of love, to collect the light which may come from modes and aspects of development and perhaps learn thus a little further about love in the Godward sense, by reaction from outward to inward, or in our old recurring symbolism, by passing from circumference to centre.

From one point of view the grades of love are many, but in heart and essence it is one thing only which turns hither and thither, as if to pour out its being. Every urge of our activity is a mode of love and every dedication has love as the root thereof. The desire for success is the doing of that well, whatever it is, which is done at all only for love thereof. It follows that love not only impels to action but is in all the *moyen de parvenir*. It is a soul of love in the poet which has given the world its song, and that which is said of this most high vocation is true of all the arts. Musicians and painters know, whosoever comes with a message, and the priest knows at the altar—if he be priest indeed

—that he has been called from the beginning in love and that this is the work of the Altar. Those who built temples of old to the glory of God in the highest and made in the doing their gifts to the world at large—these also built in love. It is the root of all the crafts, and those who pursue them apart from this their life are not in the guilds and the liveries but only cowans and hirelings.

So far concerning the love which brings forth vocations, and their name is legion, but there is that which the soul pours out to the spirit of beauty in all its kinds and degrees, the beauty which is Nature, beauty of body and mind and ineffable beauty of the heart. As expressed thus, it will be seen that it includes everything, within and without all preceding enumerations. In one of its restricted aspects, it is the response from each one of us to the appeal of the cosmos. The varieties of this are myrionymous, and in a deep sense it is the love of the spirit in man for the spirit in the great world behind its radiant veils. Where it abides on the surface of things, it is the heart's attraction towards all talismanic magic of outward appearances communicated through all the senses.

We have been contemplating many sacraments of love, outward and visible signs of its inward grace from the font of grace within us, and perhaps it has scarcely occurred to us that we are the place of its presence. The activities, the callings, the worships are all ours : we are talking therefore and only of human love, not that of seraphs before the Throne or of deified spirits in union. But permeating, encompassing and above all there is the love in its manifestation of man for man, the absorption of lovers in each other, the love between friend and friend, of parents for children. These things are also ours, and assuredly we are a house of many treasures, for these are the grades of love. But they are of love shewn forth by outflowing from the self-centre, and there is another fatal aspect of the whole subject, when there is no passage of love from subject to object, when it revolves only about and within the self. All murder, all cruelty, all hatred are modes of self-love in operation. It is the root of evil in the world, and there is none other. This is a word in passing, because in these essays I have taken out no warrant to dwell upon the dark side. But it is needful to realise that if love is life it is possible to poison life.

I have spoken of many directions to which the one thing turns and is ever the same in all, because love is one. It is always desire of attainment and fruition therein. This indeed is the whole point of my intention, for the love which turns to God is no new thing that has to be born within us. This is why the path is in reality of all things simple, and it is why also the formal, elaborate processes by which we are taught to meditate, concentrate, contemplate not only take us by a hard and long road but are liable to miss the term. The secret is only the turning of the old, old principle in yet one other direction, to that self behind the self which is called the place of the Presence, and is that of Divine Life, or the love within the life which is that of the life of love. It is sought as an object so long as the seeking lasts—or, shall I say? like an image in the mind—but because it is found within the passage from subject to object ceases at the end of all, though now in the Godward sense, as in union with the Presence, which is that of love with love.

It follows that beyond the manifest Grades of Love there is love in the plenary sense, or that which is All in all; and he in whose heart it reposes has attained God Who is within. The progress of life in this love is that which is called advancement in the knowledge of God, an exploration of the deeps and riches which He has reserved for those who love Him. The deeps and the riches are love, and these are the world and its Kingdom, which becomes a Heaven within, until such time as it shall reign also without. And this is the Day of Christ *et vita venturi sæculi*.

THE INWARD HOLY OF HOLIES

THERE is a state beyond the images, a repose of inward being, apart from action in the mind. It has been the subject of intimations from time to time in these papers, and their last message shall be concerned with it nearly and only. In so far as it can pass into expression it is a state of awareness at one's own centre, but it will be seen that the attempted formulation produces an inevitable image in which the essence escapes. There is no realisation therein of centre, circumference, height or deep, and that awareness which is perhaps the only representative word has no relation to things or objects, to modes and qualities, but is wholly and as if unconditionally within. I suppose that in the nature of things it emerges subsequently in the mind as an awareness in self, but there is no reaction on self or objective presence of the ego. It is not mind reflecting on its own being. Realisation itself is only an approximate word and exceedingly remote also, because it denotes effort, while the state is still being, outside both subject and object, as if in some middle way between this pair of opposites. It is, moreover, neither light nor darkness, which belong to the world of appearances, and it cannot be called knowing, which connotes a faculty in exercise and that upon which it acts. The state knows not this or that.

When it is entered there is no sense of beginning, middle or end, for the state is timeless. It is only on coming out therefrom that the external correspondence in event is found to be exceedingly short. But it must be understood here that in attempting to convey an impression I am under the penalty of words which fail everywhere and communicate nothing but antithesis. The state is not entered and one does not come out therefrom : we are simply in it and subsequently we are not in it, but amidst a terrible experience of lost beatitude in reality. The sense of abiding in the timeless is not with us and that of beatitude belongs to the subsequent reaction. There is no external correspondence in temporal duration because time does not measure eternity, nor is metaphysical infinity represented by extension in space.

There seems no doubt in experience that the habit of going inward into the state, when we sink willingly therein, may cause it to endure longer in respect of the time-appearance; but the inward reality is one and is not affected thereby. In itself it is full completeness, though time has measured but seconds. If we reflect in the mind thereon, whether in the aftermath or otherwise, it will be seen, I think, that we cannot have more or less of an eternal mode of being.

As I have intimated that there are certain circumstances by which we may " become " into the state—and they may be called an inward attitude—it may be that there is a part of our nature which is always sunk therein or raised into its great altitude. In the very truth it is neither of sinking nor rising, but of being and abiding simply. Ruysbroeck and others knew it, when they spoke of an apex of the soul. Eckehart knew when he alluded to the soul in its highest prototype which has never possessed therein either time or space. It was known also by the Kabalist in his ecstasy, prophesying concerning TSURE, that part or aspect of the soul which never leaves the Supernals. Except in a vocational way there is of course no part of the soul, as if it were in layers or sections and could so be divided up. It is a question of states attained. Ruysbroeck's apex is a mode of the Presence, like a Grade in an Ineffable Rite which is called the Finding of God; and TSURE is a mode of being in Godhead or of deification, as Christian mystics call it. It is as if the act of transmutation at Cana were one of its images and all our water were changed into wine of that Kingdom which is He. But our earthly symbols shine too pale and cold, or ring too false to pass as a medium of exchange at tables of Heaven.

There is a beautiful hymn beginning: " Abide with me "; and if I do not know what these words of eloquence signified to him who wrote or may spell to those who sing them, I know at least in their shining and haunting how they are translated to myself, for it is in the inward being and there and so only that

God abides. It is not therefore that we are on the altar-steps and He in the tabernacle, for we are *Tabernaculum Dei*, the Altar of Repose and the Monstrance which holds the Host. Again these are words of images, and they are scarcely true of voice in respect of the Great Reality : they are sacramental rather and communicate as such to those who can receive, making the proper distinctions, as between *latens Deitas* and *sacramentum mirabile*. The Abiding Presence is not otherwise like a Host in the Monstrance, any more than it is like the Blessed Vision of Dante. All these things are gracious figures and representations to the desiring mind, and at that a little material. There is a sense in which they are kindred to the ten, thirty and ninety days' indulgence granted poetically in certain Church dispensations and, to those who earn them worthily, sketching forth in type a spiritual reality undeclared in offices of grace and mercy : we know not what reality till something falls in the stillness, as the voice of a star, and reveals the bond of union between many simplicities without and many deeps within.

It is the beginning of discernment on that which lies within the centre of the Rose of Dante, to whom God must have opened, I think—but who can know ?—a sacred heart of knowledge ; yet how should the Italians of that day have understood, with or without him, the dark things beyond the choirs of vision, even if it was the day of Petrarch and the schools of love ? What plainer language therefore could any Dante use ? And what could the Church offer then or earlier but the transubstantiation of bread and wine, not that of the soul of man ? So the Host is placed in the Monstrance and is called Christ, looking for that hour when he who says on his knees *Adoro Te devote* shall find that Christ is within.

It is the same through all the catholic range of symbolism, awaiting the key of union. We talk of God as a King in His Heaven above us till we are able to realise that for each and all His Heaven, which is our Heaven, is only within, and that from this *centrum Naturæ concentratum* we can look abroad on the Heaven without and find that all is Heaven. *Ecce quam jucundum :* in a day like that the whole company is with us and all the hierarchies.

This state is the Inward Holy of Holies, and Shekinah is on the mercy-seat, between the wings of the cherubim, like thought and desire in transcendence, which are no longer desire and thought but an ineffable *tertium quid* in the deific nature of being. It is that state in which the hidden God of the great Latin " prose " is more hidden than ever and yet is declared for us, because we have taken off our veils and have entered into the one, true, holy and indefectible mode of faith. We have become the outward sign and God is the inward grace.

St. Thomas Aquinas tells us that objective truth is one thing, while its realisation in the subject is another. It is precisely this present barrier in the relation between God and the soul that constitutes our state of separation. So long as there is such passage from subject to object we are denied so long the direct realisation of union. It is this hindrance which has to be taken out of the way before the path of the mystics ends in the mystic term. I regard St. Paul himself as a witness to the possibility of the union when he says : " Then shall I know even as I am known." It follows that some of us dare to look beyond the Beatific Vision to that state when for each soul in its attainment God shall be All in all.

That which it has been given me to do I have done as I could to indicate some early steps in the path that leads to this end. There are no difficulties so great but love can take them out of the way. The truth is not unknowable, and it is known in love, for this is the principle of union. It is not a search pursued through any intellectual universe, or by any hard thinking on problems of life and mind. This is the crucifixion of the mind and comes to nothing, like that other crucifixion of the body in unreasoned ascetic practice. The first and only condition is the will to love the true, the beautiful and the good, understood as that One Which is the beginning and end of all. The work of the will is a continual self-suggestion towards the state of unconditional love, until a point is reached when suggestion transforms in love and the self dissolved in love passes out of sight. There is always less and less reaction of thought and will upon self as we grow in the art of God's love. This is the art of the soul and its science : our life within and without becomes,

in attaining this, a holy palace of art. By night and by day
the experience of God is with us: so is He built up within us
and we are built in Him. The external house of man and his
city become the great wonder of the house and city of God.

We know what is said by a poet, reaching out towards these
high things: "The dewdrop slips into the shining sea." But
the whole essence escapes in this utterance, regarded as the end
formulated: we are not more utterly absorbed in God than is
He absorbed in us. The doctrine of experience intervenes with
the far older formula that God is within. We do not find Him
by going from star to star, though He is there also. For us and
for our attainment, He is in the great privity of heart and mind
and soul: when these three become as one in His love He is
known and found therein. It is like a point of union between
the infinitely great and infinitely little, as if the sea within the
dewdrop. Then all high things encompass us; then mercy is
on every side; and on every side of our being, in a vibrant state
of awareness, we answer all the messages. In another sense
than that of Matthew Arnold, "the end is everywhere." It
must be so surely, for the true paths meet in God. The crown
of quest is not so far apart from any of our daily roads. The
light needs little seeking, the grace abounds truly, and ever
the will of God waits upon the wilfulness of man, till it shall
become the will to be His.

I affirm that a time comes when His is the will within us,
and those who trafficked in our temple till it became a den of
thieves are not so much cast out from courts and precincts as
removed of their own accord, with all their wares and baggage,
because there is henceforward no custom. The old Rites pass
also and the old workers of Mysteries: all things enter into
knowledge. We are henceforward neither theists nor pantheists,
because the dispensation is now that of God in experience and
not God in doctrine. According to the last and everlasting gospel
and the last valid formula *quod erat demonstrandum:* the soul
has become the Presence. And those who enter into this state
come back into the world, with the yoke of the kingdom upon
them in a law of service. Then God shall give them work. Of
such it is said in the ZOHAR that the world is sustained by the

voice of little children reading the Law. And God is known of the heart.

Unto this last I have borne my witness in the Holy Assemblies, looking towards all that which it hath not entered into the heart of man to express or conceive,

" And where beyond these voices there is peace."

INDEX

ABBA and Aíma : 57
Absolute : 106
Adam Kadmon : 58
Advent, Second : 178
Agrippa, Cornelius : 7, 65, 69
Alacoque, Blessed Margaret Mary, 195, 233
Albigenses : 7 ; Albigensian Crusade : 149, 184
Alchemy : 66, 67, 71
Alexandria, 134
Althotas : 311
Alvarez, Rodrigo : 287
Angela of Foligno, Blessed : 311
Anthony, St. : 273
Antonio a Spiritu Sancto, 198
Aquinas, St. Thomas : 36, 49, 95, 105, 128, 135, 277, 278, 279, 310, 311, 312, 328
Arnold of Villanova : 65
Arnold, Matthew : 17, 18, 19, 20, 33, 34, 86, 298, 300, 319, 329
Asceticism : 26, 27, 28, 29 ; Ascetic Path, 297
Ashmole, Elias : 225
Assembly, Holy : 7, 8, 42
Astrology : 66, 67, 70, 71
Augustine, St. : 7, 12, 56, 135, 243, 280
Austin, Alfred : 301
Ayin-Soph-Aour : 57

Baker, Ven. Augustine : 314
Barbanson : 273
Bartholomew, Massacre of St. : 184
Bartholomew of the Martyrs : 287
Basil, St. : 151, 308
Beauty and Truth : 305, 306
Bellarmine, Cardinal : 206, 208
Bernard, St. : 6, 128, 135, 174
Blake, William : 305
Blosius : 287
Böhme, Jacob : 28, 36, 39, 40, 78, 178, 179 et seq., 198, 209, 213, 217, 222, 223
Bona, Cardinal : 206, 208, 311
Bonaventura, St. : 36, 128, 135
Bonilla : 273
Book of the Dead : 111, 112
Bossuet, Bishop : 129, 186, 187, 192, 286

Cagliostro, Count : 81, 211, 212, 216, 222, 223
Calvary : 27
Carmel : 127, 283
Catherine of Siena, St. : 93, 163 et seq., 311
Character : 302
Christ, Day of : 324 ; Christ-Life : 164 ; Mystery of : 27 ; Christ Mystical : 127 ; Personal Christ : 14, 15 ; Christ Spirit : 14, 15, 185 ; Christ Tradition : 129 ; Christ within : 39 ; Manifested Christhood : 32
Church, its Hidden Mind : 16 ; Official Churches : 3 ; Anglican Church : 11, 12, 13, 242 ; Greek Church : 11, 242 ; Latin Church : 11, 12, 24, 25, 87, 93, 135, 173, 193, 199, 228, 231, 242
Cloud of Unknowing : 128, 132, 185, 313, 316
Coleridge, S. T. : 281
Conformity : 30
Consciousness : 294, 295, 296
Corderius : 317
Cornelius a Lapide : 308
Crashaw, Richard : 233, 305
Crawford, W. T. : 92
Cross : 17, 27, 203 et seq.
Crucifixion : 29, 328
Curé d'Ars : 285

Dante : 49, 50, 84, 166, 327
D'Arenthon, Bishop : 190
Davis, A. J. : 84, 85, 88
Death, Figurative : 103
Detachment : 262
Dionysius, pseudo- : 99, 133, 155, 161, 185, 274, 309, 317 ; see also 144 et seq.
Divine Aspects : 290 ; Divine Darkness : 138, 270 ; Divine Essence : 313 ; Divine in Man : 321 ; Divine Life : 320, 324 ; Divine Nature : 317 ; Divine Object : 255 ; Divine Order : 255, 256 ; Divine Spirit : 275, 281 ; Divine Understanding : 155 ; Divine Unity : 28 ; Divine Will : 186
Doctrine, Secret : 54, 99, 113

Double : 79
Douze-Tems : 200, 201, 203

ECKARTSHAUSEN, Councillor : 7, 8, 219, 220
Eckehart : 5, 13, 36, 128, 129, 147, 181, 279, 307, 310, 313, 315, 316, 326
Eleusis : 97, 108, 122, 134, 298
Elias the Artist : 307
Emerson, Ralph Waldo : 75, 219, 305
Epiclesis Clause : 292
Eschatology : 9, 13, 159
Eucharist : 9, 15, 80, 121, 179, 233
Evil, Eradication of : 27 ; Root of : 323, 324
Experience, Doctrine of : 329

FAITH, Mystery of : 11
Fall of Man : 290
Fatherhood and Motherhood in God : 55, 56, 57
Fénelon, Archbishop : 5, 129, 184, 185, 186, 187, 192, 193, 195, 196, 197, 198
Fischer, Doris : 92
Fludd, Robert : 65, 66, 72, 178, 225
Formation, Book of : 55
Fournié, Abbé : 226, 227
Francis of Assisi, St. : 180
Freemasonry : 28, 97, 211, 212, 214, 220, 221, 223, 224, 225, 226
Frothingham, A. C. : 143

GEBHARDT, Emile : 146
Gerard of Zutphen : 180, 181
Gerson, Chancellor : 128, 129, 279, 317
Glanvil, Joseph : 248
God Abiding : 319 ; God and Love : 162, 293 ; God as All : 309 ; God as the Great Symbolist : 293, 294 ; Abyssal Godhead : 156
Grace and Nature : 43, 292
Gratry, Père : 69
Gregory the Great : 146, 308
Gurney : 85
Gutmann, Ægidius : 181, 198
Guyon, Madame : 184, 185, 186 *et seq.*, 200

HELLO, Ernest : 131
Heredom : 302
Hexagram : 109, 110, 111
Heydon, John : 225
Hidden Life in God : 8
Hierotheos : 142, 143
Higgins, Godfrey : 225
Hilton, Walter : 278

Hildegarde, St. : 129
Holy Assemblies : 380
Holy of Holies : 290
House of the Lord : 293, 299
Hugh of Saint Victor : 128, 135
Huss, John : 129
Huxley, Thomas : 295
Hypnotism : 63, 77

ILLUMINATI : 218
Immanence : 291, *et passim*
Initiation : 77, 78, 81, 97 *et seq.*
Interior Life, Degrees of : 272, 274
Isaac de Loria : 222

JAMES, William : 85
Jesus of Nazareth : 15, 16, 39, 40, 42, 53, 56, 58, 59, 60, 93, 94, 138, 158
Joachim of Flora : 147 *et seq.*
John the Evangelist, St. : 35, 153
John of the Cross, St. : 7, 65, 95, 128, 134, 141, 164, 172 *et seq.*, 178, 181, 199, 209, 210, 222, 278, 287, 310, 313, 316, 318
John the Scot : 128, 135, 140, 185
John XXII, Pope : 156, 317
Julian of Norwich : 132

KABALISM : 10, 54, 55, 67, 70, 160, 182, 202, 215, 218, 222, 258 *et seq.*, 326
Karma : 14
Keats, John : 306
Kegan Paul, Rev. C. : 216
Kingdom of God : 155, 246, 311, 313, 318, 326
Kingdom of Heaven : 42, 65, 152, 193, 265, 266, 291, 295, 315, 324, 327
Kingdom of the Soul : 160
Kingsford, Anna : 145
Kircher, Athanasius : 88
Knowledge : 293

LACOMBE, Père : 189, 190, 191
Lamp of the Sanctuary : 113
Lascaris : 211
Lavater : 218, 219
Law, William : 223, 224
Lawrence, Brother : 179, 180
Lead, Jane : 222, 224
Leibnitz : 201
Lévi, Eliphas : 97
Liebistorf, Baron de : 217, 220, 221
Lodge, Sir Oliver : 92
Lopukhin : 207
Love : 262, 266, 275, 284 ; Path of Love : 261 ; Sacraments of Love : 313 ; Love of the Highest : 302 ;

Human Love : 303 ; Love of Nature, 303, 304 ; Lover and Beloved : 159, 161, 177
Lully, Raymond : 7, 264, 309

MACROPROSOPUS : 57
Maeterlinck, 131
Magic : 65, 67, 98 ; Black Magic : 222
Magnetism, Animal : 63, 77, 216, 229
Maintenon, Madame de : 191
Maitland, Edward : 64, 145
Mambrini, P. du Toit de : 198, 200, 217, 224
Man a Mystery : 302
Manichæan Sects : 7
Maria d'Agreda : 39, 222, 311
Maria d'Escobar, Ven. : 313
Marianna of Geso : 27
Marriage : 170, 171
Marriage, Spiritual : 163, 164, 165, 166, 310
Martin, Thérèse : 231 *et seq.*
Mary of the Incarnation, Ven. : 311
Meditation : 256, 257, 266–68
Merswin, Rulman : 181
Mesmer, Anton : 216, 229
Microprosopus : 58
Midrashim : 35
Miramion, Madame : 191
Molinos : 5, 7, 36, 129, 222, 278, 279, 286, 288
Monica, St. : 86
Moral Law : 245, 246, 247, 248
Moray, Sir William : 225
Moses of Cordova : 222
Mother of God : 152
Mountain of the Lord : 21, 269
Myers, F. W. H. : 85
Mysteries, Ancient and Modern : 68, 77, 78, 81, 329 ; New Life in : 103 ; Secret Rites : 98 *et seq.* ; Sacramentalism of Rites : 105
Mysticism, Western : 5 ; Greek : 5 ; Islamic : 312 ; Eastern, at large : 14 ; Subject of : 4 ; Claim of : 23 ; Light of : 69 ; Science of : 240 ; Reconstruction of : 241 ; Last end of : 15, 239 ; Mysticism and Ecclesiastical Authority : 5, 6 ; and Dogma : 95 ; and Science of Life : 33 ; and Secret of the Soul : 64 ; Second Birth in Mysticism : 103 ; Mystical Life : 62 ; Mystical Sentiment : 4 ; Mystical System : 3

NATURE : 73 ; Love of Nature : 303, 304 ; Nature and Beauty : 323 ; *see also* 290 *et seq.*

Nicene Creed : 56, 57
Nicholson, Dr. R. A. : 312
Nicolai : 218

OCCULTISM : 62, 63, 64, 70, 76, 78 ; Occult Sanctuaries : 77, 98, 112 ; Occult Schools : 80
Origen : 206

PALACE of the King : 46
Pantheism : 287, 308 *et seq.*
Paracelsus : 7, 69, 98, 113, 307
Parnassus : 300, 302
Pascal : 124
Pasqually, Martines de : 40, 65, 213, 214, 215, 217, 220, 227, 308
Patmore, Coventry : 9
Patmos : 127
Patriotism : 302, 303
Paul, St. : 21, 37, 134, 138, 140, 299, 308, 319, 328
Pentagram : 109, 110
Perfect Way : 29 ; Way of Perfection : 130, **131**
Person of **the Son** : 155
Personality, Parts of : 258–61
Peter, St. : 159
Peter Lombard : 7
Peter of Alcantara : 134
Petrarch : 327
Plato : 49, 50, 68, 250, 298
Plotinus : 10, 64, 68, 69, 106, 134, 288, 299
Poet's Gift : 301
Poiret, Pierre : 198
Pordage, John : 223
Poulain, Père : 155, 279, 310
Prayer and Love : 186 ; Prayer of Attainment : 285 ; Prayer of Rapture : 177
Presence, Inward : 21, 22, 31, 38, 128, 185, 252, 253, 269, 270, 285, 288, 290, 291, 294, 319, 320, 324, 329 ; Divine Presence in the Universe : 292, 294, 329
Proclus : 106, 135
Prototype : 155
Psychical Research : 63, 74, 81, 96

QUEST, Mystic : 82

REALISATION, Divine : 270, 284, 325 ; Realisation and God : 296 ; Realisation of Union : 295
Reality, Divine : 291
Reincarnation : 9, 14
Religion : 61 ; its True Nature : 300

Remusat, Anne Madeleine de : 314
Renan, Ernest : 149
Resurrection of the Soul : 16
Revolution, French : 211, 213, 215
Richter, Sigmund : 225
Rolle, Richard : 132
Rosenroth, Baron von : 210, 215, 219
Rosy Cross : 113, 198, 201, 202, 206, 214, 218, 225, 302
Ruskin, John : 127
Ruysbroeck, Jan van : 6, 7, 8, 13, 65, 73, 95, 128, 129, 131, 147, 153, 155, 181, 209, 210, 278, 279, 286, 288, 307, 310, 313, 316, 317, 318, 319, 322, 326

SACRAMENTS : 9, 15
Saint Germain, Comte de : 81, 211, 215, 216
Saint-Martin, Louis Claude de : 28, 65, 75, 143, 207, 208, 212, 213, 214, 215, 217, 219, 221, 223, 227, 229, 308, 310
Scaramelli : 198, 279, 317
Schram : 279
Schroepfer : 218
Secret of the King : 46
Secret Orders : 321, 329
Seership : 65
Senancour : 228, 229
Sephiroth : 55, 57, 259, 260
Shekinah : 38, 39, 58, 328
Simeon, Rabbi : 248, 250
Son, Eternal : 156
Southcote, Joanna : 227, 228
Southey, Robert : 305
Southwell, Robert : 305
Spenser, Edmund : 21, 49
Spirit, Holy : 57, 94, 127
Spiritism : 63, 77, 234
Spouse of Souls : 15
Stael, Madame de : 215
Stanislaus de Kostka : 287
Stilling, Heinrich Jung : 218
Strict Observance, Rite of : 28, 97
Surius : 131, 160

Suso : 155
Swedenborg, Emanuel : 39, 211, 212, 214, 222
Swinburne, A. C. : 305
Symbolism : 119
Synteresis : 315

TALMUD : 35
Tauler : 6, 7, 9, 36, 155, 198, 311, 313, 315, 316, 318
Taylor, Jeremy : 49
Temple, Order of : 149
Tennyson, Alfred : 288, 305, 308
Teresa, St. : 129, 130, 134, 172, 176, 177, 178, 222, 287, 310, 311, 313, 316, 318
Theologia Germanica : 181
Timothy : 138, 140, 274
Traherne, Thomas : 14
Transubstantiation : 12, 327
Trinity, Holy : 8, 12, 34, 37, 52 *et seq.*, 90, 135, 140, 156, 158
Trithemius : 7
Tsure : 259, 260, 315, 316

UNION, Divine : 25, 28, 33, 62, 69, 84, 139, 141, 152, 155, 239, 264, 267, 268, 272, 282 *et passim*

VAUDOIS : 7
Vaughan, Thomas : 225, 305
Victorines : 128, 135
Vision, Beatific : 7, 9, 14, 84, 95, 105, 138, 152, 156, 170, 247, 310, 311

WEIGEL, Valentine : 181, 198
Weishaupt : 218
Willermoz : 213, 214, 217
Word : 155 ; Word of Life : 109, 122
Wordsworth, William : 306

ZOECKLER, Dr. Otto : 200, 201
Zohar, Sepher Ha : 10, 35, 40, 55, 182, 210, 248, 251, 252, 311, 313, 329

1730 **ESPecially Irene:** A Guide to Psychic Awareness

Hughes/$1.65

1708 Ancient Mysteries of **East: Rama-Krishna**   Schure/$1.45

1709 Mysteries of Ancient **Egypt: Hermes-Moses**   Schure/$1.45

1710 Mysteries of Ancient **Greece: Orpheus-Plato**   Schure/$1.45

1711 Ancient Mysteries of **Delphi: Pythagoras**   Schure/$1.45

1712 **Light** of the Mysteries: **Jesus**   Schure/$1.45

1713 **Methods** of Spiritual Research   Steiner/$1.45

1714 **Results** of Spiritual Investigation   Steiner/$1.45

1715 **Gardening For Health:** The Organic Way (new edition)

Philbrick/$ .95

STEINERBOOK GIANTS — 6⅛″ × 9¼″ — Quality Paperbacks

G-5   A **Christian Rosenkreutz** Anthology   Allen/$7.50

G-1   Rudolf **Steiner,** An **Autobiography**   Steiner/$6.50

Additional titles in preparation. Send for complete catalog.
Rudolf Steiner Publications, Blauvelt, N.Y. 10913, U.S.A.

Steinerbooks
The Spiritual Sciences in popular paperback format, 4-3/16" x 7" rack-size

1722 **Caspar Hauser:** Enigma of a Century   Wasserman/$2.95

1729 **Queen Moo** & the Egyptian **Sphinx**   LePlongeon/$2.95

1739 **Occult & Curative Powers** of Precious Stones
           Fernie/$2.95

1737 **A Romance** of Two Worlds   Corelli/$2.45

1724 **Atlantis:** The Antediluvian World   Donnelly/$2.45

1717 **Atlantis/Europe:** The Secret of the West   Merejkowski/$2.45

1720 **Lamps** of Western Mysticism   Waite/$2.45

1733 **Paracelsus:** Life & Prophecies   Hartmann/$2.45

1718 **Ragnarok:** The Destruction of Atlantis   Donnelly/$2.45

1703 The **Unknown Philosopher:**
Louis Claude de Saint-Martin   Waite/$2.45

1723 **Zanoni:** A Rosicrucian Tale   Bulwer-Lytton/$2.45

1704 **Alchemists** Through the Ages   Waite/$1.95

1731 **Commentaries** On The Bhagavad **Gita**   Sri Chinmoy/$1.95

1716 **Cosmic Memory:** Atlantis & Lemuria   Steiner/$1.95

1702 **Count** of Saint-Germain   Cooper-Oakley/$1.95

1707 **Education** As An Art   Steiner/$1.95

1721 **Eleven** European **Mystics**   Steiner/$1.95

1705 **From Sphinx** To Christ: An Occult History   Schure/$1.95

1726 The **Golem:** Mystical Tales of the Ghetto   Bloch/$1.95

1735 The **Great Pyramid:** A Miracle in Stone   Seiss/$1.95

1701 **Meditations** on the Signs of the **Zodiac**   Jocelyn/$1.95

1732 **Mother India's** Lighthouse: India's Spiritual Leaders
           Sri Chinmoy/$1.95

1727 **Mysteries of Egypt:** Secret Rites of the Nile   Spence/$1.95

1719 **Occult Mysteries** of Antiquity   Steiner/$1.95

1728 The **Pictorial Key** To The **Tarot**   Waite/$1.95

1706 **Reincarnation** & Immortality   Steiner/$1.95

1767 **Steiner Dictionary** of the Psychic, Mystic, Occult
           The Editors/$1.95

1725 **Vril:** The Power of the Coming Race   Bulwer-Lytton/$1.95